CIVIC EDUCATION:
ITS LIMITS AND CONDITIONS

Edited by Susan Douglas Franzosa

Nine Essays by
Susan Douglas Franzosa
James M. Giarelli
Ronald K. Goodenow
Beverly M. Gordon
Richard Pratte
Betty A. Sichel
Andrew R. Trusz and Sandra L. Parks-Trusz
Donald R. Warren
George H. Wood

PRAKKEN PUBLICATIONS, INC.
1988

© 1988 by Prakken Publications, Inc.

CIVIC EDUCATION: ITS LIMITS AND CONDITIONS
Edited by Susan Douglas Franzosa
Published by Prakken Publications, Inc.,
    Post Office Box 8623, Ann Arbor, Michigan 48107
ISBN 0-911168-68-0
Library of Congress Card Catalog Number 86-63414
List Price - $20.00

In memory of Barbara Trafford Flynn (1946 - 1966)
and her commitment to justice and equality

It was a terribly severe winter in 1904. I remember picketing in front of a shop on Green Street . . . A police officer came along and said, "Young lady, it's too cold for you to stand out here so long." I told him that I wasn't cold and that it was my job to stand there just as it was his to safeguard the peace.
—Rose Schneiderman

The question is not whether we will be extremists, but what kind of extremists we will be. Will we be extremists for hate or for love? Will we be extremists for the preservation of injustice or for the extension of justice?
—Martin Luther King, Jr.

The world progresses, in the slow and halting manner in which it does progress, only in proportion to the moral energy exerted by the men and women living in it.
—Jane Addams

Contents

INTRODUCTION—Susan Douglas Franzosa 1

PART ONE: THE GOALS AND CONTEXT
OF CIVIC EDUCATION 9
    Chapter One: THE CIVIC PURPOSE
    OF EDUCATION: CIVIC LITERACY—
    Richard Pratte 11
    Chapter Two: CIVIL EDUCATION
    IN AN UNCIVIL WORLD—Donald R. Warren ... 29
    Chapter Three: EDUCATION AND DEMOCRATIC
    CITIZENSHIP: TOWARD A NEW PUBLIC
    PHILOSOPHY—James M. Giarelli 50
    Chapter Four: CIVIC EDUCATION
    FOR PARTICIPATORY DEMOCRACY—
    George H. Wood 68

PART TWO: CIVIC EDUCATION
IN A PLURALISTIC SOCIETY 99
    Chapter Five: THE USE OF CULTURAL
    KNOWLEDGE IN THE CIVIC EDUCATION
    OF TEACHERS—Beverly M. Gordon 101
    Chapter Six: WILL THE SCHOOLS REBUILD
    AN OLD SOCIAL ORDER?—Andrew R. Trusz
    and Sandra L. Parks-Trusz 127
    Chapter Seven: THE EDUCATION OF THE
    CITIZENESS—Susan Douglas Franzosa 142

PART THREE: GLOBAL THEMATICS
AND MODERN CITIZENSHIP 165
    Chapter Eight: RETHINKING THE PROGRESSIVE
    NATURE OF CIVIC EDUCATION IN THE
    MODERN WORLD—Ronald K. Goodenow 167
    Chapter Nine: CIVIC LIFE AND CIVIC EDUCATION:
    A STUDY OF CHANGING SYMBOLIC
    SYSTEMS—Betty A. Sichel 194

SELECTED BIBLIOGRAPHY—
    Susan Douglas Franzosa 217

CONTRIBUTORS 229

Introduction

By Susan Douglas Franzosa

WITHIN the last few years there has been a renewed interest in civic education. Perhaps this is because, as R. Freeman Butts has maintained, "the urge to promote civic education through the schools accelerates in time of crisis or rapid social change."[1] Butts has contributed much to the contemporary debate concerning the nature and tasks of a modern civic education. His *Revival of Civic Learning*, in which he proposes that the American public school now reclaim its historic role as civic educator, has prompted a wide range of responses from scholars in the foundations of education. Some assert along with Butts that the schools, despite what might be characterized as historical setbacks, can and should take up the task of social reconstruction by providing a uniform "civism" designed to restore a sense of democratic community and a set of core democratic values. Others, dissenting from this view, argue that a uniform civic education is untenable in a pluralistic society; that a national agreement on the content of a civic curriculum would, as it has in the past, constitute a form of cultural imperialism. Still others maintain that without dramatic social and political change in the country as a whole, an emanicipatory civic education, which is taken as desirable, is almost impossible. The schools, they argue, cannot help but perpetuate or reproduce an unjust social order.

The issues generated by the debate over civic education are not new. From Plato's concern in the *Republic* to prescribe an education that would lay the foundations for the just state, to Dewey's assertion in *The School and Society* that the public schools "will be the deepest and best guaranty of a larger society which is worthy, lovely, and harmonious,"[2] civic education has remained a foundational preoccupation of educational theorists. Central to this preoccupation is the idea that the stability, continuity, reform, and even the transformation of the social and political order depends upon the practice of a citizenship that can be learned in schools. That is, the school's creation of the good citizen has been seen as a means to the creation of the good state and good society.

Seen positively, the public school's attempt to create citizens is also an attempt to democratize the opportunities of the young to become fully entitled participants within the culture. Schooling assures social continuity and political harmony by producing a network of emotional responses and intellectual dispositions towards social and political relations. Power and identity are distributed, or at least promised, to individuals who can legitimately earn them by coming to understand, accept, and act in accord with standards of belief and behavior set by the curriculum. Seen negatively, public schooling, as Michel Foucault contends, is a disciplinary institution akin to psychiatric and correctional institutions. The schools function to coercively "normalize" individuals within the culture. The institution's role, according to Foucault, is to "introduce the constraint of a conformity that must be achieved."[3] It thus formalizes a set of knowledge codes, rules of behavior, and attitudes towards that behavior, which students come to accept as normal. Their responses to others, their public actions, and their own sense of who they are, are the results of comparisons with the norms which they come to see as legitimate as they become schooled in citizenship.

Whether the process of schooling is seen in negative or positive terms, it is difficult to avoid the realization that historical arguments and rationales for state supported schooling have been advanced as ways of reconstituting the attitudes, beliefs, and behaviors of the citizenry. Plato's *Republic,* one of the most thoroughgoing philosophical arguments for state education, is an admirable example. The realization of the good society, for Plato, necessitated that citizens be educated to fulfill specific political functions within the state. The few who were to have full access to power needed an education that would enable them to become just rulers, skillful politicians, and wise judges. Their citizenship required that they place reason before emotion, thought before action, and public virtue before private gain. They needed to be immune to the potentially violent responses elicited by poetry, music, and drama; practiced in the art of the dialectic; and knowledgeable in history, law, ethics, natural science, and mathematics. The *Republic,* then, not only characterized the qualities of mind and character, the requisite knowledge and skills, and the rights and duties appropriate to full political citizenship; it clearly articulated these characteristics as guiding principles for curriculum and pedagogy.

Within the American educational tradition we find a number of examples of reform programs for public schools that explicitly intend to work out social and political agendas by reconstituting the nature of the citizenry. Thomas Jefferson's *Bill for the More General Diffusion of Knowledge*, for example, advocated three years of publicly supported schooling for all free, white children as a way of "illuminating the minds of the people at large," and free further education for those white males "naturally endowed with genius and virtue" who could be "rendered by liberal education worthy to receive, and able to guard the sacred deposit of the rights and liberties of their fellow citizens."[4] For Jefferson, the highest form of citizenship was the reasoned exercise of statecraft and this would require an education in the classical tradition of the liberal arts. Jefferson's educational reforms were not only intended as a way of maximizing the potential of the talented few; they were also intended to transform the uneducated and potentially violent "people at large" into reasonable, patriotic, and compliant citizens.

Another useful historical example, of course, is Horace Mann's proposal for common schooling advanced during the mid-nineteenth century. Unlike the reforms advanced by Jefferson, the work of Mann and his contemporaries placed primary emphasis on the schooling of a general public in morals and manners rather than intellectual preparation for political leadership. According to Mann, the result of publicly supported schooling should be the creation of a society composed of "sober, wise, and good men," a society in which "each citizen can participate in the power of governing others."[5]

If we follow the historical thread of educational reform programs since the creation of the common schools in the United States, what we find is a series of modifications and revisions of the curriculum thought appropriate to the future citizen. Never really approaching the thoroughness of Plato's *Republic*, these modifications and revisions have alternated between emphasizing (as in Jefferson's proposals) the importance of academic subject matter or emphasizing (as in Mann's) the importance of character training. Just prior to the turn of the century, for example, students normally read didactic literature that focused on the lives of American patriots as part of their training for citizenship. By 1900, didacticism had fallen out of favor and was replaced by an effort to teach high school students more scholarly historical skills as well as political theory. By 1919, proponents of the social studies advocated focusing education in citizenship on issues of community, personal character, and vocation.

These shifts in emphasis continue to occur within the contemporary debate on the need for school reform and improvement. Yet, as Mary Anne Raywid, Charles A. Tesconi, and Donald R. Warren have argued in *Pride and Promise: Schools of Excellence for All the People,* one of the major flaws in the current debate is that it has taken place within a context framed by state and federally supported task force reports that "pay scant attention to matters of educational purpose [and] offer no vision, no anchoring goals to direct schooling in America."[6] On the surface, this is quite true. The task force reports have not seemed to address the question of "what schools are for" in any direct or thoroughgoing way. Nor have they explicitly examined the social and political implications of the changes they advocate for the individual student of modern citizenship. Instead, their concentration has tended to be on enumerating the public school's failures in quantitative form and advancing recommendations for what Raywid, Tesconi, and Warren characterize as "additive" and "piecemeal" change.

Yet, the task force reports and their current prescriptions for school improvement do emerge for a powerful ideological consensus. Their proposals for "additive" and "piecemeal" changes must be understood as just that—pieces or additions that fit within a coherent system of belief that defines the relation between school, society, and individual. In the most widely read and popular of the reports, *A Nation at Risk,* for example, what is of central concern is the restoration of national strength defined in terms of the United States' ability to compete internationally in the areas of scientific research, technological achievement, and economic production. Defined in terms of perceived national need, the school's primary goal is seen as the production of competitive, independent, yet loyal, citizens who can contribute significantly to the maintenance of the nation's international supremacy.

Within this context, individual citizenship involves acquiring knowledge in a standard core of subject matter as well as a repertoire of skills that can be translated into productive patterns of behavior within the economy. Good citizens are thus characterized in *A Nation at Risk* as those who "by virtue of their own efforts, competently guided, can hope to attain the mature and informed judgment needed to secure gainful employment and to manage their own lives, thereby serving not only their own interests but also the progress of society itself."[7] Those who fail to meet these expectations, warn the report writers, should not expect to be granted full social and economic citizenship. "Individuals who do not possess the levels of skill, literacy, and training essential to this new era will be effectively disenfranchised, not simply from the material rewards that accompany competent performance, but also from the chance to participate fully in our national life."[8]

Current scholarly interest in reconceptualizing the goals and tasks for a modern civic education has been fueled by the poverty of the reasoning and rhetoric represented in *A Nation at Risk* and the state and local educational programs it has engendered. The question now being asked by scholars of the foundations of education is how the schools might assure, rather than limit, "full participation in our national life" and foster, rather than restrict, the development of a democratic social and political order. Although emerging from divergent philosophic perspectives, critical theorists like Henry Giroux, as well as liberals like Butts, have begun to explore "the necessary and appropriate contributions of the school to the individual and society"[9] and the principles which should govern our understanding of citizenship and the requirements for civic education in a democracy.

The essays in this volume attempt to broaden as well as clarify the terms of the continuing debate on school reform and introduce alternative perspectives on the limits and conditions of civic education. In the first section of the volume, the authors focus attention on the need for a philosophically grounded and socially contextualized definition of democracy and democratic citizenship. First, Richard Pratte evaluates the parameters of the term *civism* and explores the relationship of a multidimensional civic literacy to a democratic social order. Donald R. Warren investigates the ways in which contemporary forms of privatism, elitism, and intellectual fragmentation have characterized the contemporary American social context and impeded the ability of the public schools to meet the goals of equity and excellence. The essays by James M. Giarelli and George H. Wood then examine conflicting concepts of democracy and the models they generate for citizenship education. Giarelli contends that a tacit acceptance of the assumptions of democratic elitism has caused the public school to abdicate its responsibility for "forming and reforming a public" and thus fostered a citizenship of unconscious conformity and compliance. Wood's essay extends this analysis and reviews ways that educators might counter student passivity and alienation and foster a new civic courage.

The essays presented in the second section address the socio-historical consequences of institutionalizing a core of civic virtues and a uniform civic education within a pluralistic society. Beverly M. Gordon argues that the African-American educational experience demonstrates the core curriculum's power to perpetuate negative images of minority group members and legitimate their disenfranchisement as adults. Gordon further suggests that the social theories of African-American intellectuals, which have been largely overlooked by educational scholars, have the potential to provide an emancipatory model for citizenship that would affirm cultural sovereignty and promote active civic engagement. The essay by Sandra L. Parks-Trusz and Andrew R. Trusz evaluates the class bias inherent in an attempt to restore a canonical set of civic virtues within the public school curriculum. They argue that the meritocratic structure of the schools will necessitate institutionalizing mechanisms for testing, knowledge selection, knowledge transmission, and pedagogical strategies that perpetuate hierarchical levels of civic participation. The essay by Susan Douglas Franzosa that completes this section continues the discussion of cultural diversity and pluralism by focusing on the gender bias of historic rationales for civic education and the models of the citizen they delineate.

The third section of the volume contains two essays that attempt to look beyond the limits of the current debate by posing questions relevant to a modern global citizenship. Both Ronald K. Goodenow and Betty A. Sichel advance the thesis that we are currently living in a time of radical transformation in which traditional conceptualizations of citizenship and civic education will prove inadequate. Goodenow discusses this from a historical and international perspective. First, he reviews the assumptions of early twentieth century progressive education and its provisions for citizenship education. He then suggests that current work in civic education, particularly that which is centered on resolving the conflict of citizenship and cultural diversity, would be considerably enriched by a study of citizenship programs in European and Third World nations. Finally, Sichel approaches these issues from the perspective of the philosopher. Beginning with an analysis of the Aristotelian distinction between the good person and the good citizen, she explores how the ambiguity of symbolic systems during periods of radical social and political transformation affect one's relation to community, nation, and world. Her contention is that such periods provide a dissonance that can result in rootless anomie and treason or creative engagement and civic transformation.

Notes

[1] R. Freeman Butts, *Historical Perspectives on Civic Education in the United States*, National Task Force on Citizenship Education (New York, NY: McGraw-Hill, 1977), 48.

[2] John Dewey, "The School and Social Progress," in *The School and*

Society (Chicago: University of Chicago Press, 1974), 29.
[3] Michel Foucault, *Discipline and Punish: The Birth of the Prison* (London: Harvester Press, 1977), 236.
[4] Quoted in Merle Curti, *The Social Ideas of American Educators* (Totowa, NJ: Littlefield, Adams & Co., 1968), 3.
[5] *Ibid.,* 132.
[6] *Pride and Promise: Schools of Excellence for All the People* (Westbury, NY: American Educational Studies Association, 1984), 5.
[7] National Commission on Excellence in Education, *A Nation at Risk: The Imperative for Educational Reform* (Washington, DC: United States Department of Education, 1983).
[8] *Ibid.*
[9] Henry Giroux, "Critical Theory and Rationality in Citizenship Education," in *Theory and Resistance in Education: A Pedagogy for the Opposition* (South Hadley, MA: Bergin and Garvey Publishers, 1984).

Part One

The Goals and Context of Civic Education

Chapter One

Each generation must redefine for itself what it means to be a good citizen and what education is required to help citizens play their roles effectively.

1

The Civic Purpose of Education: Civic Literacy

By Richard Pratte

ALTHOUGH most Americans sense that they live within an extremely complicated political system and suspect that much of what is thought and done within this sphere is promoted by consideration of less than high citizenship motives, the relationship of good citizenship, or civism, to political life has remained murky. The problem has been compounded by the fact that few social groups have access to the sustained means for effective participation in public policy-making. Although numerous writers have addressed the issue of democracy's need for an education that prepares citizens for taking an active and effective role in public life,[1] today's students seem ill-prepared for the intelligent and effective exercise of citizenship. Within this context, it is imperative that educators consider the issues of civism and civic literacy. Recognizing that the problems of effective citizenship are many and complex, I will deal with the following questions: Should civic education be given a central place in the curriculum? What legitimately defines the parameters of civism? Does civic education require a distinctive mode of literacy—civic literacy?

The Place of Civic Education in the Curriculum

The question: Should civic education be given a central place in the curriculum? might strike some as flippant and irresponsible for, they would assert, isn't it abundantly clear that schools were begun and are maintained for this very purpose? That is, isn't it the case that being a responsible citizen takes a special knowledge, say, of the constitutional system and of the guarantees of the Bill of Rights, and to teach this knowledge most effectively is a basic charge assigned to the schools? In other words, developing in the young the skills and knowledge of responsible citizenry is the responsibility of those charged with conducting public education in this country, and that charge rests squarely on teachers and schools along with the lesser charged private voluntary organizations: Boy Scouts, Girl Scouts, religious groups, civic bodies, the family, and the community

Patently, it is foolhardy to argue against the foregoing. No nation-state has the luxury of turning out graduates who do not understand how its political and social system works. Clearly, the schools are expected to play a major role in shaping the young into responsible citizens. The question, then, is answered in terms of recognizing the fact that schools are expected to systematically produce citizens with a strong sense of responsibility regarding the principles, concepts, and precepts of American democracy, and who are expected to be fully committed emotionally and attitudinally to use their knowledge and skills through their participation in the society as informed, rational, responsible citizens. This charge to the schools is the primary reason why a system of schooling is maintained at public expense. Consequently, the question of why civic education should be given a preferred position in the curriculum is answered. Civic education is a mandated element of the curriculum: it is obligatory that the nation's schools enhance the level of citizenship by preparing youth to become responsible citizens.

But what is not answered in the foregoing is: What is the status of civic education? What shape or form is civic education to take in the schools? Here is the gut issue. A renewed effort to place civic education in a central position in the curriculum calls forth the salient question of what is to "count" as good citizenship. Thus, the prior question is this: What is good citizenship? Clarification of this point seems absolutely vital.

What Is Civism and Where Is It to Be Found?

The term *civism* is a term found in ordinary speech, and we may say very generally that *civic* refers to, or pertains to, a city, municipality, or to citizenship and citizens. Being civic minded, for example, is to be concerned with the well-being of the city or municipality. Hence, *civism*, a term closely related to *civic*, has to do not only with citizenship but with a particular form of citizenship; namely, good citizenship.[2]

It remains to be asked, however: What is to "count" as good citizenship? One person may have a particular conception of good citizenship and another a quite different conception. Hence, what is to count as civism is not readily agreed upon, although there are those who refuse to recognize this fact. They offer arguments against the background of a particular conception of civism with or without realizing that civism is an essentially contested concept both in terms of its criteria and its application. These sweeping pronouncements invite us to agree that civism has been properly defined, or more simply, that civism ought to be so properly defined, whatever anyone might wish or think desirable in the matter.

On the other hand, others recognize the essential contestability of civism and claim that attempts to define the term are doomed to failure. Such pronouncements attempt to bulldoze others' positions into a single corner. Both approaches preempt the need for rational debate and the result is that civism, both as a concept and as an element of school study, has been largely ignored by scholars, the public, and policymakers until quite recently.

It is obvious that the problem of what is to count as civic education presupposes that the community underwrite what it wishes its citizens to be. It is equally obvious that, in the nature of the case, such a position, if achieved, has to be presumed rather than explicitly formulated here since the status and program of civism today are problematic. Concerned scholars argue among themselves regarding the need for civic education in the schools, some contending that school funds need not be allocated for the civic education of children because they believe the public life of the citizen is education enough. Others, while in fundamental agreement that civic education is needed, argue regarding its proper content.[3]

Civic education, we are reminded by R. Freeman Butts, must be a part of American schooling. He contends that the
> goal of civic education for American schools is to deal with all students in such a way as to motivate them and enable them to play their parts as informed, responsible, committed, and effective members of a modern democratic political system.[4]

Butts further suggests that while this goal can be achieved in a number of different ways, all civic education curricula should include "basic aspects of political values, political knowledge, and the skills of political participation needed for making deliberate choices among real alternatives."[5]

He lists ten requisite political values that must underlie the curriculum for civism. Five of these tend to support pluralistic tendencies or the goals of *pluribus*: freedom, diversity, privacy, due process, and international human rights. Five others support unitary tendencies or the goal of *unum*: justice, equality, authority, participation, and personal obligation for the public good. The ten values are organized into a set which Butts calls "A Decalogue of Democratic Civic Values."[6]

Butts, or anyone who sets out to reflect upon civic education, has to face, as he or she does so, a question of provisional definition. But to offer a decalogue of political values is not to provide a definition of civic education. There is considerable doubt, in fact, whether civic education can ever be finally or conclusively defined.[7] Every month new proposals appear, and very quickly responses appear which challenge these. And herein lies the problem.

Because civic education is a normative set of ideals, really political values, any proposal will evoke questions about it which are difficult, if not impossible, to answer. To attempt to spell out the proper or true definition of civic education is, it would appear, wrongheaded. Any attempt in this regard would be no more than to proffer a normative set of values or ideals.

Clearly, then, the issue is not one of determining what civism is. Civism is good citizenship and we determine this through an activity of linguistic study. Rather, the problem is one of determining what is to count as civism, and this involves choosing among competing conceptions of civism. The place to begin our examination of what counts as civism is the public sphere for, as reflection will show, the public sphere is the social space where civism is reflected in its many guises.[8]

Civism and the Public Sphere

The moment we mention the word *civism* a score of ideological ghosts rise to obscure our vision. Without careful attention, the search for civism could draw us imperceptibly into a consideration of the logical consideration of various ideas—such as authority, freedom, responsibility, and consent—and away from the facts of human activity. It is better to start from the latter and see if we are not then led into an idea of something which will turn out to implicate the parameters which define civism.

The proper place to look for the parameters that define civism is the public sphere. While the phenomena of the public sphere vary immensely with time and place, they are not hidden from us although they are very complex. They are facts of human behavior accessible to human observation and testing. Thus, the existence of a multiplicity of competing civisms should be seen as summaries of what is rather than what ought to be. The characteristic of such positions is that they are the characteristic phenomena of civic activity. Hence, the wrong place to look for the parameters that will define civism is the realm of principles, viewpoints, and high-sounding notions which are conceived in the minds of individuals and which are supposed to produce a particular kind of society. If we look, instead, at the public sphere we see civism in action or inaction. When we seek for civism in a society, we find it not in supermundane slogans but embodied in a level or range of public sphere activity engaged in by citizens. A realistic regard for the facts compels us to conclude that the public sphere is a consequence of the actions of people acting effectively or ineffectively with regard to the well-being of a city or municipality. In principle and in practice, a public sphere in which citizens confer, defend, and justify political action or inaction is what we mean by civism. Thus, civism is a consequence of the public sphere, deriving its vitality from the legitimizing force of the public sphere.

By public sphere, then, I refer to a realm of social life—a social space—in which something approaching public opinion can be formed and exercised. The norms of the public sphere may be such that the public can confer and act in an unrestricted fashion; that is, with the guarantee of freedom of assembly and association, and the freedom to express and register their opinions about matters of the general interest. On the other hand, the public sphere may be a realm in which questions of political life cannot be discussed openly, debate is not allowed, free argument is punished, and public actions are restricted.

Thus, the level and range of civism are bound by the norms of proper engagement in the public sphere. This point makes no judgment about the quality of the norms of the public sphere. What it does is focus our attention upon what the public sphere is.

It is not my purpose to fully trace the origin and development of our idealized political democracy or assess our basic democratic norms as embodied in the Constitution and legal codes; that is a task beyond the scope of this paper.[9] What I intend to note is that democratic norms exist and that they serve both in a legal and moral nonneutral way to help secure a public sphere in which citizens act. They exercise their abilities, values, and capacities as their conceptions of good citizenship allow, both rationally and irrationally, agreeing or disagreeing as to whether any particular conception of citizenship is acceptable.

Historically, American polity developed out of a commitment to a democratic participatory ideal that took form when English political norms and legal institutions were adapted to the harsh, pioneer conditions of American colonial and frontier existence. Idealized democratic principles in themselves may never have given rise to a public sphere of neighborly sociability and self-governing community. However, forms such as the town meeting, with its face-to-face relationship in which the general interest was pursued in a disinterested fashion, did emerge. A political ethic, based on lived patterns emanating from the family and community and historically linked to English common law, did coalesce to forge a general norm for civism.

Deeply embedded in this early concept of civism were standards of decency which included the judging of behavior such as public drunkenness, wife beating, physical mistreatment of children, brutality to animals, and unnecessary violence as morally wrong, although the observance of these standards was far from universal. Additionally, the concept of civism accepted distinctions and behaviors based upon race, religion, social class, age, gender, and ethnicity. The concept of civism thus existed without regard to individual capacity and service to society.[10]

What is important to grasp is that the self-regulating autonomy embodied in face-to-face participation was limited to those who were generally of high standing, people of the community with education and wealth. The public sphere operated on a mixture of restricted participatory politics, public opinion, and fairly homogeneous values, and was populated with private individuals who promoted and shaped a particular civism, believing themselves to represent the general interest. Armed with what they took to be the best understanding of the general interest, they sought to change society into a realm of private autonomy free of an overriding political inference and sought to transform the State into an authority that was restricted to a limited number of functions merely supervised by the public sphere. Ideally, the transformation of self-interest into the general interest was the function of the public sphere. Civism, which was thought to have been the measure of such a general interest, was thus guaranteed.[11]

The Public Sphere Today: A Unidimensional Civism

A grimness sets in when we examine the status of the public sphere today. Following a line of thought laid down by Dewey, we might argue that the public sphere has been eclipsed.[12] He noted in the late 1920s that the public sphere, as an arena of political activity, was less and less involved in political processes having a direct bearing on the public's well-being.

Dewey observed:

> In spite of attained integration, or rather perhaps because of its nature, the Public seems to be lost; it is certainly bewildered. The government, officials and their activities are plainly with us. Legislatures make laws with luxurious abandon; subordinate officials engage in a losing struggle to enforce some of them; judges . . . deal as best they can with the steadily mounting pile of disputes that come before them. But where is the public which these officials are supposed to represent? . . . Is the public much more than what a cynical diplomat called Italy: a geographical expression?[13]

And,

> What, after all, is the public under present conditions? What are the reasons for its eclipse? What hinders it from finding and identifying itself? By what means shall its inchoate and amorphous estate be organized into effective political action relevant to present social needs and opportunities?[14]

In effect, Dewey addressed the problem of a public unable to perform its political responsibilities because of rapidly changing economic and social conditions. Chief among these were the expanded role of the government, the growth of large-scale economic organizations, the breakdown of face-to-face relations in town and cities, a press that was less and less involved in political affairs, and the emergence of trained specialists as "managers" of political affairs.[15] These and other considerations precluded the raising of political and practical governance from large segments of the public sphere. By implication, the individual social actor was increasingly less able to practice effective civic participation.

What was significant about these conditions for Dewey was the way the role of the public had been altered. No longer was the public sphere under the control of individuals committed to promoting control over events in the general interest. No longer was the public a competent and decisive force within the civic order. At the core of this problem, Dewey claimed, was the creeping erosion of the functioning of the public sphere: the realm of intelligent problem solving. For Dewey, the eclipse of the public was put thus: "There are too many publics and too much of public concern for our existing resources to cope with."[16]

Today, even more than in the 1920s, society is characterized by large-scale economic organizations, multinational cartels, increased state intervention to stabilize the economy, an expanding role of research and technology, and the preeminence of the role of instrumental reason or technical decision making in social life. Further, there has been an increased subjectivizing and relativizing of morality, the conceding to each individual that his or her opinion is as valid as all others. These and other present-day factors have radically altered an already divided and troubled public sphere.

Moreover, a dominant force at work today in the public sphere is the ready acceptance of the legitimacy and value of state intervention in the interest of minority or special-interest groups' demands. The public sphere has become a field for the competition of interests, particularly ethnic and racial groups' interests. This has fostered a trend toward a pluralism that shows little regard for the general interest of the society as a whole. With the blending of the public and private realms, not only do political authorities assume certain functions in the sphere of the marketplace; but, conversely, social groups now assume political functions. This leads to a kind of "refeudalization" of the public sphere. In other words, large organizations, be they economic, social, or a mixture of the two, strive for a kind of political compromise with the government and with one another, avoiding a consideration of what might be in the larger public interest.

In this situation, the public sphere increasingly operates under direct political regulation. This amounts to a repoliticalization of many social institutions; the power that once operated indirectly over the decision-making process is superceded by the more visible hand of the state. The more active role of the state in adjudicating many demands, however, is fraught with danger. If social and political stability is to be maintained, the state takes on a peculiarly negative character, oriented toward the avoidance of risks and the elimination of dangers to the system both economic and political, not toward the realization of a clearly stated general or public interest. Practical goals conceived in terms of solutions to technical problems dominate. The tasks facing those who make decisions are believed to be those that can be solved only by research and technology—by experts. The public sphere loses its function of decision making about practical problems since the public cannot be expected to understand the complexity of problems. Hence, civism is reduced to making plebiscitary decisions about alternative sets of leaders who are believed to truly understand the role of research and technology in decision making. The public sphere, once a social space concerned with providing an arena for making decisions about practical goals and the general interest, has become an arena for the selection of administrators who will employ technicians/experts to guarantee the solution of technical problems.

The deterioration of civism to its unidimensional function of plebiscitary decision making is the major problem of society today. Under present circumstances, the public seems to have no special insight into the competence of political candidates, because to judge, say, a federal, state, or local candidate presupposes some consensus or criteria of evaluation. The evaluation of political leaders, even if agreed upon criteria were available, is extremely difficult because candidates are "packaged" by mass media manipulators and their public opinion research. A well-run political campaign amounts to managing the media and maintaining a public relations "image." Yet, polls, samples, and surveys do not constitute a public sphere; they represent only mental images. One fact is obvious, namely, that the public sphere is weakened by confusing mass opinion for public opinion. Hence, the entire democratic ideal is sorely tested, and as citizens we may be on the verge of a rude awakening to the fact that an enlightened citizenry is a mere myth today.

The realization of this situation entails overcoming the alienation between the citizen and the public sphere or political community. To achieve this goal means effecting concrete changes in the relations between citizens and the state. The problem is thus a search for conditions under which the unidimensionality of civism may be eliminated in favor of a multidimensional civism.

In the search for the conditions under which competing conceptions of civism may function, we proceed on the assumption that there is a need to revitalize publics or groups acting *qua* groups—that is, real behavioral manifestations of good citizenship must be legitimized as public sphere activities. In effect, the public sphere must be strengthened. We need to revitalize representative institutions, electoral institutions, and establish the conditions necessary for an informed citizenry, all presently a sham of political democracy.

Education for a Multidimensional Civism

To begin this project, we must come to grips with the problem of civic provision. Civism as a goal of education is required from a democratic society's need—all future citizens must have a civic education. That is, the assumption is that the future citizen's right to play a meaningful role in society is the basis for civic education. The assumption of a citizen's right to a meaningful role in society subsumes the whole topic of civic education. Hence, the citizen's identification, loyalty, and commitment to society are the result of civic education. Here is one sense of equality in education—the form of civic provision—where all children, conceived as future citizens, have the right to obtain the goods and services of society, where the school helps citizens to gain the necessary prerequisite for these, and where the society is best served if citizens are taught what they need to know in order to obtain these goods and services. Schools cannot make available what citizens must know on the criteria of social standing or the economic status of parents.

The aim of education in a democracy, civic literacy, is to help students to know how to be citizens first and workers, managers, professionals, and so on only afterward. The curriculum should not provide a privileged access to citizenship, for some but not for all. As an equalitarian enterprise, it should strive to provide equal results—a civism available to all. The ethical ideal of such an enterprise is one of service: the placing of the expertise of teachers at the service of students for some larger purpose or interest—the general good.

But there is a nagging problem, namely, an inequality of knowledge resulting from a "scientific" view of decision making which makes public choices extremely complicated and dependent on expert information. When experts stress the problem of complexity in public choices, seeking to use surveys, research, computer analysis of data, etc., they erect a barrier between the public and public policy making. In this instance, experts—rather than the electorate—rule. One remedy for this situation is to raise the competence of the public in science, stressing science in education—preparing citizens through scientific training. Unfortunately, however, such training may become obsolete by the time students attain full voting status in society. Education in science must, it would seem, be supplemented by the continuous transmission of information and the education of adults, and this is no small task, but a necessary one if the public is expected to be competent in choosing means and ends in the public arena.

Here is the rub! Equal access to citizenship requires a common schooling paradigm. As an educational goal, civism is not concerned with the education of presidents, statesmen, diplomats, and the like; it is restricted to preparing students for good citizenship. This being the case, some agreement on what the common currency of political and social life is and how this is to be dealt with in the teaching/learning situation is a basic stumbling block in achieving civism. We must not lose sight of the brute fact that civic education can be a coercive business. There may be no avoiding that, but it may be both politically and morally disastrous if the fact is not readily grasped. School personnel alone cannot be expected to develop, organize, and deliver a general curriculum in civism. Entire communities, really publics, must be alerted to the need for underwriting what they wish civic education to be.

What is needed to develop a full-blown and defensible position on civic education is to make a commitment to a democratic society the focal point. This means, among other things, that the question of where the proper boundaries are to be drawn between the political and nonpolitical, between instructing and indoctrinating students, raises issues that are themselves of political as well as instructional significance. As communities seek to clarify their goals for civism, there may be a real and indissoluble conflict of political as well as educational values. This last point is of very great importance for civic education.

That we live in a constitutional democracy is a fact. Recall that it is also a fact that, whatever else people may disagree about, they agree on the crucial importance of school in the preparation of youth for the duties of citizenship. These facts cannot be ignored. They come together in the contribution to be made by basic schooling to civic life, in which each individual fulfills the obligation of the highest political office in a constitutional democracy: that of citizenship. We are citizens of the United States and we the citizens *are* the government of the United States.

This last point is crucial. If we take seriously the democratic ideal—that a democracy is government of, by, and for the people—then officeholders we elect to head our local, state, and federal offices are not the government; they are only the executors of the people's government. A democratic polity, at least in theory, is coextensive with self-government; it calls for citizen conduct that moves our nation in a more just, reasonable, and responsible direction. In such a social order, an adequate schooling for exercising the political privileges and responsibilities of citizenship requires the steady improvement of the citizens of the state. If we wish the citizens of our nation to be just in making laws, reasonable when making decisions, and responsible when ruling and being ruled, then they must learn a civic literacy—that is, how to live by democratic civic values.

Civic Literacy and Persistent Questioning

Teaching for civic literacy is to educate with the end in view of making inchoate democratic attitudes, beliefs, sensibilities, and commitments actual. Civic literacy includes, among other things, the theme of persistent questioning in the quest for a democratic polity. A civic literacy must be invented to provide certain fundamental attitudes and dispositions, certain ways of proceeding, so that students may learn and come to understand the process by which democratic society is structured, and how a democratic consensus is built. Further, students need to attain the skills to take part in consensus building, and to link these to the dominant political and economic issues of the day.

The theme of persistent questioning in the quest for a democratic polity is extraordinarily important for civic literacy. How we understand it will influence the relative weight we give to our teaching of civic literacy, the place of civic literacy in a democracy, the importance of civic education as opposed to teaching basic subject matter, and the relative flexibility we will allow teachers in accommodating local, regional, national, and transnational differences. These, of course, are important matters. But if the goal of civic literacy is to have its due influence in determining the structure of the polity, then we must understand the theme of persistent questioning.

The first point to grasp is that democracy and democratic processes are never givens. They can never be taken for granted. They must be contested for and won against great odds. What is democracy's greatest enemy? A cognitive inertia, a blasé attitude, which assumes that democratic institutions and processes are part of the natural order of things.

Taking these comments together, it looks as if something extremely valuable is lost whenever democracy is taken for granted. We embrace the institutions of democracy without understanding how they came into being and for what reasons. On another tack, however, something else is jeopardized when we come to regard democracy as established doctrine to which no question mark can ever be appended. That is to say, should civic education exclude as one of its essential tasks the serious questioning of the meaningfulness of democracy itself, then we risk in civic education a minimal standard of informed and rational decision making. We are merely producing doctrinaire democrats. In other words, the question: Should civic education include as one of its essential movements the serious questioning of the meaningfulness of American democracy itself? is important. But the question is not altogether well put. One might ask rather: Under what conditions can serious civic education include a persistent questioning of American society? This question is of immense importance and deserves serious attention.

First, the question that belongs to an exhibition of civic education is, at the same time, an exhibition of civic literacy. Students must be taught the concepts and strategies of persistent questioning. As Dewey said, "We have the physical tools of communication as never before. . . . Without such communication the public will remain shadowy and formless."[17] It is clear, however, that Dewey did not foresee the power of the media in organizing a political agenda as well as diffusing others. In other words, there are managers of societal attitudes and norms. To a large degree, control of media results in a managed communication product. This is not to talk about censorship in its "vulgar" form, as state censorship, but the vesting in the media of the authority to judge public repute, political credibility and legitimacy, as well as being the locus for determining truth and falsity.

Our dependency on the media managers must be reduced because it impedes the development of aware publics taking active, effective, unreserved roles in creating public policy. Let us say it as plainly as possible: an undistorted, nonideological media is not possible, but its domination may be subverted by the public's demand for a critique of its management. The school's focus on censorship as an intervening variable standing between the inputs of the media and established institutions on the one side and, on the other, the public's behavior in everyday life and politics, could bring about a real gain and make the public sphere an effective lever in political decision making. This strategy, of course, requires of teachers a discerning eye, a communicative competence, and skepticism regarding the products of the media. Above all, teaching emphasis must be given to the role of institutions, connecting media products and the goals of economic institutions. In focusing on the special role of the media as a source of decision making, small group discussion, face-to-face communication, is essential. Such communication can, and commonly does, serve as an instrument of counterpolitics. It can foster a critical view of the media and implant a new set of information at variance with those supplied by the dominant media. In short, people appear to be much more influenced in their political decisions by face-to-face contact than by the mass media directly.[18] This being so, the public sphere cannot be declared an obsolescent social structure.

If this is accomplished within the curriculum, then there should be an active study of the work produced. It should have to do with connecting national and international successes and failures, the fortunate and not so fortunate, of praise and pride for those who have labored—sometimes in the face of great odds and adversity—to improve society, which is an essential component of good citizenship, of the tentative status and uncertain standing in the larger world of democracy and democratic process. This focus of questioning the managed account of democratic tradition would create a common ground or union that transcends the mere plebiscitary function of today's civism, drawing from the elements of language, history, religion, art, cultural diversity, and other areas.

Disputes about civism are, at the deepest level, interpretations of that union. But unless teachers are free in the classroom to examine and critically teach different conceptions of the union, to practice inquiry and discussion so productive of the spirit of union and intelligent participation in the democratic process, an unidimensional civism will prevail. Teachers must resist the demand to reduce civic education to a mere drill—and so must the students—or, better, the parents of the children must resist, insofar as they are politically alert and capable.

In sum, the debate about the union is obviously critical, and that is the burden of the point here. The point is that the public schools should be training grounds for citizenship, not for predetermined types of citizenship—little automatons eager and willing to give another life for their country, or alternatively, unwilling to fight for anything. We must grasp the point that the nature of civism, and thus the civic education it requires, changes over time, just as demands upon citizens alter under the press of new circumstances. Each generation must redefine for itself what it means to be a good citizen, and what education is required to help citizens play the role of citizen effectively.

Conclusions

The foregoing suggestions for bringing about a revitalized public sphere and hence an active, informed civism are all necessary conditions, but they are not sufficient to the development of an informed multidimensional civism and civic literacy. However difficult it is, and perhaps strictly speaking impossible, to eliminate unidimensional civism, the decisive problem is this: how to make face-to-face communication an effective force in strengthening the capacity of the public for rational judgment and free it from the control of external or built-in censors. Clearly the school must play a central role. Its products, future citizens, are a key source of restraint and control over political representatives. That is, there is no contradiction in asking school personnel to work on two levels simultaneously, to consider competing, contradictory civism views, identifying, discussing, and evaluating them, while appreciating all the time that these very views may help to create greater ruptures and divisions within the society. Within the doom the latter seems to place on the former, there are spaces and potentials for producing viable public policy. For example, we need to hold our politicians in suspicion, but not contempt, rather than the politicians holding the public in suspicion and contempt. Moreover, to contract out of the messy business of the day-to-day problems of civism is to deny the active, contested nature of civism; to condemn students to the status of passive recipients of indoctrination; or to turn the control of society over the the "managers." To refuse the challenge of preparing students who can engage in counterpolitics is to deny the continuance of political life and democratic society themselves. Such a refusal will prove to be a theoretical as well as a practical failure.

A civic literacy embodying persistent questioning turns attention to the civic core of subject matter, to the analysis of practices, forms of life, and economic and political meanings of society's organization and institutions, helping students to see what underlies and is presupposed by the civic study of subject matter. They will ask how such social practices arise, are sustained, and change. Do they express ideologically frozen social relations of organization? Do all attempts to explain social and political life presuppose that we accept *de jure* standards of what is proper and reasonable behavior? Why do standards that appear so obvious and basic resist our realization that they are always open to rational criticism?

The development of civic literacy necessitates that educators assume the responsibility of helping students grasp the dialectical relationship of good citizenship and societal context. A persistent questioning of social change and politics would open students to a larger history, to a new consciousness of everyday life. The student of such a civic education will come to understand the necessary tension between short-term political actions taken in good faith in relation to barely understood aspects of societal growth and transformation and their unpredictable long-term outcomes. There is no reason why we cannot ask those who work in schools to operate under the tension of the relationship between two levels in their activity. Whether this approach will be successful is not predetermined, but the public sphere will be strengthened and, inevitably, so too will the possibilities for the practice of civism. This is no small task, but it is one of the things the members of a democratic society owe one another.

Notes

[1] In the late 1970s several national organizations expressed concern, really a sense of urgency, over the status of civic education in the United States, among these were: the American Bar Association through its Committee on Youth Education for Citizenship, the Danforth and Kettering Foundations, the U.S. Office of Education's Conference on Citizenship, and the National Council for the Social Studies, whose special meeting on the topic resulted in the publication *Building Rationales for Citizenship*, Bulletin 52, 1977. See also, National Assessment of Educational Progress, *Education for Citizenship: A Bicentennial Survey* (Citizenship/Social Studies Report No. 07-CS-01, Denver: NAEP, Nov. 1976). Moreover, recently R. Freeman Butts has presented his views concerning the need for civic education through the schools before several professional organizations such as the American Association of Colleges for Teacher Education, Society of Professors of Education (SPE), and the John Dewey Society. He has called for the examination of assumptions and a basic rationale for young citizens-in-process in the schools.

[2] *Webster's New International Dictionary*, 2nd ed. (Springfield, Mass.: Merriam-Webster, Inc., 1958), 492-93.

[3] See R. Freeman Butts et al., *Civic Learning in Teacher Education*, Ayers Bagley, ed., SPE Monograph Series (Minneapolis, Minn.: University of Minnesota College of Education, June, 1983); George H. Frederickson, "The Recovery of Civism in Public Administration," *Liberal Education* LXVIII (Winter 1982): 343-357; and Richard C. Remy, "Criteria for Judging

Citizenship Education Programs," *Educational Leadership* 38 (October 1980): 10-11.
[4] R. Freeman Butts, *The Revival of Civic Learning: A Rationale for Citizenship Education in American Schools* (Bloomington, Indiana: Phi Delta Kappa Educational Foundation, 1980), 123.
[5] *Ibid.*
[6] R. Freeman Butts, "The Revival of Civic Learning Requires a Prescribed Curriculum," *Liberal Education* 68, no. 4 (1982): 392.
[7] See, for example, how this issue is treated in "The Civic Education of the American Teacher," *Journal of Teacher Education* XXXIV, no. 6 (November-December, 1983).
[8] A public sphere is constituted by the process of various publics or social groups participating in creating public policy.
[9] In the Greek *polis* every man—that is, every free citizen—was a *Zoon politikon*: the social and political were inextricably fused, and there was no separate sphere of the "political." Private and public life were not distinct, and the only private individuals were those who, as slaves, lacked public status as citizens altogether.
[10] John Dewey, *The Public and Its Problems* (Chicago: Swallow Press, 1927); Walter Lippmann, *The Public Philosophy* (New York: Mentor Books, 1955); Nancy F. Sizer and Theodore R. Sizer, eds., *Moral Education: Five Lectures* (Cambridge, Mass.: Harvard University Press, 1970); Robert H. Wiebe, *The Segmented Society: An Historical Search for the Meaning of America* (New York: Oxford University Press, 1975); and Charles A. Tesconi and Van Cleve Morris, *The Anti-Man Culture: Bureautechnocracy and the Schools* (Urbana, Ill.: University of Illinois Press, 1972).
[11] C. Wright Mills, *The Power Elite* (New York: Oxford University Press, 1966); Robert Heilbrenner, *Business Civilization in Decline* (New York: W.W. Norton, 1976); John Schaar, *Power and Community: Dissenting Essays in Political Science* (New York: Vintage Books, 1970); and William M. Sullivan, *Reconstructing Public Philosophy* (Berkeley, Cal.: University of Caliornia Press, 1982)
[12] John Dewey, *The Public and Its Problems* (Chicago: Swallow Press, 1927), see Chapter IV.
[13] *Ibid.*, 116-17.
[14] *Ibid.*, 124.
[15] Dewey said, "It may be urged that the present confusion and apathy are due to the fact that the real energy of society is now

directed in all non-political matters by trained specialists who manage things, while politics are carried on with a machinery and ideas formed in the past to deal with quite another sort of situation" (*Ibid.*, 123).

[16] *Ibid.*, 126.
[17] *Ibid.*, 142.
[18] P.F. Lazarsfeld and Herbert Menzel in W. Schramm, ed., *The Science of Human Communication* (New York: Basic Books, 1963), 96.

Chapter Two

The aim of civic education is to enable young Americans to perform their public roles with understanding and courage. This requires the moral authority marshalled through the educator's shared commitment to inquiry and the advancement of human understanding.

2

Civil Education in an Uncivil World

By Donald R. Warren

THE appeal for renewed emphasis on civic education in the United States coincides with the drive for educational excellence. Both efforts pursue admirable goals, and yet both risk the further separation of public schooling from the world in which adults work, build families, take their leisure, and function as citizens. As in all such matters affecting educational purpose, complex contextual factors warn that obvious problems may be other than they seem. The popular response suggests that calls for excellence and citizenship training in schools relieve widely held concerns. But if they constitute answers, what are the questions?

The "rising tide of mediocrity" detected in American public

schools by the authors of *A Nation at Risk* occurs pervasively.[1] Commercial television, for example, offers a daily fare of amateur photography, inept directing, bathetic scripts, and undisciplined acting. American automobile manufacturers routinely blame their failures on careless, unmotivated workers, but the cars themselves offer bleak testimony to the power of the profit motive and the effects of untested, shoddy designs. Defined as heightened skill, intelligence, and understanding, excellence is an unusual attainment. One can note its absence in almost all institutions, religious and secular, public and private, commercial and nonprofit. Focusing on schools, advocates of a drive for excellence can easily overlook this ubiquitous mediocrity. To the extent that they do, their efforts will fail to explain educational conditions or to devise effective strategies for improving them.

Like excellence, good citizenship seems to represent an unassailable ideal. Not everyone, however, agrees on the goals that translate excellence from a general aspiration to an agenda of action. One point is clear. Whether the object of reform is an individual, a group, or an institution, excellence can be inspired or elicited but not imposed. It emerges as a function of motivation and commitment to the highest standards of achievement. So it is with good citizenship. Thus, basic questions regarding civic education need to be addressed. What is its purpose? Who determines its content? What agency or institution is responsible for it? What criteria are applied in assessing its results? Answers to these questions have provoked political debate in the United States for two centuries. The lack of closure has resulted in part from conflict among Americans over the notion of citizenship. Political theory aside, the pushes and tugs of American political life have revolved around a tension between idealistic national commitments and pragmatic compromises. Long ago, Americans endorsed both George Washington's promise that a homogeneous citizenry would strengthen "our prospect of permanent union" and Thomas Jefferson's trust in individual liberty.[2] We understood the intent of Benjamin Rush's proclamation that "every man in a Republic is public property" and excused his hyperbole.[3] The tension has remained unresolved. At certain times and in some contexts, unquestioning loyalty to the nation seemed appropriate. More often, the issues were clouded. Since some events and conditions have justified dissent or civil disobedience as an expression of patriotism, does good citizenship require the capacity at least for effective social criticism? Such a question penetrates an apparent consensus to reveal basic complexities in any effort to school future citizens.

Some of us would emphasize civic education as a way to achieve social cohesion, others connect it to the freedom of individuals to speak their minds and seek self-fulfillment, and still others want it somehow to serve both goals. If these were the only options, devising goals and content for civic education would be relatively easy. The choices become more complicated and more fateful, however, because they include the programs of advocates who, in the service of a partisan political agenda, seek to impose their concept of citizenship and their cutural values on others. Constitutional principles and democratic processes, as thoughtful Americans know, are open to various interpretations. What qualifies as civic education to the best-intentioned and most vigilant citizens among us can appear to other well-meaning folk as cultural dominance or even brainwashing. Like Janus, the Roman god of doorways and gates, civic education in a democratic society apparently must face in several directions simultaneously. The simile is apt. In the United States, citizens function as guardians of divergent ideals. This is why civic education is best approached as persistently problematic, a knot to be worked at but not untangled.

Empirical evidence helps to explain the current revival of interest in civic education. Assessments of student achievement in social studies reveal that students are not well informed about governmental roles and functions in the United States.[4] They have trouble identifying their political leaders, describing how federal or state laws are enacted, or recalling major events in American political history. Typically, they lack detailed knowledge of the United States Constitution and cannot recognize once-familiar passages from the Declaration of Independence. As Judith Torney-Purta and her colleagues have found, American students are not alone in their relatively low levels of civic learning.[5] International assessments have reached similar conclusions about students in other countries.

Opinion and attitudinal surveys have gathered equally troubling data on the civic values espoused by students and on their interest in political participation.[6] High school and college students seem to be more committed to personal goals and material rewards than to social concerns. They demonstrate limited understanding of democratic values and admit to feeling unconstrained by the canons governing democratic processes. On the other hand, they are responsive to political slogans and real or imagined threats to national honor.

Such findings raise the spectre of uninformed and disengaged citizens. A more fundamental threat to democracy cannot be imagined, but whether it can be routed or deflected by a pedagogical process is not so clear. Current features of American political life suggest difficulties of another order or at least ills that are not susceptible to educational remedies alone. This chapter discusses three: privatism, elitism, and intellectual fragmentation. Each has stimulated interest in civic education. Each suggests purpose and content for such an enterprise. From somewhat different angles, each sheds light on the public philosophy, the amalgam of common sense and popular mood that animates the current practice of citizenship in the United States.

Privatism

Robert Coles defines *privatism* as "the insistent emphasis on self."[7] Transforming solipsism into a social ethic, it tailors community values to fit individual preferences. There are numerous indications of its growing presence in American life.[8] Evidence suggests that the career choices of youth are being driven increasingly by promises of income and status. Colleges and universities experience privatism in the form of pressure to dismantle general education requirements because students and faculty view them as irrelevant to the acquisition of technical skills. A recent report on the "shopping mall high school" describes the influence of consumerism on the forms and purposes of American secondary education.[9] If young people are drafting their priorities narrowly, adults are equally focused on security, career, and job advancement. In their emphasis on immediate profits, large and small corporations display similar attitudes and behavior. The concepts of public service and responsibility do not appear currently to have a strong claim on the popular imagination.

Coles attributes an almost clinical preoccupation with feelings as an expression of privatism.[10] The popular media, the prevalence of self-help books, and ordinary language reflect a general interest in personal appearance and individual needs. We have become, Coles complains, a people committed to "talk," but we have little interest in listening and seem to be losing the ability to keep silent. We want to "talk out" our problems, describe our diets or our sex lives, clarify our motives, and express our opinions. We buy countless manuals and guides to train ourselves to engage in this "psychological chatter" in more self-satisfying ways. Ironically, privatism is a public affair.

R. Freeman Butts's call for a renewal of civism in the curricula of schools, colleges, and universities seeks to reverse the trend toward privatism.[11] He is particularly concerned about strengthening the civic education of teachers. He traces the current rise of privatism to the 1960s, which he interprets as a time of consensus-shattering protests and single-issue movements. According to Butts, youthful challenges to authority and established values fragmented the American political community. The right to privacy took on corrupted meanings that glorified personal pleasure and isolated the individual within a seamless cloak of self-justification. "Doing one's own thing," at best a cryptic proclamation, served both to defend and define the self. For Butts, privatism is pluralism run amok. Racial and ethnic groups, women and men, and all manner of single-issue advocates sought to advance their own interests without regard to the social impact of their efforts. Individual careerism became a logical, if blatant, manifestation of these centrifugal developments.

Coles agrees with this reading of the rise of privatism.

> Is it making too brash a leap to say that there is a connection between, on the one hand, the insistent emphasis on self... and, on the other hand, the proliferation of single-issue political activity, whereby one gives one's all to what one feels most strongly about, and the devil with any notion of a larger personal, never mind social, responsibility? A long question, but I've heard it reduced all too readily to a terse statement, indeed: I'm in this struggle because it means a lot to me; it's where I'm at.[12]

Connecting privatism to pluralism and, tacitly at least, to political dissent poses several troubling concerns. As a bundle of psychological phenomena, privatism is easily diagnosed. It is the self talking and listening primarily to itself. It is the ideology of self-contained subjectivity, which ultimately exiles the capacity to transcend personal feelings, to explore other territory. It revels in self-aggrandizement and consumerism. Privatism is individuality benumbed by sensitivity training and the insatiable quest for possessions. To answer Coles' question differently, the leap from such abstracted selfhood, the person without a world, to any socially responsive form of political activity is not too brash; it is inconceivable. Privatism is a refutation of citizenship.

That, of course, is one of the points underscored by Butts and Coles. They acknowledge that privatism has social consequences but insist that these public effects tend to be uncivil. Unchecked by such moderating influences as deference to the opinions and well-being of others, ambiguous circumstances, or the likelihood of unexpected and undesirable outcomes, privatism justifies the fanatical pursuit of a social goal that appeals to the acting self. Privatism can also assume social forms of political participation. Collaborative efforts or "movements" enhance its social effects but do not alter its anticitizenship character. Citizenship, in Coles' view, is responsible political behavior, a mode of action in which the desire of individuals or groups to control is in turn balanced by their willingness to be governed.

Privatism as the antithesis of citizenship can be readily detected after the fact. The centrifugal effects of self-centeredness on society tend not to be subtle. In some cases they can also be anticipated. The advocates of educational excellence who openly stress the importance of individual academic achievement intend to weaken the school's socializing capability. On behalf of intellectual rigor, they deny the value of social experiences to students, especially unplanned and extracurricular ones, and they denigrate those kinds of intellectual development that occur most effectively in social settings.[13] Learning about critical thinking or citizenship, for example, is enhanced through interactions with other students. Peer tutoring in any subject results in learning for both students.[14] In place of such cooperative achievement, some proponents of excellence endorse competition for grades and for high scores on standardized achievement tests as useful preparation for professional and economic success. Those who win have proved themselves to be resourceful, self-reliant, and independent. Those who are less successful or who lose also benefit because competition itself is edifying. Taxpayer revolts, which have attracted national attention since the 1970s, can also reflect an explicit affirmation of privatism. In this case, individual earnings rather than academic achievement become the resource to be conserved for personal use. The social value of learning or of paying taxes seems not to be a primary consideration.

Not all single-issue causes end predictably in social disintegration, and not all arise from privatism. Or to make the same point in different terms: Some social disintegration advances social welfare. It has become fashionable to see a connection, perhaps a causal one, between the social reform efforts of the 1960s and the materialistic individualism of the 1980s.[15] Each certainly has had destabilizing effects, and each has challenged accepted notions of the general welfare. Yet, they reflect quite different public philosophies and perpetuate divergent social values.

The effort to end the *de jure* segregation of black people rested on constitutional and humanitarian principles. It intended to change the law of the land and the hearts of people. Admittedly, it sought to enhance the sense of self-worth of black people but not in order to protect some threatened privilege. Against political opposition, social custom, and personal prejudice, the civil rights movement arguably may have changed individual feelings, but it certainly altered the law in extending the benefits and responsibilities of citizenship to an excluded group. In its wake followed waves of similar efforts on behalf of women, American Indians, Spanish-speaking peoples, and descendants of other immigrant groups. The resulting flurry of activity sought equality of opportunity in schools, the workplace, and American political life. To an unprecedented degree, pluralism was advocated as an enriching cultural and national resource.

Other instances of political dissent and advocacy also occurred in the 1960s. Among young people, the most pervasive focused on the war in Vietnam. By the end of the decade, virtually every section of the country had been touched by the antiwar sentiment. It pitted college administrators against students, faculty members against each other, and adults against young people. Before the effort dissipated in the early 1970s, national political leaders and a wide array of citizen groups had joined the debate. At once excessive and poignant, the peace movement spawned a culture of protest that challenged the authority of cherished institutions, including the presidency, organized religion, and the family. During this period, other groups formed to promote the rights of handicapped people, to oppose or support abortion, and to protect the natural environment.

Because of the intensity of these various movements, because they coincided, and because communications technology permitted news of protest activities to be disseminated quickly, widely, and vividly, concern arose about the cohesiveness of American society. Indeed, it seemed to be falling apart with no center powerful enough to balance or moderate the contending forces. Vietnam War protests provoked counterdemonstrations, and groups of white people organized to oppose civil rights for black people. While no group demonstrated against handicapped people, public and private grumbling could be heard about the costs of making buildings and transportation systems "barrier-free" and of "mainstreaming" handicapped children in schools. Extremists surfaced in most of the movements. Especially shocking were the terrorist tactics visited upon civil rights activists, the peace advocates and anti-abortionists who resorted to violence, and those who greeted returning veterans from Vietnam as though they were responsible for a shameful and unnecessary war.

In this era of painful and dramatic dislocations, demonstrations and rhetoric that became undisciplined, fanatical, or uncivil, to use Coles' word, offered evidence of a less honorable motivation at work than a social conscience. Nevertheless, only by distorting the meaning of both terms can political dissent be classified as privatism. The latter, in fact, can be understood as the inability to tolerate the former or to appreciate its positive social significance, except where personal privilege is threatened. More than in the protests themselves, one explanation for the growing strength of privatism can be found in the reactions to political dissent. As the civil rights movement collapsed into conflicts among races and ethnic groups, a fundamental democratic principle suffered in the process: the belief that compromising the rights and responsibilities of an individual or group imperils the liberty of all. Privatism rejects such a commitment, often in defense of a superficial tranquility. More direct explanations of its rise, however, can be identified. Unstable economic conditions in the 1970s, triggered in large measure by inflation-abetting expenditures on the Vietnam War, turned individuals and families inward. Jobs, personal income, pensions, individual aspirations, and other strategies that were designed to bring or to protect financial security became dominant concerns. Assassinations and political scandals, including the threatened impeachment of the President, further undermined the capacity of elected officials and traditional institutions to exert moral authority. From both economic and political fronts, the American people received a similar message: You are on your own.

Civic education can offer help of a limited sort, if the point is to turn private-centeredness inside out. Privatism and dissent are alike in at least one respect. Both can be partially explained as reactions to political and economic realities and to the extent to which these conditions are perceived as malleable. Pedagogical strategies undertaken in lieu of any effort to heal social fragmentation can be expected to treat symptoms only.

Elitism

Elites acquire status and authority through inheritance, sponsorship, individual achievement, or, as some research has shown, sheer luck.[16] Elitism, on the other hand, reinforces economic and political structures and conventions that protect privilege. It fosters a celebration of social alienation and can provide the basis for an organized opposition to distribution systems and policies that reward merit. The issue elitism raises in a democratic society is not whether elites ought to exercise power—they do and will—but whether their influence and leadership can transcend the boundaries of self-interest. The answer to that question has become ever more uncertain. The problem is not merely that the acquisitive tendencies of elites have grown stronger, although given the rise of privatism that is a plausible explanation. In addition, the legal and policy constraints against elitist goals and strategies have weakened. Under the Reagan administration, particularly, antidemocratic tendencies have surfaced across a broad range of domestic policies. Retreats from governmental advocacy of civil rights, consumer interests, and environmental standards can be noted. The notion of "social security" is under attack, not only as it applies to the elderly but also in regard to unemployed workers, single parents, dependent children, and medium to low income farmers. Direct federal aid and tax benefits to corporations and large land-holding farmers have increased dramatically.

Elitism is also evident in the area of education. Research and conventional wisdom agree that educational opportunity and attainment in the United States have tended to vary positively with social and economic status. Reforms begun in the 1960s were attempts to dislodge this correlation as it pertained to minorities and low-income families in urban and rural settings. Head Start and federal efforts begun under the Elementary and Secondary Education Act of 1965 represented vehicles of equal educational opportunity.[17] Aid was targeted for those groups who traditionally had been ill-served by schools. However well intended, the efforts rested on a flawed assumption, namely that inclusive schools could produce more equitable social structures. Actually, the assumption was not so much flawed as untestable in the short run. The reformers and policy makers wanted immediate and quantifiable positive results. They expected to see rising levels of achievement among children from low-income and minority families. What they heard was bad news. The achievement gap between middle- and lower-class students remained. Measured student learning reflected family background.[18] Although the only way to measure the quantitative robustness of that finding was through intergenerational studies of the new programs' effects, the results dampened the reformers' enthusiasm and closed legislative pocketbooks. The turnaround occurred during a short span of less than five years, from 1966 to 1970. The first "graduates" of Head Start programs were still in elementary school when the retreat from equal educational opportunity was sounded.

The systematic testing of students' academic achievement also began during this period. Results over the next decade showed declines across the whole range of school subjects. New reforms proposed a "back to basics" curriculum and "competency testing" of students' cognitive development.[19] In 1983, these efforts coalesced under the "excellence" banner with the publication of *A Nation at Risk*. If Americans must choose between excellence and equity, the argument went, they must opt for the former or risk losing the economic and ideological competition with other countries. Public schools must serve the needs and aspirations of the ablest students. They must set higher standards of achievement, require more work in mathematics and science, and establish longer academic years and longer school days. In short, schools must be tougher.[20]

A group of conservative educators has suggested that one goal of such efforts should be to redefine equity. They oppose investing more heavily in the education of "limited groups of students" than in the education of "healthy children."

> Even if a pupil is doing reasonably well, such competency does not necessarily justify depriving him [or her] of help so that a less successful learner can be given extra help. The "reassignment" in such a case deprives the able pupil of his [or her] opportunity to move from competence to excellence. In addition, the money and resources being thus reallocated do not belong to teachers, pupils, or parents. They are the money and resources of voters and taxpayers. There needs to be some connection between the welfare of these "paying" groups and decisions on school expenditures.[21]

In a few sentences, this statement manages to recast taxpaying from a social and public act to a private one and to distort fundamentally the concept of the public school. Beyond its antidemocratic sentiment lies a misconception of the educational process. To grasp the latter, one has only to imagine a teacher trying to make the proposed "allocation" of time and resources among actual students in a classroom on a given day.

No one who cares about the quality of American education can quarrel with the spirit of a call for excellence. School curricula certainly should be rigorous; standards should be constant and high; and policies and teaching practices should not permit students, even tacitly, to avoid intellectual labor. More to the point, schools should be places that induce learning, and school personnel should be enabled to devise ways to reward their students' academic initiative and success. Given the country's democratic commitments, however, there can be no choice between educational excellence and equality of opportunity. Excellence that is exclusionary by design promises only to exacerbate social fragmentation and to set the stage for subsequent explosions of undisciplined pluralism. To be effective, strategies to achieve educational excellence must be responsive to the variety of interests, aspirations, learning styles, and capabilities represented among the American people. Attending to this diversity pedagogically would make excellence a meaningful goal and a unifying principle. On the other hand, an excellence agenda that values labeling and sorting students more highly than educating them, not only misses its mark, it damages young people and puts the nation at risk. Fundamentally antidemocratic, it also reduces the ideal of civic education to a sham and a delusion. Educational and democratic principles aside, there are neither economic nor pedagogical reasons for forcing a choice between excellence and the deliberate attempt to be equally concerned about the educational advancement of all students. In fact, successful schools can be identified across the country that have effectively merged excellence and equity.[22]

The threat of elitism becomes especially clear when one tries to match the proposed curriculum reforms with job-market data. The message from several state legislatures and governors and from countless national reports is clear. To secure their own and the country's economic future, students need to know more mathematics and science. They must be familiar with computers and possess "higher order thinking skills." As educational goals, these would be foolish to reject. As preparation for employment for the majority of students, they are at best misleading. Job-market projections indicate that a dramatic growth in the number of "high-tech" positions will occur, but they reveal as well that for most Americans employment opportunities will be found increasingly in the service industries, which require little preparation in advanced skills.[23] Higher-paying specialized positions will not be prevalent. In light of these data, if the great majority of American young people complete the "more rigorous" high school curriculum, they will find themselves mistrained for the available jobs. More likely, they will simply drop out of high school in growing numbers as they come to understand economic realities. In either case, prospects for domestic health and tranquility are not bright—an increasingly bimodal workforce, sharply divided by status, income, job satisfaction, and probably race.

This depressing scenario does not lie in the distant future. As a recent survey of employers of high school graduates suggests, it is a present reality. Robert L. Crain sought to identify the traits of high school graduates considered extremely important by company personnel responsible for hiring them.[24] The national survey of over

4000 employers found that none of the reforms proposed in *A Nation at Risk* ranked high. Good grades, graduation from a quality school, mathematical background, or critical thinking skills were not thought to be especially important. Rather, employers wanted dependable employees who would come to work regularly and on time, accept supervision, display other "proper attitudes," and work well with people. Reading skill at the level of difficulty offered in a daily newspaper and the ability to use basic arithmetic completed the employers' list of preferred traits. As Crain notes, these findings conflict sharply with the criticisms of public schools emanating from the business community. They also confirm suspicions about the elitist intents of the excellence movement.

As a democratic society, the United States does not assign jobs, status, or income to its citizens, but it can attempt to equalize access to these opportunities. To the extent that it is successful, it provides a unifying center of policy and principle for its diverse population. In the short run, schools likewise have no role in the assignment of social class status. Students attend school in the shadow of their parents. Over time, aggregate data show, years of schooling explain some of the gross differences in job status and income among white male age cohorts. Reflecting job-market inequities, the relation of educational attainment to economic benefit for women and racial minorities has been weaker. Crain's findings warn that education's contribution to status and income could become increasingly problematic. Although inclusive schools cannot produce an inclusive society, his data suggest that schools can promise at least limited economic rewards if they function as inclusive educational institutions and if, in doing so, they can be prevented from simply mirroring present market conditions in their curricula and expectations. Unless their task is merely to reproduce and reinforce existing social class patterns, public schools must find ways to challenge and stretch all students intellectually.

Such an educational mission provides a rationale for civic education. One could argue that the form and substance of inclusive schools demonstrate civic education in a democratic society. Since their aim is the opposite of elitism, their mission needs to be informed openly and directly by what Henry Giroux calls "the principles of critical literacy and civic courage."[25] The specific task of civic education in schools is to apply these principles across the curriculum in order to prepare all students for effective democratic participation.

Elitists are likely to oppose any such effort. They can see that politically literate and courageous citizens promise them no benefit and considerable aggravation. Even without opposition, civic education of this quality will be difficult to realize. It requires a combination of intellectual resources currently scattered among disparate disciplines and academic enclaves.

Intellectual Fragmentation

A civic education that intends to prepare students for effective participation in a democratic society occurs throughout a curriculum. It is not assigned exclusively to particular courses or teachers. To be sure, students can acquire knowledge about systems and institutions of government that has been organized as a course. This is the traditional mode in which civic education is offered in elementary and secondary schools.[26] But, students' understanding and appreciation of democratic values and processes are strongly influenced by the teaching methods and classroom procedures they encounter in all their courses. Some evidence suggests that students become more interested in political participation as a result of teaching methods that solicit their opinions and require them to analyze content in class discussions.[27] These findings are not limited to civics courses.

What students more typically encounter in school is not a curriculum but a collection of courses.[28] That they satisfy core requirements in particular subject areas does not alter this essential character of school learning. Students must earn credits in English, mathematics, science, and social studies, for example, but rarely is there any attempt to integrate these requirements. For younger students, the unifying element may be a teacher who is responsible for most subject areas. For older students, even that influence is absent and fragmented learning is reinforced by a faculty of specialists who lack the time or inclination for the collaborative curriculum planning necessary to demonstrate connections among seemingly disparate courses and subjects.

The reforms currently proposed as part of the excellence agenda reflect intellectual fragmentation and seek to strengthen its influence on schools. The divisions cut in two directions. Content is isolated within broad subject areas. In addition, teaching method is separated from considerations about content and consigned to a subordinate role, thus implying pejorative distinctions between cognitive development and knowledge of the ways learning is acquired. The proposals also suggest a hierarchy of subjects, with mathematics and science raised to preeminent positions. The current advice to prospective secondary school teachers is to become content specialists, but they are warned that specializations in mathematics and science may earn them higher salaries because such skills are in greater demand than teaching expertise in, say, history or literature. The advice is commonsensical and shortsighted. The warning is an assault on teacher morale and collegiality. Granted, teachers must "know something," but how they teach also directly affects student learning. Effective teachers are not merely content specialists. They require expertise in learning theory, pedagogy, evaluation, and the social and cultural influences on student ability and motivation.[29] In short, they must be prepared to organize and present content for particular students. Furthermore, if their expertise pertains only to specialized knowledge in a particular subject, they will be ill-equipped to help students acquire a broad sense of education or draw resources from several subjects in analyzing nonacademic, i.e., real, problems. The ability to do the latter, of course, is the ultimate achievement of an educated person, or citizen.

The compartmentalization of school learning within subjects mirrors the intellectual fragmentation of higher education.[30] The arts and sciences disciplines consist of fields and subfields of study characterized by esoteric languages and research methodologies. The emphasis on research and publication has accelerated the trend toward specialization. As a result, universities have difficulty organizing a curriculum of liberal education. With academic departments and faculty groups competing for student enrollments, the general studies requirement found on most campuses resembles a peace pact among warring factions more than a defensible program of core courses.[31] Scholarly and curricular collaboration across departments is difficult enough, but advancing specialization has also divided departments internally. If members of a history, English, or physics department cannot communicate with each other and have little interest in listening to colleagues with different scholarly foci, they are not well prepared to develop core courses on behalf of their respective departments.

The effects of intellectual fragmentation on the world of scholarship have been noted in the decline of narrative history, the rise of empirical case-study research throughout the social sciences, and the virtual disappearance of systematic philosophy and theology.[32] Large-scale theoretical work in the humanities or in the sciences is rarely seen. Scholarly undertakings that cut across specialized fields require not only academic preparation that is at once broad and deep, they also evoke an element of selflessness. They require that scholars individually or as collaborators forgo the security of narrow expertise and the rewards of specialized reputations.

Recent developments in the field of history illustrate the new directions in policy and curriculum that are needed to address intellectual fragmentation. Over the past two or three decades, historians have produced new knowledge, tapped fresh documentary and statistical sources, and adapted social science methods and techniques for use in historical inquiry.[33] The results in the field of United States history alone have been striking. We now have detailed knowledge about the lives and contributions of racial minorities, women, and other previously unrecognized participants in the American past. Regional and urban studies have made possible a richly textured understanding of the nation's history. These achievements, which can be attributed principally to sharply focused research, have rendered untenable the unidimensional narrative that once passed as American history. There are those who mourn this loss and who seek to recover the familiar account, but, as Thomas Bender advises, the conceptual and methodological challenges posed by the splintering of American history permit no simple or single response. Fragmentation in history, he observes, "is a phenomenon that may represent a disintegration of the civic sense as much as purely intellectual trends in historiography."[34] U.S. Secretary of Education William J. Bennett has argued that United States history should provide "a story that applies to us all."[35] For purposes of civic education in particular, he insists, we need a common history again. The difficult task, however, is to conceptualize themes for such a synthesis that capture what we now know about our country's variegated past. The cure for historical fragmentation is not to be found in a consensus narrative formulated in a previous, presumably ideal, era. That story no longer holds power for a very good reason. It is not true enough.

Intellectual fragmentation, Bender seems to be suggesting, is the academic equivalent of privatism. It has two powerfully negative effects on civic education. First, collaborative planning of curriculum by faculty is rendered difficult because their individual expertise moves on vertical continua. They are unlikely to know how to talk with each other. Their preparation has not equipped them for professional collaboration, and the monetary and status reward systems of their institutions provide them at best with weak incentives for doing so. These conditions prevail in higher education and are only slightly less dominant in secondary schools. At both levels, civic education can be expected to be classified as merely another specialization. As such, it can contribute to students' cognitive development, but cognitive development alone leaves to chance their understanding and appreciation of democratic values and processes and their interest in political participation.

Second, and more fundamentally, intellectual fragmentation

depletes the resources needed for conceptualizing the goals and assessing the results of civic education. The problem is fundamental because civic education in a democratic context requires hard intellectual labor. Myriad interests and issues must be considered: pluralism and union, dissent and loyalty, individuality and commonality, freedom and responsibility. These are dynamic principles of citizenship to be applied in particular, changing circumstances. They are not fixed categories or static dichotomies. Beyond matters of content lies the difficult work of formulating pedagogical strategies that reflect democratic values and processes. The final challenge comes in efforts to evaluate the results of civic education. No standardized test is equal to the task, because the aim of civic education exceeds quantifiable academic achievement, important as that may be in preparing informed citizens. The aim is to enable young Americans to perform their public roles with understanding and courage. These several tasks require both the wide range of resources available in the various disciplines and also the moral authority marshalled through a shared commitment to inquiry and the advancement of human understanding. For the present, no such unified vision is available to guide civic education. The danger this poses within a democratic society is that the notion of citizenship will be so simplified or distorted that it cannot withstand the corrosive effects of privatism and elitism.

Marie Wirsing insists that none of these current trends is new. She traces privatism to the prenational period of American history and adds that it "forms the heart of the free enterprise system itself."[36] She finds elitism, too, has been ever present, arguing that throughout the country's history it has sought to supplant the diversity of interests protected by representative democracy with consensus values reflecting established distribution of political and economic power. Although intellectual fragmentation may be a recent phenomenon, she sees hints of it in the long-standing susceptibility of American intellectuals to the attractions of privatism and elitism and in the recurring attempts by scholars "to tell us what our national purposes are."[37]

Wirsing helps us understand the extent to which privatism and elitism are embedded in American history. She also locates their common origin in economic self-interest. From there they develop in different directions, at least in a democratic society. Unrestrained, privatism moves towards materialistic anarchy, whereas elitism can flourish only in the context of a contented majority. Neither can withstand a civic education that promotes critical intelligence and political courage if it is accompanied by economic and political reform. A civic education of this sort encompasses studies of American government, including constitutional principles and political institutions, and it organizes opportunities throughout the curriculum for students to experience democratic participation. It prepares citizens for their individual roles in affirming and enriching democratic community. It gives meaning to the tradition of informed consent, which guides voting behavior; protection of individual freedoms; commitment to public responsibility; and the other forms of political action needed to sustain a democratic society such as ours. In these ways, and in the present period especially, civic education can combat the fragmenting effects of privatism, and it can dispel the passivity encouraged by elitism. Civic education programs can also induce the collaborative curriculum planning among teachers and faculties and the education policy reform that are needed to overcome intellectual fragmentation.

This chapter includes references to the growing body of empirical research on effective civic education in a democratic society. These findings, however, cannot determine the purpose of such an enterprise. This more fundamental assignment entails continuing conceptual work. Civic education occurs in an uncivil world. If we mean it to serve individual self-interest, we strengthen the lure of privatism at the expense of building democratic community. On the other hand, if a renewed emphasis on civic education masks a desire to promote conformity, or even a mild docility, it represents a retreat from historic democratic commitments and a preference for the disenfranchising effects of elitism. In some historical periods, civic education is not necessarily the solution if the perceived problem is a disintegrating polity. The latter may not be pathological; it may rather signal an awakening public conscience. But, if the question concerns a disempowered or somnolent citizenry, civic education may indeed provide a partial answer.

Notes

[1] National Commission on Excellence in Education, *A Nation at Risk: The Imperative for Educational Reform* (Washington, D.C.: U.S. Department of Education, 1983).

[2] James D. Richardson, ed., *A Compilation of the Messages and Papers of the Presidents: 1789-1908*, Vol. 1 (Washington, D.C.: Bureau of National Literature and Art, 1908), 202 and 409.

[3] See Benjamin Rush, "Of the Mode of Education Proper in a Republic," in Dagobert D. Runes, ed., *The Selected Writings of Benjamin Rush* (New York: Philosophical Library, 1947).

[4] Judith V. Torney, A.N. Oppenheim, and Russell F. Farnen, *Civic Education in Ten Countries: An Empirical Study* (New York: John Wiley and Sons, 1975).

[5] Torney, Oppenheim, and Farnen; see also, Marshall William Conley and Kenneth Osborne, "Political Education in Canadian Schools: An Assessment of Social Studies and Political Science Courses and Pedagogy," *International Journal of Political Education* 6, 1 (April 1983): 65-85; and Joseph P. Farrell, "The IEA Studies: Factors That Affect Achievement in Six Subjects in Twenty-One Countries," *Teachers College Record* 79, 2 (December 1977): 289-297.

[6] William B. Fetters, George H. Brown, and Jeffrey A. Owings, *High School Seniors: A Comparative Study of the Classes of 1972 and 1980* (Washington, D.C.: Government Printing Office, 1984). Also, Arthur Levine, *When Dreams and Heroes Died: A Portrait of Today's College Student* (San Francisco: Jossey-Bass, 1980).

[7] Robert Coles, "Civility and Psychology," *Daedalus* 109, 3 (Summer 1980): 140.

[8] Dean R. Hoge and Teresa L. Ankney, "Occupations and Attitudes of Former Student Activists Ten Years Later," *Journal of Youth and Adolescence* 11, 5 (October 1982): 355-371; Leon McKenzie, "Adult Life Goals and Program Planning," *Lifelong Learning* 7, 3 (November 1983): 20-23; and Donald B. Holsinger and David W. Chapman, "Students' Occupational Aspirations and Choice of College Type," *College Student Journal* 18, 1 (Spring 1984): 87-93.

[9] See Arthur G. Powell, Eleanor Farrar, and David K. Cohen, *The Shopping Mall High School* (Boston: Houghton-Mifflin, 1985).

[10] Coles, 131-141.

[11] R. Freeman Butts, *Teacher Education and the Revival of Civic Learning* (Minneapolis: Society of Professors of Education, 1982); also R. Freeman Butts, *The Revival of Civic Learning: A Rationale for Citizenship Education in American Schools* (Bloomington, Ind.: Phi Delta Kappa Foundation, 1980).

[12] Coles, 140.

[13] Linda Darling-Hammond, *Beyond the Commission Reports: The Coming Crisis in Teaching* (Santa Monica, Cal.: The Rand Corporation, July 1984); Diane Hedin, "The Impact of Experience on Academic Learning," IRE Report #9 (Boston: Institute for Responsive Education, 1984); Linda M. McNeil, "Teacher Culture and the Irony of School Reform," in Philip G. Altbach, Gail P. Kelly, and Lois Weis, eds., *Excellence in*

Education: Perspectives on Policy and Practice (Buffalo, New York: Prometheus Books, 1985), 183-202.

[14] Questions about the efficacy of peer tutoring in higher education, at least in a European setting, are posed in Maurice L. deVolder, William S. deGrave, and Wim Gijselaers, "Peer Teaching: Academic Achievement of Teacher-Led Versus Student-Led Discussion Groups," *Higher Education* 14, 6 (December 1985): 643-650.

[15] In their refined analyses, Butts and Coles avoid simplistic notions of historical causality, but see Diane Ravitch, "Forgetting the Questions: The Problem of Educational Reform," *The American Scholar* 50 (Summer 1984): 329-340.

[16] Christopher Jencks et al., *Inequality: A Reassessment of the Effect of Family and Schooling in America* (New York: Basic Books, 1972), 3-15.

[17] For a review of these reform initiatives, see Robert L. Church and Michael W. Sedlak, *Education in the United States: An Interpretive History* (New York: The Free Press, 1976), 431-473.

[18] The most influential study was James S. Coleman et al., *Equality of Educational Opportunity* (Washington, D.C.: Government Printing Office, 1966); but see also, Alice M. Rivlin, "Forensic Social Science," *Harvard Educational Review* 43, 1 (February 1973): 61-75.

[19] See Walt Haney and George F. Madaus, "Making Sense of the Competency Testing Movement," *Harvard Educational Review* 48, 4 (November 1978): 462-484.

[20] See Business-Higher Education Forum, *America's Competitive Challenge: The Need for a National Response* (Washington, D.C.: The Business-Higher Education Forum, 1983).

[21] Quoted in *Education Week*, 5 September 1984, 12.

[22] Larry K. Brendtro and Arlin E. Ness, *Re-educating Troubled Youth: Environments for Teaching and Treatments* (New York: Aldina Press, 1983); and Joan Lipsitz, *Successful Schools for Young Adolescents* (New Brunswick, N.J.: Transaction, 1983).

[23] See the analysis by Henry A. Giroux, "Public Philosophy and the Crisis in Education," *Harvard Educational Review* 54, 2 (May 1984): 186-194. Also, W. Norton Grubb, "The Bandwagon Once More: Vocational Preparation for High-Tech Occupations," *Harvard Educational Review* 54, 4 (November 1984): 429-451.

[24] Robert L. Crain, "The Quality of American High School Graduates: What Personnel Officers Say and Do About It," Report

Number 354, Center for Social Organization of Schools (Baltimore, Md.: The Johns Hopkins University, 1984).

[25] Giroux, 193.

[26] The tradition is longstanding. See Howard E. Wilson, *Education for Citizenship: Report of the Regents' Inquiry* (New York: McGraw-Hill, 1938).

[27] Judith Torney-Purta, "Psychological Perspectives on Enhancing Civic Education Through the Education of Teachers," *Journal of Teacher Education* 34, 6 (November-December 1983): 30-34.

[28] See Ernest L. Boyer, *High School: A Report on Secondary Education in America* (New York: Harper and Row, 1983); John I. Goodlad, *A Place Called School: Prospects for the Future* (New York: McGraw-Hill, 1984); and Theodore R. Sizer, *Horace's Compromise: The Dilemma of the American High School* (Boston: Houghton-Mifflin, 1984).

[29] David C. Berliner, "Laboratory Settings and the Study of Teacher Education," *Journal of Teacher Education* 36, 6 (November-December 1985): 2-8.

[30] Mervyn L. Cadwallader, "Destruction of the College and the Collapse of General Education," *Teachers College Record* 84, 4 (Summer 1983): 909-916; Tom Meisenhelder, "Ideology of Professionalism in Higher Education," *Journal of Education* 165, 3 (Summer 1983): 295-307; and George J. Papagiannis, Steven J. Klees, and Robert N. Bickel, "Toward a Political Economy of Educational Innovation," *Review of Educational Research* 52, 2 (Summer 1982): 245-290.

[31] Two recent studies provide analysis of curriculum and policy issues in American higher education: Frank Newman, *Higher Education and the American Resurgence* (Princeton, N.J.: Princeton University Press, 1985), a report by the Carnegie Foundation for the Advancement of Education; and Study Group on the Conditions of Excellence in American Higher Education, *Involvement in Learning: Realizing the Potential of American Higher Education* (Washington, D.C.: U.S. Department of Education, 1984).

[32] For the impact on history, see Bernard Bailyn, "The Challenge of Modern Historiography," *American Historical Review* 87, 1 (February 1982): 1-25.

[33] Thomas Bender, "Making History Whole Again," *The New York Times Book Review*, 6 October 1985, 1 and 42-43.

[34] Bender, 1.

[35] Quoted in *Education Week*, 5 September 1984, 10.

[36] Marie E. Wirsing, "The Revival of Civic Learning: A Critique," *Journal of Teacher Education* 34, 6 (November-December 1983): 62.
[37] Wirsing, 64.

Chapter Three

Democracy is now widely understood as a mechanism for legitimating a leadership elite and citizenship is understood as the obligation to support the state by acting on proscribed and granted rights.

3

Education and Democratic Citizenship: Toward a New Public Philosophy

By James M. Giarelli

UNDERLYING all debates, historical and contemporary, about the purposes of schooling, the content of the curriculum, and the preparation of teachers, lies an essential truism about the nature of education and its relationship to social life. Education is the primary means for the conversation, creation, and criticism of culture. Thus, as a society decides on how it will educate its members, it is undertaking to define its own future. Saying this, however, makes it clear that education is always intensely and significantly political, for it is about the forming and re-forming of our public, our community, our polis. It is a sign of the times, perhaps, that calling something "political" gives it a bad name, connoting power grabs, manipulation, and trickery. By calling education inherently political, however, I mean simply that it concerns all the people in their capacity as citizens and members of a civic community. In this view, education is the preeminent public concern, it is the people's business.

However, in recent years, a serious and sustained consideration of the civic purposes of education has been neglected. The National Commission on Excellence's report, *A Nation at Risk*, serves as a telling illustration of this tendency among the latest spate of educational criticisms and calls for reform.[1] In this report, the purposes, needs, and vocabulary of a civic community are replaced by those of a commercial and corporate culture. With culture thus redefined, the task of education becomes one of providing individuals with marketable capacities and skills in order to insure the preeminence of American capitalism in international competition. There is a powerful political intent here, to be sure, but except for occasional slogans and platitudes, the report is silent on the notion of education preparing intelligent and humane citizens for public life in a democracy.

This neglect of the civic purposes of education has not been confined only to reports from special commissions. The twentieth century has seen an ever-increasing tendency toward specialization among educational scholars as well. One result has been a de-emphasis on the formulation of theories of education that analyze schooling as a normative and historical agency of social reproduction and renewal. A recent National Society for the Study of Education *Yearbook*, for example, suggests that the main development in philosophy of education since midcentury has been the shift from a public to a specialized professional orientation.[2] The public philosopher who saw educational problems as reflections of tensions originating in the cultural practices of an evolving historical tradition, who used the resources of cultural understanding synthetically to situate these problems, and who sought to develop a vision of what the good life is and ought to be, is all but *passé*. To be "deeply concerned and thoughtfully reflective about fundamental aspects of educating in our time" is no longer enough, nor a requirement, to be accepted as a professional philosopher of education.[3] Professional philosophers of education, in contrast, are trained in the techniques of philosophical analysis and logic, working on problems arising from the scholarly literature, and aiming at the piecemeal elucidation and clarification of linguistic and logical ambiguities. Philosophy of education, as a professional discipline, has largely given up the subjects and tasks of a public philosophy. There have been recent efforts to write and think publicly and philosophically about education—two of which I will treat later in this essay—but they are sketchy and inadequate.

As both educators and citizens, then, the need for critical and rigorous thinking about the civic purposes of education is evident. In this essay I will explore and critique what I consider to be the dominant twentieth century models of citizenship and citizenship education. My vehicle will be the idea of a public philosophy. Although there are several different conceptions of what a public philosophy is, some of which I will discuss, William Sullivan's description serves as a worthwhile beginning. In his view, a public philosophy is a system of beliefs and communicative practices through which a society can develop and maintain a widely shared sense of political meaning and direction.

> A public philosophy could provide expression for the meaning and worth of the political commitments embodied in republican institutions and mores. . . . It is a tradition of interpreting and delineating the common understandings of what the political association is about and what it aims to achieve.[4]

In a democratic society in which common projects are taken to be achievements of an active and enlightened citizenry, "a public philosophy is both a cause and an effect of awakened discussion of those things most important and at issue in the life of the nation."[5] To serve as the basis for public debate and conversation, a public philosophy cannot be reduced to slogans or formulaic theory, but rather must be rooted in the concrete problematics of daily social life. A public philosophy gives expression to the moral understandings and political skills required to be a member of many diverse communities. A public philosophy in this sense embodies a conception of citizenship and can provide a foundation for a model of citizenship education.

The need to reconstruct a public philosophy is an especially urgent contemporary task. My argument will be that the history of twentieth century social, political, and philosophical thought has been one of flight from, and assault on, the idea of a public philosophy. One consequence of this development has been an eclipse of any meaningful notions of the public and the citizen, or any basis for understanding education as an arena for the reconstruction of social experience for the purpose of enabling and liberating imaginative communal action. As a result, we have been left with a "new public philosophy" in which ethics has become economics, democracy has become decision making, and politics has become public administration.[6] This ideology cannot support a substantive commitment to education for democratic citizenship.

In the remainder of this essay, I will provide a brief historical account of public philosophies in the history of educational thought, critique the "new" public philosophy for its antidemocratic and anti-educational implications, and critically assess some recent efforts to develop a public philosophy of education. Finally, I will discuss some of the theoretical foundations for the development of a democratic public philosophy and their implications for citizenship, education, and the preparation of teachers.

Public Philosophies in Educational Thought

Despite what professional philosophers have said, those interested in believing that education has something fundamental to do with the cultivation of a state of mind and set of social practices that speak to the possibilities of a better society and way of life for humankind can take some solace in knowing that the "classics" in the history of educational thought always have been public philosophies of education. Thus, Plato's arguments against democracy were part of an effort to provide a legitimation for a kind of social life in which individuals could find a meaningful place in just a polis.[7] For Plato, democracy—in its radical sense of direct rule by the many—violates the fundamental principle of justice by treating unequals equally. As we know, Plato believed humans fell into categories of competence and nature, therefore, for one to be able to do what one could do *excellently*, one had to do that for which one was best suited and not all were suited to govern. For Plato, democracy accorded equal freedoms and rights to all desires and thus equated the "higher" desires for reason and truth with the "lower" desires of the appetites and senses. Democracy, in his view, led to hedonism, a focus on the pleasures of the moment, instability, reckless change, and, most importantly, disharmony. While modern democratic theorists reject Plato's crude divisions of classes according to fixed natures and question harmony and stability as absolute ends of social life, we can see that in a number of important respects, his scheme is reproduced under a veneer of modern social science in many contemporary liberal notions of equality of opportunity.[8] And, while many, including notably his pupil Aristotle, reject Plato's idealistic derivations of public principles, we should recognize the enduring nature of the problem of finding some means for expressing and justifying a sense of shared life.

Where Plato was responding to the instability of the life around him, Rousseau responded to the decadence and stifling artificiality and uniformity of eighteenth-century European social conventions.[9] For Rousseau, democracy required a healing education which would return man to his original nature and restore his self-reliance. Men would then give up their dependence on institutions which had, under the guise of protection, ruled by taking away individual freedom and control.[10] Emile's education is the cultivation of the democratic personality. Rousseau tried to show that an "ordinary boy," Emile, could be the moral and intellectual equal of Plato's philosopher-king, thus giving evidence for the possibility of democracy.

Closer to home, and perhaps our most relevant beginning for a discussion of the development of a public philosophy of education, is John Dewey.[11] Like all enduring thinkers, Dewey rejected the given categories of his age and sought a reconstruction of meanings rooted in social experience. For Dewey, philosophy was a civic enterprise, the discipline that teaches the community how to govern itself, and in this sense he saw philosophy as educative. For Dewey, the problems of life were not found in the abstract dichotomies of individual vs. society, public vs. private, or citizen vs. person, but rather in the nature of the interactions in which these terms represent phases in a continuum of experience. For Dewey, a democratic public philosophy had as its center an educational theory, where an educational theory expressed the possibilities for meaning and action in the social continuity of life. Dewey spoke of democracy, then, not as a form of government, but rather as a way of life, a fundamental attitude toward nature and our fellows marked by generous and nondeferential relations. The cultivation of this attitude required the democratization of education, its processes, aims, and methods. Thus, Dewey's educational prescriptions all centered on social means based on the ideas of interaction, cooperation, and communication. He advocated a curriculum derived from lived social concerns that would give people more power over their experiences now and in the future, and he favored the use of qualitative evaluation standards based on communal purposes in the creation of social and educational policy. In short, democracy for Dewey was a way of life, a public philosophy.

We can call Dewey's view of democracy *developmental democracy*.[12] He argued that the case for democracy was that it alone among possible social and public arrangements allows for the fullest development of individual personality. In a democracy, the values of individuality and community are synthesized, each enabling the fullest extension of the other. Human beings are thought of not as

consumers and appropriators of culture and nature, but rather as
creators and developers. The good society is one which permits and
encourages thoughtful and creative participation. Citizenship entails
both the right to share equally in the *distribution* of public goods and
benefits and the right, and indeed the obligation, to participate in the
production and valuation of what is to be counted as the public good.
Education for democratic citizenship demands democratic educational environments in and outside of school. Democracy is an
educative arrangement, more important for what it does *to* us than
for us.

Dewey's failure to challenge seriously the social relations of a
changing capitalist system by developing a sophisticated analysis of
class relations and historically conditioned inequalities resulted in
serious problems in developing the theoretical and practical bearings
of his social theory.[13] The momentum of capitalist social and productive relations toward fragmentation, isolation at the interpersonal
level, and monopolization and corporatism at the economic and
political levels thwarts the kind of reciprocal interactions of sharing
and communication which enable self- and social development.
Dewey was not sanguine about the existing state of democracy, but
his "method of cooperative intelligence" proved less influential in
guiding social and institutional policy than he had hoped. Its acceptance had little chance in a social structure which systematically
narrowed the possibilities for imaginative expression to personal,
rather than public, arenas. Thus, it was not Dewey's developmental
democracy, but rather the theory of democratic elitism which
emerged as the public philosophy which best accommodated the
political, social, and educational needs of the emerging corporate
capitalist state.

We can find the roots of democratic elitism in Walter Lippmann's
writings, especially in *Essays in the Public Philosophy*. For Lippmann, a public philosopy was "the legal and moral basis, or principle, on which the power of the political class rests."[14] A public
philosophy provides the principles and criteria by which the decisions of government are guided and justified. Lippmann's own
attempts to find these principles in natural law and the Bill of Rights
were important to the development of the dominant "new" public
philosophy. However, more important, because more basic, was the
shift from a democratic public philosophy as a way of life—an
educative arrangement, a vision of the polis as paideia—to a set of
principles for guiding and justifying governmental actions. The idea
of a public as a social group living in and through an ethos of shared
meanings, and of a citizen as a producer and developer of these

meanings, gave way to an abstract procedure for legitimating public decisions through private means. That is, democratic elitism as a public philosophy justifies power and settles questions of public authority by parceling out public authority to private parties. It solves the problem of public authority be defining it away. Although the substantive foundations of the theory of democratic elitism have changed since Lippmann, its basic structure and assumptions remain and set the problems for contemporary politics and civic education. Once democracy is made into a mechanism controlled by elites to insure the smooth functioning of existing institutions, democracy's radical moment, its capacity to educate for citizenship, is vitiated and the public awaits only the articulation of the interests of the next new hegemonic class to give substance to democracy's lifeless form. Thus, whether Plato, Rousseau, or Dewey were right or wrong, it is important to understand how democratic elitism, as a "new" public philosophy, is radical in its silence on the problems, such as citizenship, with which the older public philosophies had to deal.

This new public philosophy has been the working model for modern political and social science. Indeed, we might say it allowed the development of these disciplines. Whether we call it interest-group liberalism, democratic or pluralist elitism, or equilibrium democracy, its foundational principles are the same. It assumes that society is composed of individuals of competing interests, thus, there is a need for mechanisms of negotiation, and it assigns to an elite of "leaders" the ability and right to adjudicate among these interests and thus govern. Democracy in this view is a method for choosing and authorizing governments and not a way of determining a state's moral ends. That determination is the province of governing elites. Democracy thus becomes a way to choose between competing elites. Citizens do not decide on issues and elect people who will act with them, rather they choose on the personal and persuasional attributes of people who will decide for them. Thus, democracy becomes a mechanism to register the desires of people as they are, not to contribute to what they might be or might wish to be. Freedom, then, defines, within certain circumscribed limits, what we already have, not the power to become something other than what we are. In this model, democracy has no intentional educational content. It is important for what it does for us, rather than to us. In short, for the democratic elitists, democracy is a market mechanism with citizens as consumers, politicians as entrepreneurs, and voting as the purchase of products.

Education for this kind of democratic citizenship is obviously much different than for Dewey's developmental democracy. The most important requirement for this kind of life is to be adept at market relations, and education serves to create consumers and separate out elites. As portrayed in *A Nation at Risk*, the modern world is a global village marked by a competition for the domination of the markets in products and ideas. The new material of international commerce is knowledge, learning, information, and skilled intelligence. Learning is an "investment required for success" in this new age, and the purpose of educational reform is to develop and channel the raw material of intelligence in such a way that the nation can remain competitive in world markets and thereby benefit all of its citizens.[15] To prepare citizens for a society guided by this type of public philosophy, educational institutions typically focus on curricula that can foster a consumer culture. The emphasis is on training in instrumental interpersonal relations and adaptation to market norms, the accumulation of products, development of a limited range of technical decision-making skills, lowering of expectations for participation in public life, and a cultivation of the personal.

This new public philosophy is grounded in the language and assumptions of positivistic and economistic thought and, as such, it cannot nurture a civic ethic. It consequently narrows the meaning of *public* education. Instead of a public philosophy which connects the personal and political themes coursing through lived social experience, we get a depoliticized and mathematized language which masks power by presenting what are essentially public moral and political choices in the form of private economic choices. As Sheldon Wolin writes of the implications of this development:

> If, as philosophy has taught us, the limits of our language are the limits of our world, and if, as the linguists say, language sets limits to what we can think, then the change in public discourse implies that some of the things the old language was suited to express and emphasize are being lost or downgraded by a new public vocabulary, while some things which may have been devalued by the old vocabulary, or discreetly veiled, are being exalted.[16]

Restricted to the assumptions and vocabulary of a new public philosophy, we find ourselves unable to talk and teach sensibly about our shared lives.

For example, the term *public* in public education has at least three referents. The first and most obvious is to the group being educated, the constituency. The more important referents are to the methods or processes by which cultural capital and knowledge claims are justified and transmitted, and to the aims of the enterprise. That is, public education does not refer merely to a kind of education that serves a public. Rather, it expresses the idea of something to be formed—a public—through communicative practices in which all can participate. The new public philosophy gives up on the idea of public education as an intentional agency popularly controlled and directed for the purpose of forming the states of mind and social practices necessary for living in a voluntary social association. It gives up on the task of promoting common sense, literally, the sense needed to live in common.

The new public philosophy, whether expressed in "liberal" Lester Thurow's idea of a "zero-sum" society or in conservative Reaganomics' cost-benefit analyses of everything from school lunches to nuclear war, devolves into a Hobbesian conception of society in which "the Good" becomes "the goods" and we struggle against each other, either individually or in our interest groups, for a maximization of means. In this view, as Wolin explains, there are "only winners and losers; there is no basis for common action, only threat, inducement, or corruption. When the economy becomes the polity, *citizen* and *community* become subversive words in the vocabulary of the new political philosophy."[17]

Given this analysis of the contemporary crisis in public authority and the failures of the dominant public philosophy, from what possible models of citizenship and civic education have we to draw? Before turning to some suggestions for reconstituting a public philosophy in a way which will make the ideas of citizenship and civic education more accessible for democratic social practice, I will discuss briefly two recent attempts to look publicly and philosophically at education, Eva Brann's *Paradoxes of Education in a Republic* and Harry S. Broudy's *Truth and Credibility: The Citizen's Dilemma*.[18]

Brann's argument is that an intelligent understanding of the role education plays in the conservation and criticism of a republican culture requires analysis of the intellectual paradoxes inherent in the founding documents. She is led, then, to an examination of the writings of the founding fathers as expressed in such documents as the Constitution and the Declaration of Independence. She finds perennial tensions in these writings, grouped around the ideas of utility, tradition, and rationality. Confining herself to the classical texts, she considers the dilemmas suggested by each ideal and presents a logical but decontextualized intellectual resolution.

The weakness of Brann's analysis derives from the way she formulates her problematic. She tells us that in thinking about education we must avoid all problems having to do with society. "The social construction of educational problems, at least, is usually a futile misconstruction."[19] As she sees it, the problem confronting educators is that schools have failed to transmit the best of Western cultural tradition and sentiment and have not produced highly literate readers of the accepted canonical literature of Western democracy. Her problems are intellectual, they are problems of words in books. Thus, the solution to the problem of citizenship education is to get students to read the hundred great books of the Western intellectual tradition. For Brann, "to have an education is to know how to read."[20] Thus, citizenship education is learning how to read the books that constitute the republican tradition. Further, according to Brann, this course of study can only go on in the college years. Schooling before college is preparation, after college, it is professional training. The liberal arts college is the source and means of citizenship education: a leisured interlude of literate activity between childhood and professional training.

While there is some nostalgic appeal in the kind of historical and philosophical sensibility which Brann advocates, her model of citizenship makes no connections between the intellectual understandings of ideals and their possible translation into living practices and actions in a community. Nor is her model for educational practice workable. What is to be done with all those who cannot, or do not, have a leisured interlude for literate activity? Brann dismisses these concerns, however, and asserts that we must start somewhere and, in any event, these are social-political concerns—questions about participation and equality—and not educational questions.

A democratic society which invests each of its members with at least the opportunity for more than formal political equality (i.e., educational, moral, economic) cannot tolerate this elitist notion of liberal education, not because of its "liberal" nature, but because of its restricted range and access. As a public philosophy of education, then, Brann offers a classical model of liberal education which serves the few for a short time in the interest of maintaining a social hierarchy through an educational meritocracy. While it may be that a reverence for the republic and a respect for our institutions will come naturally from a reflective education for those who enjoy these benefits,[21] it is just as natural to assume that the sentiments of those citizens excluded will be marked less by reverence and respect than by resistance and rejection.

Broudy in *Truth and Credibility: The Citizen's Dilemma* presents another alternative. He begins with Dewey's "amazing proposition" that a democratic society could be governed by an enlightened citizenry and that a system of schooling, guided by reason and science, could produce such a citizenry. For Broudy, the problem is that this model of school life assumes a public life which no longer exists. The question for the citizen in contemporary society, as he sees it, is not "What can I believe?" but "Whom can I believe?"[22] Truth, knowledge, and reason may give us warranted assertions, but a democratic social life is based on warranted commitments. In short, according to Broudy, we face a problem of too much knowledge without the necessary understanding, courage, and insight to choose to act on it for communal purposes. What is needed, then, is a way to unify truth and credibility to furnish the ground for some unified version of the public good. Broudy seeks such a principle in the domains of existential truth and remoralized knowledge. The remedy for the arbitrary narrowing of relevance that our knowledge seems to have is to broaden the context of our problems so that their ramifications in the various value domains are discovered. The acquisition of credible knowledge as a ground for warranted commitment depends on an awareness and disclosure of motives as well as facts, where purity of heart, sincerity, and authenticity are more important criteria than objectivity and replicability. Broudy asserts that the question for citizenship education which legitimizes personal belief as well as reason is: What are we willing to live our lives for? To live with the idea of a common good, we must believe in a set of stable norms, even though they may not be true, and live our lives as if they were. These kinds of beliefs are the products of tacit knowlege, the consequences of existential choices by a self, straining for consistency of commitment and assertion. Broudy argues that it is through these individual acts of will that individuals form a view of democracy to which they can be existentially committed; committed, that is, to "The American Creed." The curriculum which best promotes this kind of character and choice is the liberal arts seen as a form of general education. Thus, Broudy's final prescription is for general education which fosters personal optimism and through which we will choose a general, commonly held belief in The American Creed.

There is much to be said for Broudy's analysis. Commitment to a life of common projects and shared meanings does involve a cultivation of sentiments and beliefs inaccessible through purely rational means. However, he sees education as the accumulation of warranted propositions which reduces knowing to an achievement of static norms rather than an activity designed for the securing of values in lived existence. His analysis masks the relation of knowledge claims to patterns of social reproduction and domination.

Further, his recommendations for schooling offer no new directions for civic education. Calls for a general education in the liberal arts have historically been advanced during periods in which educators have been unable or unwilling to connect the characteristic experiences of concrete social life to school curricula. "General education," in any case, is an amorphous and problematic term which Broudy's analysis does little to clarify. It is not clear, for example, why a general education curriculum will necessarily be more open to the kind of pedagogy which legitimizes personal beliefs or leads to a common commitment to The American Creed. Then, too, we need to consider exactly which American Creed Broudy has in mind. Does he mean that students will naturally come to believe in, and act in accord with, the Puritan ethic; the radical democratic principles of Jefferson and Paine; the *Pax Americana* imperialism of Monroe, Wilson, and Kennedy; the "society is a business" ideology of Coolidge and Reagan? Again, we are given a remedy without the hard work of uncovering the connections between the progressive elements of what has passed for The American Creed and the possibilities of a more democratically committed social and personal life. Fostering personal optimism in students may be a worthwhile goal, but in the absence of powerful ideas and clear commitments, optimism can be foolhardy. Broudy's model of citizenship has important individual elements, but their significance and coherence are lost when combined in an unmeasured eclecticism.

Toward a Public Philosophy of Education

Walter Feinberg has written
> The major question for contemporary education is how the interpretive and value functions of general education can be re-established at a time when the dominant code provides legitimacy to the idea that public participation is reducible to market participation.[23]

In a culture where the philosophical foundations of a public, civic consciousness are largely eclipsed, where the terms citizen and community are reduced to slogans, where claims to patriotism have been captured by conservatives, and where education is seen as a technical problem of information processing, where are the sources for the reconstruction of a democratic public philosophy? While the works of Brann and Broudy are important for their attempts to transcend the narrow professional paradigm in which most educational debate is conducted, their usefulness for developing a new democratic public philosophy is limited by their uncritical acceptance of many of the ideological assumptions of current social and educational thought and practice. In contrast, many radicals and radical educators of different varieties, in their sincere and necessary effort to critique existing educational theories and practices and develop understandings of the school as part of a larger socio-economic system, have often described a world devoid of doubt and the possibility for democratic praxis. On the one side, we seem to have uncritical hope, on the other, hopeless criticism.[24] The contemporary challenge of building a public philosophy, and with it a renewed sense of citizenship and civic education, will require an approach that joins the language and methods of opposition and critique with the language and methods of hope and reconstruction. We can begin this task through a radical analysis of the language of democracy. By "radical" here I simply mean an attempt to get at "root" meanings.

Democracy refers to a situation in which the people have power. It is not the name for a political system, institutional arrangement, or form of government. When democracy does become defined in reference to an existing political system, the task of democracy tends to become one of preserving and defending the state. This perverts the democratic sense of democracy as the critique of centralized, institutional authority or power. This is not to suggest that democracy is like anarchism, for anarchism seeks to destroy power and, in its radical individualism, what it means to be "a people."[25] Democracy refers to a situation where the people have the power to choose, act, and speak, thus democracy is at the root of all governmental power, rather than a consequence of state-proscribed rights and privileges. Democratic patriotism, then, is the feeling of loyalty that binds the people together, not the love of institutions. Thus, citizenship is a political virtue which expresses a commitment to, knowledge of, and ability to stand for the people as a whole.

I am suggesting here that a progressive model of citizenship requires that we make a clear distinction between the people and the state or government.[26] When good citizenship is defined solely in reference to the state's need for continuity, our definition of citizenship is confined to the legal obligations and rights granted to persons by a state. That is, the determining characteristics of the good citizen become those consistent with the state's self-preservation and maintenance. Citizenship defined in reference to the people or the public, in contrast, expresses a commitment to the kind of civic activity which will protect and advance the kind of polity which depends upon one's involvement in its common concerns. That is, the citizen is seen as a participant in a collective undertaking, not merely a bearer of formal rights and obligations.

Dewey helps us to understand the importance of this distinction in

The Public and Its Problems. For Dewey, all distinctions were based on an analysis of consequences. The state grows out of the need to regulate the consequences of human interaction within the social context. The import of Dewey's analysis is the recognition of the distinction between the state and other forms of social life, such as family, friends, and voluntary associations. These forms of social life, and not the state, are the primary arenas for the cultivation of democratic sentiments and habits. As the consequences of transactions in these arenas affect a wider sphere, they contribute to the formation of a public. Eventually, the public effects the formation of a government which administers the consequences of these transactions in the community as a whole. The public, however, is continually changing in its ideals and aspirations, while political forms tend to become static and rigid. Dewey writes

> Inherited political agencies . . . obstruct the organization of a new public. They prevent that development of new forms of the state which might grow up rapidly were social life more fluid, less precipitated into set political and legal molds. <u>To form itself, the public has to break existing political forms</u>... By its very nature, a state is ever something to be scrutinized, investigated, searched for. Almost as soon as its form is stabilized, it needs to be remade. Thus the problem of discovering the state is not a problem of theoretical inquirers engaged solely in surveying institutions which already exist. It is a practical problem of human beings living in association with one another, of mankind generically.[27] [Emphasis added]

One of the most profound educational changes in this century, and one that is reflected in the changing conceptions of what a public philosophy involves, has been in the relationship of the public educational system to the state. As I argued earlier, a dominant "new" public philosophy has emerged that identifies with the principles that guide and justify governmental power. Democracy is now widely understood as a mechanism for legitimating a leadership elite, and citizenship has been defined as the obligation to support the state through acting on proscribed and granted rights. Within this context, the civic purpose of public education has become identified with the promotion and maintenance of existing political forms rather than a process of forming and re-forming a public, and teachers are being trained as servants of the state educational apparatus, instead of agents of the public. The curriculum in civic education is thus reduced to a mixture of ritual, myth, and abstracted content and is seen, with some justification, as an irrelevant and bothersome requirement to be met as painlessly as possible so as to get on to the information needed for life in the real world.

If we take seriously the distinction between the public and the state and the root meanings of democracy, a different conception of public and civic education is possible. A democratic public life requires an effort to find a commonality of purpose and interest and a commitment to integrative action as the means for overcoming existing political forms so as to reconstitute new public forms. In this view, to be a citizen is to be a breaker and maker, as well as a finder and user.[28] If citizenship is seen as an expression of the quality and intention of our activities in a variety of social relations (e.g., church, family, workplace), a wider realm of meanings and experiences can be drawn on for the development of civic consciousness. This suggests that education for citizenship today needs to be rooted in the characteristic activities of a universe of social experiences and forms and that it should be directed at promoting the capacity for constructive resistance, where this entails both the ability to critique existing political forms and the imagination and fellow feeling to envision new public forms and participate in their development.

In this view, teachers should be prepared to be public educators, not merely technical arms of the state. As public educators, teachers must be prepared to confront the state where necessary, not for personal or ideological reasons, but as part of their civic responsibility, the formation of new publics.

Our task as citizens and as public educators is to find the spaces existing in all institutions which permit the democratic sense, the power to rule ourselves and engage in generous and nondeferential relations with others, and to develop and make these spaces wider arenas for public power. These democratic and educational struggles for individuality and community within the "little traditions" of social life are incomplete in themselves and await generalization, but they provide the necessary starting point for the reconstruction of a more truly democratic public philosophy and view of civic education without which the larger tasks will be impossible.

Conclusion

A good deal of this essay has been devoted to a consideration of the language with which we express our political understandings. It was argued that the vocabulary of democratic elitism, the dominant "new" public philosophy, restricts and skews the meaning of democracy and citizenship and makes the development of a truly democratic civic consciousness and public education impossible.

It has been said that democracy begins in conversation and there is some truth to this. This essay argues that this kind of public and democratic conversation and the issues which it raises have largely been avoided, obscured, or distorted by proponents of a democratic elitism and the civic curriculum this new public philosophy of education has legitimized. Further, the "professionalization" of the philosophy of education has limited our ability to adequately critique this dominant public philosophy or propose an alternative foundation for civic education. The calls for a return to an education framed by the canons of classical liberalism and the great books clearly accede to a democratic elitism and do not take seriously the problems of a culture in which many ordinary citizens feel alienated and disenfranchised and in which the idea of a public education itself is under attack. Dewey's work, at the least, gives us a more promising starting point for a reconstruction of the essential categories and meanings necessary for a public, democratic educational conversation

Still, we must be clear that the struggle for democracy and democratic education is not over meanings alone. Rather, it is over the power to make meanings, to confirm and deepen our experiences in and of community, and to insist upon a difference between what is and what could be. These are matters of democratic practice. There is, however, a relationship between meanings and democratic practice, and the unfinished business of civic education is to make this connection stronger and more fruitful.

Notes

*Parts of this paper are drawn from a presentation on education and democratic citizenship delivered at the National Council for Social Studies Annual Meeting in Boston, November 1982. I would like to thank Henry Giroux for developing some of the themes of that presentation in his "Public Philosophy and the Crisis in Education," *Harvard Educational Review*, Vol. 54, no. 2 (May 1984). This essay has benefited from his ideas.

[1] *A Nation at Risk. The Imperative for Educational Reform*, The National Commission on Excellence in Education (Washington, D.C.: United States Department of Education, 1983).

[2] *Philosophy of Education 1980*, Jonas F. Soltis, ed., Eightieth Yearbook of the National Society for the Study of Education (Chi-

cago: University of Chicago Press, 1981).

[3] Jonas F. Soltis, "Philosophy of Education Since Mid-Century," *Teachers College Record*, Vol. 81, no. 2 (Winter 1979): 128.

[4] William M. Sullivan, *Reconstructing Public Philosophy* (Berkeley: University of California Press, 1982), 9.

[5] *Ibid.*, 10.

[6] Sheldon S. Wolin, "The New Public Philosophy," *Democracy*, Vol. 1, no. 4 (October 1981): 23-36.

[7] *The Republic of Plato*, translated by Francis W. Cornford (London: Oxford University Press, 1973).

[8] For a good discussion of the liberal ideal of equality of opportunity, see Walter Feinberg, *Reason and Rhetoric* (New York: John Wiley, 1975).

[9] Jean Jacques Rousseau, *Emile, or On Education*, introduction, translation, and notes by Allan Bloom (New York: Basic Books, 1979).

[10] It is important to note that for Rousseau "man" is *not* a generic term. See Jane Roland Martin, "Sophie and Emile: A Case Study of Sex Bias in the History of Educational Thought," *Harvard Educational Review*, Vol. 51, no. 3 (August 1981): 357-372.

[11] The best sources for this aspect of Dewey's thought are: *Democracy and Education* (New York: Free Press, 1966); *The Public and Its Problems* (New York: Henry Holt, 1927); and *Reconstruction in Philosophy* (New York: Henry Holt, 1920).

[12] C.B. MacPherson, *The Life and Times of Liberal Democracy* (Oxford: Oxford University Press, 1977).

[13] See Feinberg, *Reason and Rhetoric*; and Samuel Bowles and Herbert Gintis, *Schooling in Capitalist America* (New York: Basic Books, 1976).

[14] Walter Lippmann, *The Public Philosophy* (Boston: Little, Brown & Co., 1955).

[15] *A Nation at Risk*, 6-7.

[16] Wolin, "The New Public Philosophy," 27-28.

[17] *Ibid.*, 36.

[18] Eva Brann, *Paradoxes of Education in a Republic* (Chicago: University of Chicago Press, 1979); Harry S. Broudy, *Truth and Credibility: The Citizen's Dilemma* (New York: Longman, 1981).

[19] Brann, *Paradoxes of Education*, 2.

[20] *Ibid.*, 16.

[21] *Ibid.*, 147.

[22] Broudy, *Truth and Credibility*, 22.

[23] Walter Feinberg, *Understanding Education* (New York: Cambridge University Press, 1983), 232.
[24] As Freire writes of the sectarian of the right or the left: "They both suffer from an absence of doubt." *Pedagogy of the Oppressed* (New York: Continuum, 1981), 23. See also, George H. Wood, "Beyond Educational Cynicism," *Educational Theory*, Vol. 32, no. 2 (Spring 1982): 55-71.
[25] Charles Douglas Lummis, "The Radicalism of Democracy," *Democracy*, Vol. 2, no. 4 (Fall 1982): 9-16.
[26] This is developed further in James Giarelli, "The Public, the State, and the Civic Education of Teachers," in Ayers Bagley, ed., *Civic Learning in Teacher Education*, Society of Professors of Education Monograph Series (Minneapolis: Society of Professors of Education, 1983), 33-36.
[27] John Dewey, *The Public and Its Problems*, 31-32.
[28] See Giarelli, "The Public, the State, and the Civic Education of Teachers."

Chapter Four

If, as I believe, an historical period now exists within which educators could perform a vital role in the development of participatory democracy, their actions must be consistent with that goal.

4

Civic Education for Participatory Democracy

By George H. Wood

CIVIC education in any democratic society involves a fundamental paradox. On the one hand, the public school is expected to devote its energies to socializing children for the status quo. On the other hand, democracy implies the right of citizens to alter that status quo in ways which they see fit. This paradox is intensified in an American culture which attempts a system of political equality, i.e., democracy, within a system of economic and resultant social, cultural, and political inequality, i.e., capitalism. This has resulted in civic education which, rather than obtaining its promise of a literate, thoughtful, and perhaps even compassionate citizenry, operates to emphasize the routine, rewards rule-governed behavior, and values conformity over independence.

A wide range of scholarship has pointed out the "reproductive" nature of much of what schools do.[1] Generally put, the argument is that schools operate in ways that prepare students to accept a place in our stratified social order. Working through a variety of means—ideological biases in textbooks, ability grouping, teacher behaviors, and class-biased uses of language—the reproductive functioning of schooling is seen to limit challenges to the existing social order. Recently, the almost functionalist nature of reproductive arguments has been challenged by those arguing that schools are in fact sites in which a dominant ideology may be contested.[2] Both lines of research have helped us go well beyond traditional understandings of classrooms where children are assumed to learn a sequence of value-neutral and socially necessary concepts, facts, and generalizations. However, lacking from most of this discussion, has been an analysis of what democracy means and how competing visions of democracy necessitate alternative forms of civic education.

The purpose of this paper is to suggest how educators concerned with educating for a democracy might move beyond what I have called "radical educational cynicism"[3] by claiming a participatory vision of democracy to guide their practice. To do this, I will first examine both protectionist and participatory democratic theory, locating current civic education reality within the former and its promise within the latter. I will then turn my attention to how civic education might be transformed in order to generate civic courage (the courage needed to live and act democratically in what is fundamentally an undemocratic society) in our students as well as in ourselves as educators.

Establishing what we mean when we talk about democracy is essential to defining the role of civic education. What does it mean to invoke democracy as an organizing principle for social life? Leaving aside the question of institutional structures, can we establish the theoretical and normative parameters within which democratic life is to occur?

Democracy is frequently invoked as both an organizing principle for our collective social lives and as a rationale for public education. Yet, often absent from discussions relying upon democracy, is a definition of the concept itself. It is seemingly assumed that the way our social and political structures currently function suffices as an operational definition of democracy. What this assumption misses is the fact that competing interpretations of democracy exist, each with its own normative framework within which the democratic or antidemocratic nature of social institutions can be judged. The two major versions of democratic theory with which I will be concerned are the classical, or participatory, and the contemporary, or protectionist. Before moving to a discussion of schooling for democracy, the nature of democratic theory will be outlined and an attempt to claim one as a legitimate basis for civic education will be made.

The Protectionist Paradigm For Democracy

Contemporary democratic theory was developed in an attempt to eliminate the perceived instability of classical democratic theory. According to Pateman, recent democratic theory has at its heart two crucial concerns.[4] First, classical theory, which rested heavily upon public participation in the governing process, is thought to be obsolete due to the inability of the populace to participate politically. A second concern is a fear of totalitarianism which is based upon the belief that mass participation in political affairs would precipitate a collapse into instability. These arguments derive from an analysis of the experience of the Weimar Republic in which it is claimed that increased political participation by low socio-economic status groups, who supposedly did not possess democratic attitudes, brought about a collapse into totalitarianism. How is this argument translated into democratic theory for the modern world?

Primarily, contemporary democratic theory has rested upon the tenets of empirical science. Schumpeter first argued that classical democratic theory rested upon empirically unrealistic grounds which ignored undemocratic attitudes among the populace.[5] Given such an attitudinal problem, fundamentally a desire to absolve oneself of decision-making responsibility in favor of the decisions of a "leader," Schumpeter proposed that democracy could best function as a competition for public support between decision makers. Thus, classical theory was abandoned for a theory based upon the popular selection of elite decision makers (who mirror members of the economically elite classes) as opposed to direct decision making.

Continuing the transformation from participatory to protective democratic theory, Berelson, in agreement with Schumpeter, argued that not only were the masses willing to abdicate decision-making responsibilities, they were politically apathetic.[6] He asserted that since citizens take little or no interest in decisions which do not directly influence them, nonparticipation takes on a positive dimension as it prevents those with limited interest and expertise from creating undue stress on the system. He concludes that by limiting demands and thus conflict, the stability of the democratic system is preserved. In fact, those very elements which he believed to have the least democratic attitudes, lower socio-economic status groups, participate less than anyone else as they have less at stake (generating more apathy) than other segments of the populace.

Dahl completed the transition of democratic theory from participatory to protectionist.[7] His argument was that the most important or distinguishing element of a democratic system is the election process through which non-elites choose governing elites. These representatives of the public then set and act upon a political agenda through which all major decisions are made. The role of the public is to verify that the political elite is protecting self- or group interests. In this way, democracy is best seen as a protectionist scheme devoted to the selection of elites who protect the rather stable interests of the electorate. The role of the citizenry in this model is the making of leadership choices, not decisions themselves, in order to protect their perceived interests.[8]

Not only are citizens removed from direct decision making in protectionist theory, the very range of what are considered political issues is severely limited. Those issues which deal with the very structure of the capitalist order—private ownership of capital, distribution of income and wealth, plant relocations, etc.—are deemed outside legitimate political debate. Rather, the interests to be protected must operate within existing economic structures. That is, the dual concerns of stability and efficiency dominate contemporary theory. The assumption is that excessive debate over the very nature of the economic system would not only threaten the system's stability, but it would hamper the efficiency of the economic machine.

The argument can be made that contemporary democratic theory is an accurate description of the current American political context. Indeed, those who gain the least from the current economic and social order are the least likely to vote. The social system is thus guaranteed relative stability as issues of concern to nonvoters, which might involve an alteration of existing economic structures, are not addressed. Additionally, the role of citizens in Western democracies is largely limited to attendance at the ballot box. Direct action on social issues—such as picketing, protesting, and democratic take-over—is widely discouraged as counterproductive or only symbolic. Finally, while voters may pick political leaders, they are mute when it comes to the selection of economic decision makers.

Most recently, such an analysis of democracy has been put forth by one of America's leading conservatives, George Will. Will argues that nonvoting citizens exercise their civic virtue by indicating general satisfaction with the way things are. Further, a nonvoting norm prevents the intrusion into the electoral process of those with a nondemocratic attitude. Will asserts that recent attempts to increase voter turnout are wrongheaded and can only lead to a repetition of the experience of the Weimar Republic. The best democracy seems to be the least democracy according to Will.

> In two presidential ballotings in Germany in 1932, 86.2 and 83.5 percent of the electorate voted. In 1933, 88.8 percent voted in the Assembly election swept by the Nazis. Were the 1932 turnouts a sign of the health of the Weimar Republic? The turnout reflected the unhealthy stakes of politics then: elections determined which mobs ruled the streets and who went to concentration camps.
>
> The fundamental human right is to good government. The fundamental problem of democracy is to get people to consent to that, not just to swell the flood of ballots. In democracy, legitimacy derives from consent, but nonvoting is often a form of passive consent. It often is an expression not of alienation but contentment . . . the stakes of our elections, as they affect the day-to-day life of the average American, are agreeably low.[9]

Current democratic theory and practice are locked within a protectionist rationality. That rationality favors limiting participation in governing processes to the elite and narrowing the scope of those issues deemed relevant to the stability of the political process. The social tool of our protectionist theory is becoming all too clear. Millions of the culturally disenfranchised have recognized that they are not wanted or needed by the political system and have abandoned it. Elections have become merely fund-raising contests and politics seems to be mainly an attempt to bring out the darker side (the racist, sexist, fearful, selfish side) of the electorate's protectionist nature.

Later it will be argued that public schooling in the United States has chosen to educate within this protectionist framework. Perhaps this would be a reasonable model if there were no alternatives. However, the protectionist framework is only one way of perceiving our collective democratic heritage. In what follows I will discuss an alternative version of democracy that can be used as an organizing principle for public education.

The Participatory Paradigm for Democracy

An alternative understanding of democracy is the classical, participatory framework upon which the dream of American democracy rests. Pateman demonstrates such a framework's rationale from Rousseau's *The Social Contract*: (1) participatory systems are self-sustaining because the very qualities required of citizens, if such a system is to work, are those that participation itself fosters; (2) participation increases one's "ownership" over decisions thus making public decisions more easily acceptable to individuals; and (3) participation has an integrative function—it helps individuals establish the feeling that they belong. The premises of this framework were elaborated by John Stuart Mill in the mid-nineteenth century and G.D.H. Cole during the first decades of the twentieth century.[10] Mill argued that the primary consideration in judging a society or government to be good was the effect that that system had upon individuals. Rather than concern himself with efficiency, as contemporary theorists tend to do, Mill argued that participatory democracy fostered within individuals the psychological attributes needed in self-governance. Mill, and later Cole, argued that these characteristics are best developed at the local level. Through local participation, citizens come to their own decisions on an immediate level and develop those skills and attitudes necessary for self-governance at the national level.

What is meant in referring to attributes needed for self-governance? Mill argued that an active character would emerge from participation and Cole suggested that a nonservile character would be generated. What this meant to Mill and Cole was that individuals should have the confidence that they, indeed, are fit to govern themselves. The term often utilized to describe such a state is a sense of *political efficacy*. That is, as Campbell *et al.* have pointed out, the belief that individual political action does have an impact on decision making is accompanied by the belief that it is worthwhile to perform one's civic duties.[11] And, indeed, there is empirical evidence to suggest that participation does enhance feelings of political efficacy. Studies by Almond and Verba, Carnoy and Shearer, and those cited by Wirth, point out that participatory models in local governments, workplaces, and associations do lead to higher levels of participation in national politics.[12] In all of these studies, local participation in self-governance increased the sense of control over the immediate political environment and a concurrent desire to participate in controlling the national political agenda.

Let us be clear about what is meant in these studies when the term participation is utilized. Three conditions must be obtained. First, the participants must be in the position of decision maker rather than decision influencer; second, all participants must be in possession of, or have access to, the requisite information on which decisions can be reached; and third, full participation requires equal power on the part of participants to determine the outcome of decisions. When individuals experience participation in this sense at a local level, the research suggests that they will gain a greater sense of political efficacy in the national arena.[13]

This implies that, contrary to claims made by contemporary protectionist theorists, democracy best functions as a lived process of participation. This is a process in which citizens do not merely choose between elites but actually transform themselves by contesting and debating public issues. This was the original vision of democracy upon which the foundations of our political practice were laid. Additionally, as has been pointed out in Wirth's review of workplace democracy, the classical participatory framework provides a vision of democracy which continues to be relevant.[14] It humanizes shared social spheres, empowers democratic citizens, and leads to more effective and efficient decision making. Most certainly, ongoing debate on how much participation is to be facilitated in our evolving society is necessary.[15] The point here is that participatory theory more clearly describes the principles of a democratic society than does protectionist theory.

Educators need to realize that the social, or civic, role they play depends upon the conception of democracy, participatory or protectionist, they choose. This is a choice between two polar opposites. On the one hand rests a conception of democracy in which the civic participation of the minority elite is crucial and the nonparticipation of the ordinary person is necessary to maintain the system's stability. On the other hand, democracy is conceived as encompassing the broadest participation of the people working to develop political efficacy and a sense of belonging in order to further extend and enhance civic participation.

It is the participatory vision of democracy which this essay embraces as the normative framework for civic education. The rationale for such a claim is threefold. First, our collective heritage rests upon a vision in which it is the evolving right of individuals to, as equals, govern themselves. This is most certainly the intent of those revolutionary claims for "no taxation without representation," "all men are created equal," and the principles of self-government put forth in Thomas Paine's *Appeal to Reason*. To argue against the distinctively American claim that the sovereign individual is an equal among equals is to opt for what Ryan has called "false equality" under the guise of equality of opportunity.[16] Second, the evolution of democracy in its best sense has been to broaden political participation. The expansion of the franchise, the passage of civil rights legislation, and the establishment of public boards in charge of social services are all examples of an ongoing evolution. As such, they act out the promise of democracy and, as pointed out above, fundamentally improve the quality of public decision making. Third, only participatory democracy makes possible the fundamental moral endeavor of schooling in a democracy in which the empowerment of "ordinary men and women to come to believe in their own right and power to have an increasingly greater say over what kind of society they must live and work in" can take place.[17] The conceptual framework of protectionist democracy, limiting as it does both the range of issues and actors in political dialogue and action, denies educators such a role and demeans our efforts into mere vocational training. Only the participatory vision of democracy necessitates a liberal education in its fullest and richest sense as it demands an informed, active, insightful, compassionate, and courageous citizenry.

Civic Education for Protectionist Democracy

As mentioned earlier, reproductive educational theorists have been instrumental in exposing the current social role of public education. This work has illuminated four functions of public education. First, it seems clear that traditionally the schools have operated to support and legitimate the dominant cultural, social, and economic order. This is not a remarkable finding. What makes it important are the aspects of the social order that seem most clearly embedded within the school's curriculum. In a state which pays frequent lip service to political equality, the schools instead reinforce political, cultural, social, and economic inequality.[18] One of the most crucial current roles of public schooling seems to be the reproduction of an unequal social order.

What are the messages that schools convey to students that lead them to accede to the legitimacy of existing social relations? This query leads us to the second lesson one can take from reproduction theorists. Schools teach a limited, very limited vision of democracy. By removing economics from politics; imposing only particular cultural configurations as being appropriate; limiting student and teacher participation in school decision making; glorifying a hierarchical, rule-governed administrative organization; and removing from the curriculum any mention of citizen action or resistance, schools limit our vision of democracy to an occasional trip to the ballot box. Gone is the active participant: enter the passive consumer. Through adopting this protectionist, as opposed to participatory, sense of democracy, schools often play a social role characterized again as supporting the existing social order, even when doing so is not in the best interest of students.

The third lesson taken from reproductive theory is that the positivistic and pseudoscientific most often define the parameters for teaching and learning in schools. Curriculum reflects only "truths" handed down from authorities in the field. Knowledge is reified and human agency is removed from considerations of how one "knows." A steady stream of objective facts are given to students who are never encouraged to see knowledge as a contested terrain. Teaching as well ceases to be a creative activity, but is instead a cookbook process based upon "scientific" methods. As Apple has pointed out, the curriculum often reflects a world where all the important issues are resolved and is thus "teacher-proof."[19] Creative thought, critical inquiry, and reflective thinking then all seem unnecessary in a society where problems are defined as merely technical. Within this context, the school works to depoliticize questions of value, social policy, and cultural goals by substituting a faith in science and technology. The resulting conclusion is that these twin cures for all of our ills are not subject to citizen control, but are best placed in the hands of experts removed from the political sphere. Again, schools function to support the dominant, unequal social order by limiting the democratic sphere to choices between competing elites, not between competing social visions.

Finally, reproduction theories illuminate the ways in which schooling elevates particular cultural forms at the expense of others. Choices made about modes of speech, thought, behavior, and even history fall under the rubric of neutral cultural norms. While the school claims to be merely presenting a previously agreed upon and generally resolved cultural heritage, it is, in fact, doing cultural violence to the diverse traditions children bring to school. By reflecting the supposed norm, which operates within the larger framework of political and social power, the cultural traditions of children outside this norm, especially traditions of political resistance, economic conflict, and social creativity, are seen as deviant and are at best rejected. This process has been described in the work of social linguists who have linked language forms to social power.[20] More importantly, the notion of cultural capital—those meanings, symbols, and objects that legitimate particular forms of social action or inaction—helps us understand the role schools play as cultural moderators. Moderating the struggle between oppressed and dominant cultures, schools lead students to see the dominant culture as the norm and any lived cultures that vary from that norm as deviant.

Thus, successfully schooled students may reject their own heritage and take a second-class position in a culture imposed upon them.

Only by ignoring the unequal outcomes of schooling, as demanded by the culture at large, can educators continue to play the civic role currently employed. This is not to argue that educators have, in fact, literally abandoned their charges to serve the needs of the state. Rather, by serving the state, they seem to believe that they are meeting the needs of the students in the best possible manner. Schools, operating as quasi-reproductive institutions, work to produce students "safe" for protective democracy. Endorsing a system of limited democracy, giving the impression that all "real" knowledge is objective and thus best used by impartial technocrats to solve public problems, and legitimizing a culture that comfortably functions in such a limited democracy, schools are working to encourage passivity as a civic virtue. This is even more clearly seen in examining what currently passes for "civic education," the schools most direct attempt to shape our social and political relationships.

In the area of what is currently referred to as civic education, the current social role of schools presents itself most clearly. Civic education has generally come under the banners of either citizenship transmission or a social science approach.[21] In both models, knowledge is assumed to be value free and democracy a concept limited to only a few public spheres. With the former, the idea is that students will learn, through reading or a simulation, the appropriate role of a citizen. Such a role is best demonstrated by Remy's *Handbook of Citizen Competencies* in which the emphasis seems to be upon making citizens safe for democracy.[22] This is done by only endorsing political tools and citizen activities, such as voting, letter writing, interest group formation, and the like, which fit within the current protectionist democratic rationality. In addition, lower socioeconomic status groups explicitly feared by contemporary protectionist democratic theorists for their destabilizing impact upon the system are seldom, if ever, addressed.

The protectionist framework of the citizenship transmission model is further illustrated in the explicit content of citizenship education programs. Witness the emphasis upon choosing leadership elites wisely and holding them responsible. Seldom, if ever, is the content of such programs devoted to the actual making of decisions. The focus is on the once-removed step of choosing the decision makers. Secondly, the social studies content in general is only filled with examples of great men and/or women making decisions—never examples of common people cooperatively working together to change their lives and circumstances through direct decision making.

Third, the Western democratic system itself is removed from scrutiny. Once it passes muster in comparison to Soviet totalitarianism (not to be confused with South African authoritarianism) the protectionist democracy of the West is fully embraced. Nary a word is mentioned in the curriculum of the potential contradictions between capitalism and democracy, the need of the system for nonparticipation, or the limits on decision making.

The social science model, while it goes beyond the notions of citizenship transmission by seeking to make students active and creative thinkers, recycles the very assumptions of citizenship transmission it seeks to redress. This is because notions of critical thinking and social conflict slip away before the priestly chairs of the specific experts. While claims are made that students "choose" solutions in response to the social problems about which they are inquiring, in fact, the technocratic solutions proposed by experts are the only logical choices offered. Thus, social problems are not resolved on a historical, political, or normative terrain in which varying notions of right and wrong are put forth outside of objective scientific discourse. Instead, students face a cookbook approach in which only certain types of knowledge are deemed legitimate and solutions to problematic situations are judged on their technical rather than humane merits. For example, Fenton's *Comparative Political Systems: An Inquiry Approach* claims to use concepts of leadership, ideology, and decision making to compare a variety of political systems. Yet, as Popkewitz points out in analyzing Fenton's work, the deck is "stacked" in order that students reach judgments approved by the author.

> For example, dichotomy is established between the leaders of the Soviet Union and the United States. The personal characteristics of the U.S. political leaders are characterized as energy, tact, ability to tend to many things at once, ability to operate effectively under tension, and so on. On the other hand, a Soviet leader is described as "not given to resistance, who is a little above average in energy and intelligence and below average in imagination." Under the guise of "social therapy," a dichotomy is established which seems to prevent critical scrutiny rather than nurture it.[23]

How is it that an educational program such as civic education, stemming from a genuine desire on the part of educators to help students as "educated citizen(s) act upon an unswerving loyalty to democratic ideals,"[24] turns out to serve such a limited conception of democracy? Again, we come face to face with the paradoxical nature of education's civic role: in attempting to serve students, the overriding logic of the state directs educators to work at fitting students to pre-existing roles in the cultural, political, and economic matrix of postindustrial capitalism. Of course, to adopt such roles may, on the surface, make a great deal of sense. But, in the long run, the roles and actions endorsed and embraced limit and perhaps destroy the abilities, hopes, potentialities, and dreams students have for a better world. Thus, within these two models, civic education functions to reproduce the established social order through limiting the sphere of democratic operations and further refusing to develop the skills needed by democratic citizens to critically examine claims to objective truth, to challenge the opinions of experts, and to utilize their own histories in both opposing the dominant order and building a new one.

Any suggestions that such models are soon to be repudiated by schools is belied by recent government-sponsored reports on the future role of the schools. Dominating the popular press and current presidential rhetoric is the claim that "our educational foundations are presently being eroded by a rising tide of mediocrity threatening our very future as a nation and a people."[25] To combat this feared flood, a program of "New Basics" is recommended. The ways in which this program of "New Basics" would merely extend the current social role of schooling as described by reproductive theorists are most clearly seen in the recommendation dealing with science and social studies.

> 3. The teaching of science in high schools should provide graduates with an introduction to: (a) the concepts, the processes of the physical and biological sciences; (b) the methods of scientific inquiry and reasoning; (c) the application of scientific knowledge to everyday life; and (d) the social and environmental implications of scientific and technological development. Science courses must be revised and updated for both the college-bound and those not intending to go to college. An example of such work is the American Chemical Society's "Chemistry in the Community" program.
> 4. The teaching of social studies in high school should be designed to: (a) enable stu-

dents to fix their places and possibilities within the larger social and cultural structure; (b) understand the broad sweep of both ancient and contemporary ideas that have shaped our world; (c) understand the fundamentals of how our economic system works and how our political system functions; and (d) grasp the difference between free and repressive societies. An understanding of each of these areas is requisite to the informed and committed exercise of citizenship in our free society.[26]

Returning to the lessons gained from the reproductive theorists, the ways in which such proposals operate are quite clear. First, they would only operate to reinforce the dominant society by linking politics with the economy (recommendation 4a and 4c) and setting up our society as "free" and thus superior to all others (recommendation 4d). In addition, the very content of such curricular programs would be dictated by those who have the greatest stake in containing democratic inquiry so as to leave their own actions beyond control (i.e., the American Chemical Society).

Second, the notion of democracy would be limited to current conceptions of protectionist democracy. Stressing the present system's "long-standing" nature (recommendation 4b), its ability to provide everyone a "place" (recommendation 4a), its comparatively positive nature (recommendation 4d), the message is that there is no need for expansion or change of the current model. In fact, the very notion of change, struggle, or even revolution, as democratic tools is totally absent.[27]

Third, the conception of knowledge here is locked within the positivistic notion of objective facts. The solution to social problems rests within the correct, objective application of science (recommendation 3a and 3b). The scientific knowledge to be used is, of course, objective, rational, and true, conforming to a positivist notion of science (recommendations 3a and 3b). Nothing is said here which could lead us to believe that the knowledge is at best problematic, and that the positivist notion of science itself is not generally accepted.[28] Rather, truth exists in a vacuum, to be merely passed on and absorbed.

Fourth, the recommendations seem to occur in a cultural vacuum in which only one cultural tradition of knowing (recommendation 3b) and of social organization (recommendation 4b) is acceptable. These recommendations are silent on the existence of oppositional culture. In fact, the very idea that students come with divergent cultural backgrounds is totally overlooked throughout the monolithic structure proposed for schools. Looking at the report's recommendations as to standards, what is most striking is the reliance on standardized testing and uniform objectives. What this means, when put within the framework of the report's curricular recommendations, is an educational arena in which students are evaluated solely on their ability to reproduce precisely the knowledge, values, and cultural symbols of the dominant culture.

Yet, the recent spate of such reports may prove advantageous to educators desiring to relocate the role of public schooling within the best intentions of democratic empowerment. Public interest in public education is increasing. A primary concern among many parents is the inability of public schooling to give their children the benefits promised; simply stated as a better life. Educators might seize the moment, work with parent groups to help locate this failure within the relationship of schooling and the dominant social order, and present the alternative of educating for participatory democracy. Such a relationship should be informed by Johnson's following argument.

> Being actively educative is not just a question of "carrying a policy to the public" or destroying myths about public education. It involves research, centering around particular struggles and local issues. It involves making links with other local agencies—researchers, community activities, black groups, women's groups—not to take them over, but to learn from their experiences and practices.[29]

In so doing, educators might be able to better come to the defense of public education. They might fend off attacks that only insist on more of the same and argue that schools do have a definite social purpose defined by the imperative to create a literate, democratic, and active citizenry. Thus, public welfare is the legitimate social role of schooling in a democratic society.

Civic Education for Participatory Democracy

If schools and educators are to recognize their potential to serve students, liberating them from a tacit acceptance of the assumptions of protectionist democracy, it will require that educators themselves display and instill in students a sense of civic courage. As defined by Giroux, civic courage means helping students gain the willingness to act as if they were living in a democratic society. At its core, this form of education is political, and its goal is a "genuine democratic society, one that is responsive to the needs of all and not just to a privileged few."[30]

It is important to note at this juncture that, while utilizing the arguments of reproductive theorists, I am not willing to accept what seems to be their rather functionalist conclusion that public schooling can do no better than reproduce the existing social order. While reproductive theorists have helped reveal the deeper structures of the hidden curriculum, linking them with the dominant rationality of the state, they have also limited insight into schooling. More precisely, what is missing in reproductionist theory is a consideration of the role of human agency. Extensively argued by Giroux and others, this suggests that reproductive theorists have an all too passive notion of human beings.[31] Locked into their structuralist understanding of society, they look at schooling as if it were a black box. Students enter and passive workers emerge. But, how the process occurs, what actually happens within the school walls, escapes the reproductive theorist's gaze. Thus, in spite of the insights provided by reproductive theory, there seems to be no alternative empowering role for schools to play.

As an alternative to reproductive theory, resistance theorists, through observing actual student behavior in the schools, suggest that a variety of things happen to school messages that are completely unintended.[32] First, these covert messages are often directly rejected through patterns of student deviance that often replicate shop-floor worker resistance. Secondly, they are often merely ignored in a passive fashion as students are unwilling to engage themselves at all in the educative enterprise. Finally, students create their own cultural structures which they use to defend themselves from the imposition of the schools. The unfortunate side of this oppositional behavior is that these students often reject the very tools, for example, literacy, available for their own liberation. Thus, they are indeed condemned to life on the margin.

This is not to suggest that resistance theory has resolved all the problems of understanding cultural and social reproduction through schools. In fact, many resistance theorists tend to glorify the oppositional behavior of students regardless of moral implications or political consequences. Thus, sexist, racist, and violent behavior is at times suggested to be the key to liberation. One suspects that an unwillingness to criticize such behavior as counterproductive and antisocial stems from a fear of imposing values upon students and thus behaving in ways already deemed unacceptable when carried out by schools at the present time. This avoids the fact that schooling, regardless of its master, is always a form of imposition. Dewey was one of the first to argue that such imposition is possible in the name of a democratic society for educators who believe that there is a better world possible and that schools can play a role in bringing about that world.[33] The task is to locate a pedagogy that redirects self-defeating oppositional behavior toward self-affirming democratic empowerment.

The primary function of such a pedagogy would be the empowerment of youth as future citizens. How might we educate the young so as to facilitate their active participation in self-governance? What might be the elements of the school curriculum which would enable students to function as democratic citizens? Developing such a pedagogy requires retaining what is useful from reproductive theory and acting upon the possibilities offered by resistance theory. What follows is informed by the understanding that schools always operate within an existing social reality, but that men and women can alter reality to mirror what they favor as a possibility.

With respect to pedagogy for democratic participation, it is important to note at the outset that what is to be suggested here is not a full-blown and predetermined curriculum. To suggest such would only be one more step in the devaluing of teaching and would most certainly be debased into mere cookbook practice. What is suggested are parameters for educators concerned with democratic empowerment. If, as I believe, a historical period exists within which educators could perform a vital role in assisting in the development of participatory democracy, their actions must be consistent with that goal. In what follows, the case will be made that an academic program consisting of critical literacy, diverse cultural heritages, exemplars of the democratic spirit (or civic courage), and a system of democratic values form the necessary conditions for an education that could foster civic courage.

A pedagogy of critical literacy must begin with what parents have long understood: the necessity for basic academic skills. The transformative power of basic academic skills was proposed by no less a radical democrat than Antonio Gramsci.[34] He recognized that the creation of a counterideology which embraced widespread democratic participation required that citizens be able to manipulate communicative and analytic symbols in ways that enable them to challenge the dominant elite. It is not possible for students to comprehend a new world view, to critically analyze their place in society, and to resist in a positive way the demands of a fundamentally unequal social system without having obtained basic academic skills. This is not to argue for the totality of the basics, overwhelming every other facet of the curriculum, or for a rote memory approach that merely forces the students to accept—predigested—the rudiments of workbooks, dittos, and drills. Rather, it suggests that basic literacy skills—understood as the comprehension, not merely memorization, of the way in which language, numbers, and logic function—can serve as the foundation of the schools' civic curriculum.

Such an understanding would move beyond mere literacy to critical literacy if schooling in the basics could be informed by the work of Paulo Freire.[35] Working with impoverished Brazilian peasants, Freire drew directly from their experience to teach academic skills. Rejecting a "banking approach" to education utilized by most programs for basic literacy, he felt that information could not be deposited in students' heads for withdrawal later, but should be drawn out of their daily lives. Of course, the dominant reality for Freire's students was their economic, political, social, and cultural oppression. It was by concretizing these experiences through the written word that peasants not only learned how to read but how to oppose the structures enslaving them. This is critical literacy: students gaining a critical consciousness of the world about them while obtaining basic literacy skills.

For students in this country, a similar program of critical literacy needs to be undertaken. To enable students to attain the literacy skills needed for democratic action, critical literacy work could help students uncover the reality of current social relations. With students in our schools, Kohl suggests an approach similar to Freire's.

> Perhaps the most important thing we can do at present is point out . . . and expose our students to the biases of texts in all subjects as well as in the structure, management, and financing of schools . . . The system itself is an object worth studying with our pupils. Let them find out what it is, how it works, who serves it, and whom it serves. Let them research and find out for themselves, and let us as teachers and educators find out for ourselves, since often we are as ignorant as our students.[36]

Beyond the school, students can use the conditions of their daily existence in the search for critical literacy. Uncovering the ways in which particular social and economic decisions are removed from democratic control, students can name, and thus potentially oppose, limits on democracy. An example from recent work conducted with teachers in Appalachia illuminates this.[37] While the Appalachia region is rich in natural resources, its people continue to be among the poorest in the country. One of the main tools used to exploit the region is known as a broad-form deed, clauses of which entitle those holding the deed to remove minerals in any way they see fit, including strip mining. Further, many of these mineral rights deeds grossly undervalue the raw materials to be removed. Utilizing these deeds as a basic element of the curriculum, one can teach reading, vocabulary, math, law, and economics while, at the same time, fostering a consideration of how these documents deprive the people of the region of their rich birthright. Additionally, exploring how these documents are able to survive legal challenges and do not become a part of political discourse, not only teaches "subject matter" but raises questions about the legitimacy of the entire political system. Thus, students become critically literate, not only able "to read" and "do math," but able to penetrate the very structures which oppress them. This is an example of a first step towards a pedagogy for democratic participation.

If students are to develop the civic courage that makes it possible for them to participate democratically, it is necessary that they understand their own histories. When students become aware of the worth of their own histories, they can come to value their own perceptions and insights. They will not have to rely upon the history of the dominant culture to validate their experiences and truths. Rather, they can look to themselves as useful members of a cultural tradition that empowers them to speak with their own voices. This has indeed been the experience of minorities in this country as they have worked to recover a sense of their own worth and an understanding of their value to the culture at large. Teachers need to incorporate such a historical perspective within the curriculum for all children so that this sense of self-worth will permeate their social actions.[30]

Such work, which celebrates the contributions of working people, women, and minorities to our general cultural pool, would provide students with their own "cultural capital." While cultural capital has traditionally been utilized to understand how students stockpile the symbols, meanings, understandings, and language of the dominant culture, here it is being argued that students could stockpile an alternative "bundle" of cultural capital which could empower them to act in their own interest. These symbols would be taken from the "peoples' histories" of groups and individuals who have strived and are striving to expand the meaning of democracy. Existing curricular materials which focus on the struggles of American men and women to expand the terrain of freedom and to improve the quality of their lives could operate to change the current way students are led to view social history as linear, conflict free, dominated by white males, and occurring almost without human agency.[39] This alternative stock of cultural capital could indeed encourage and empower students to speak with their own voices as they link their own reality to the struggles for a possible alternative future by others.[40]

It is not enough, however, to merely arm students with a new academic cultural history. If they are to transform rejection into resistance and action, educators concerned with participatory democracy must arm students with the understanding that there are other ways to organize social life. Allowing students to continue to think that current social arrangements are merely "natural" and historical resistance an anomaly causes the critical moment of moving from critique to change to be lost. Instead, students become distrustful, angry, and cynical due to the unfounded supposition, found throughout the curriculum, that change always occurs in an orderly and linear fashion. Students are then deceived into believing that they can only alter existing social arrangements by voting in preferred ways. What this misses are the powerful forces lined up behind the status quo, ready to defend current arrangements in the face of any frontal attack. In presenting alternatives, teachers should honestly face the fact that change only occurs with struggle and sacrifice, and hope that their students can act accordingly.

But, act in the name of what? Currently the curriculum offers no alternatives to our accepted order. As Kohl suggests, teachers should be prepared to present to students, both through example and study, alternatives to the existing order.

> The most important educational thing we can do is have our students understand that socialism, communism, anarchism, and other noncapitalist forms of organizing human life are serious, and must be thought about; and that people have a right to choose the social systems they believe will meet their needs and the needs of their communities. Young people also ought to be given an opportunity to know that people fight for such abstractions as justice and for such concretions as the eliminations of poverty and oppression.[41]

Drier suggests that students be exposed to attempts in the Third World to transform a harsh reality into a humane society as examples of what people, through cooperative action, can accomplish.[42] Making the connection between the Third World and our technological society can be enhanced by exploring examples of similar social alternatives in this culture. Examples range from the publicly owned and operated plants and utilities in the United States that provide products and services at significantly lower costs and with more efficiency than privately owned utilities to such large-scale projects as Canadian socialized health systems, England's nonprofit housing system, and Sweden's mass transit system.[43] Coupling these sets of examples together provides alternatives to the existing order, illuminates the possibilities of genuine power sharing, and demonstrates the means by which alternatives arise and take their places in a transformed state.

Beyond the analysis of systems, lies the analysis of values that are conducive to civic courage. Butts has proposed a schemata of civic values that are conducive to a democracy.[44] These include justice, freedom, equality, diversity, authority, privacy, participation, due process, personal obligation for the public good, and international human rights. Indeed, these values do form the nucleus for a democratic society. But, if students are to truly understand their worth, they need to see how these values are, or are not, enacted in the culture. Through the examination of their own lives and those of others, students should evaluate the forces that limit and those that foster justice, freedom, and equality. Further, students should be given examples of lives lived in pursuit of these goals by peoples of both sexes, all colors, and every creed. Thus, they will be given not only the tools for transformation, but the alternatives available, values to strive for, and perhaps the courage to undertake the role of living and behaving democratically in an undemocratic society.

At this point, it is important to note that students confronted with such a curriculum might reject participatory democracy. They might take a cynical route, claiming that, given current limits on political power, citizen participation makes little if any difference. Responding to such a claim requires teachers to draw upon both historical and current reality. The recent history of the Vietnam War era demonstrates graphically how citizen action altered public policy. The current nuclear freeze campaign, while not yet successful, has not only affected the administration's arms policy but has made nuclear armaments a key issue in recent elections. Citizen action has sometimes forced power sharing and had dramatic effects across the nation. Cynicism is factually unsound and teachers are obligated to point this out to their students.[45]

Alternatively, students may argue that the populace is indeed incapable of sharing power democratically, necessitating the adoption of a less democratic but more efficient political system, for example, fascism. The obligation of the teacher is again to confront students with the historical and current reality of such claims. Would they be willing to live in Hitler's Germany or Mussolini's Italy? At what cost did these cultures achieve their so-called efficiency, and at what were they efficient? How does the claim to efficiency made by more authoritarian systems square with current social practices? What does one do with evidence that, in many cases, greater participation leads to greater efficiency? Finally, can those systems which blatantly override the right of the individual be considered consistent with the credo and founding documents of our republic? Raising these issues potentially deepens students' understanding of democracy as shared power and offers them a realistic choice of alternatives.

What is missing from many proposals for the schools' role as civic educator is the fact that teachers teach by example. If the school is to act for a democratic transformation, teachers will have to behave consistently with shared power goals both inside and outside of their classrooms. In their classrooms, they will have to avoid belittling students and devaluing their cultures and celebrate with them the wealth of their diversity. They will have to be willing to look deep into the structures of oppression, see how they inform their own practice, and search for alternative classroom practices consistent with democratic values. Taking seriously the democratic values listed above, can teachers treat children in ways that demonstrate those same values? Taking for example the value of equality, can teachers overcome the class-biased ways in which the children are treated and curriculum is parceled out?[46] With the value of participation, can teachers allow students a meaningful role in making classroom decisions? Can they share power within the classroom and school? Only when teachers can replicate these values in the classroom will students take them seriously.

Outside of the classroom, teachers need to demonstrate both a genuine concern for children and the civic courage they are attempting to instill in students. If they are sincere about adopting a civic role for schools which embraces participatory democracy, they need to have the civic courage to act for children now. Currently, teachers' unions are primarily interested in teachers' working conditions, and professional associations are most interested in establishing legitimacy and furthering subject areas. These are certainly important goals, yet it is relatively rare to find teachers actively working through their organizations for the welfare of children. Campaigns against child abuse and for adequate child nutrition, housing, and health care are most often carried on outside of the educational community rather than within it. Such campaigns would certainly call into question the dominant social reality and be challenged by those with political power. Educators, by taking on such struggles, would demonstrate both to students and parents the very civic courage they are attempting to instill.

Through this combination of pedagogy and action, educators can work to turn student resistance into action for participatory democracy. This would be the most valuable role educators could play in this democracy. By working within the possibilities of education, teachers could build a definitive, justifiable social role for the schools. Then, schools and educators within them, working toward democratic empowerment, could justify their claim to being the social agency primarily concerned with the welfare of children. Otherwise, educators should admit that their main allegiance is to the state and that their social role is to reproduce the unequal social order that hides itself behind the guise of democracy.

Conclusion

I am not naively optimistic that civic education can or will be transformed in the ways suggested here. Nor do I believe that schools alone will alter existing social, political, and economic relationships. We have too often relied solely upon children to restore a world order damaged by adults.[47] However, schools will certainly be an essential part of any attempt to develop and instill the civic courage needed to reclaim our democratic heritage. Thus, I contend that educators can play a distinct and vital civic role by developing in children the skills and attitudes necessary to live democratically. Further, teachers as citizens have a valuable role to play in directly altering the current social order, working for a society in which justice and democracy have real meaning.

As Connell et al. have argued,

> Education has fundamental connections with the idea of human emancipation, though it is constantly in danger of being captured for other interests. In a society disfigured by class exploitation, sexual and racial oppression, and in chronic danger of war and environmental destruction, the only education worth the name is one that forms people capable of taking part in their own liberation. The business of the school is not propaganda. It is equipping people with the knowledge and skills and concepts relevant to remaking a

dangerous and disordered world. In the most basic sense, the process of education and the process of liberation are the same. They are aspects of the painful growth of the human species' collective wisdom and self-control. At the beginning of the 1980s it is plain that the forces opposed to that growth here and on the world scale are not only powerful but have become increasingly militant. In such circumstances, education becomes a risky enterprise. Teachers too have to decide whose side they are on.[48]

I have argued that educators, out of moral obligation to their clients, children, must side with such growth and thus participatory democracy.

I am struck by two limitations of the foregoing argument. First, do teachers currently in the field or preparing to enter the field have the potential to take on the role I described? There are times when my answer to this question is an unequivocal no, when I witness teachers demeaning children, belittling parents, avoiding political and social action, and, in general, teaching their subject rather than teaching children. And yet, I do believe that most teachers enter teaching because they are concerned about children and the lives they lead. This concern gets lost in the technocratic rationality of teacher preparation, the mundane duties enforced on teachers, and a lack of professional rewards and esteem. Teachers are not inherently better than any other occupational group when it comes to reacting to the reality of the workplace.[49] Thus, their often destructive actions must be seen within the reality of their jobs and education.

As a beginning step towards changing this reality, I believe it is necessary to take seriously the recommendations of Goodlad and others with regard to the conditions of teaching.[50] Teachers should be released from all extraneous duty, empowered to deal directly with curriculum, be given more time for research and development, and be paid a reasonable wage. Further, teachers should be entitled to a career ladder which rewards good teaching.[51] Finally, teachers who are unfit for duty should be removed from classrooms through evaluation by either more adequately trained and screened administrators or committees of administrators, teachers, and parents. If we seriously expect teachers to play a vital social role, it is necessary that that role be allowed through the structure of the job. Not all teachers will respond to such a change in conditions in the ways suggested. But, coupled with the changes suggested for teacher education above, the hope is that many teachers will respond by taking the responsibility for an empowering civic education.

The very question of state funding of education raises the second limitation. Is it true, as has been suggested by many writers, that schools can do nothing but serve the needs of the state as long as it pays the bills?[52] Earlier it was argued that internally schools do not work in a lockstep manner with the demands of capitalism, as suggested by reproductive theorists. Here I want to suggest that what much of the criticism of state domination misses is the great degree of potential local autonomy schools have. Local school authorities, or school boards, have jealously guarded their authority to hire staff, set curriculum, and manage the local schools. Only in a few states has this authority been overridden, and even such mandates as competency testing have been left to local authority. This is not to deny that school boards often abandon their authority to school administrators or are controlled by the most conservative elements in a community. What it does mean is that educators must take seriously the political potential of school boards and work to populate them with individuals who will join the struggle for a new social order.[53]

Even given these limitations, and the schools' history of dashed promises, it is imperative that educators strive to claim a civic role for schools that speaks to the best of our potential. Today the world is a fearful place for children. Not only is real life terrifying, wars, crime and domestic violence all too common; but fantasy, as represented by the cultural regulator television, is itself a frightening world full of guns, gratuitous violence, and useless consumption. Even more unnerving is the feeling that nothing is to be done in the face of this ruthless world.

But that, ultimately, is the promise of democracy: that people can and should control their own destiny. The only justifiable role for schools in our democracy is to equip students with the tools necessary to do this. This means teaching students the civic skills to critically analyze the ways in which present structures prevent our taking control of our collective destinies. Further, it means equipping students with the knowledge that they and their culture are important. Finally, it means instilling the values necessary in a participatory democracy and the civic courage necessary to act upon those values. It is only when educators see and act upon these proposals that civic education can justifiably lay claim to its urgent, unique, and crucial mission: preparing children to act democratically in an undemocratic society. When educators so act, they will ultimately have to side with children against the state, an act demanding civic courage of them as well.

Notes

* The author would like to acknowledge the thoughtful comments of Marcia Burchby, Ralph Page, Crystal Gips, Paul Bredeson, Joe Burnett, R. Freeman Butts, Charles Tesconi, Donald Warren, and Susan Franzosa. An earlier version of this paper appeared in *Educational Theory* 34, 3 (Summer 1984).

[1] Such work includes, but is not limited to, S. Bowles and H. Gintis, *Schooling in Capitalist America* (New York: Basic Books, 1976); M. Apple, *Ideology and Curriculum* (Boston: Routledge and Kegan Paul, 1979); M. Apple, ed., *Cultural and Economic Reproduction in Education* (Boston: Routledge and Kegan Paul, 1983); P. Bourdieu, *Outline of Theory and Practice* (Cambridge, England: Cambridge University Press, 1977); and P. Bourdieu and J.C. Passeron, *Reproduction in Education, Society, and Culture* (London: Sage, 1977). See H. Giroux, "Theories of Reproduction and Resistance in the New Sociology of Education: A Critical Analysis," *Harvard Educational Review* 53, 3 (August 1983): 257-293, for the most comprehensive outline of this work.

[2] There is not space here to discuss in full this evolution of critical educational theory. Readers should consult H. Giroux, "Theories of Reproduction and Resistance"; G.H. Wood, "Beyond Radical Educational Cynicism," *Educational Theory* 32, 1 (Spring 1982); and "Schooling in a Democracy: Transformation or Reproduction?" *Educational Theory* 34, 3 (Summer 1984), for a more complete description.

[3] G.H. Wood, "Beyond Radical Educational Cynicism."

[4] C. Pateman, *Participation and Democratic Theory* (Cambridge, England: Cambridge University Press, 1970).

[5] J.A. Schumpeter, *Capitalism, Socialism, and Democracy* (London: George Allen and Unwin, 1943).

[6] B.R. Berelson, "Democratic Theory and Public Opinion," *Public Opinion Quarterly* 16, 3 (Fall 1952): 313-330.

[7] R.A. Dahl, *Preface to Democratic Theory* (Chicago: University of Chicago Press, 1956).

[8] G. Sartori, *Democratic Theory* (Detroit, Mich.: Wayne State University Press, 1962).

[9] George Will, "In Defense of Non-Voting," *Newsweek*, 10 October 1983, 96.

[10] J.S. Mill, *Collected Works* (Toronto: University of Toronto Press, 1965) and *Essays on Politics and Culture* (New York: Random House, 1963); G.D.H. Cole, *Social Theory* (London: Methuen,

1920).
[11] A. Campbell, G. Gurin, and W. Miller, *The Voter Decides* (Chicago: Row and Paterson, 1954).
[12] G.A. Almond and S. Verba, *The Civic Culture* (Boston: Little, Brown & Co., 1945); M. Carnoy and D. Shearer, *Workplace Democracy: The Challenge of the 1980's* (White Plains, N.Y.: M.E. Sharpe, Inc., 1980); A. Wirth, *Productive Work—In Industry and Schools* (New York: University Press of America, 1983).
[13] H. Boyte, *The Backyard Revolution* (Philadelphia: Temple University Press, 1980).
[14] Wirth, *Productive Work*.
[15] J. Cohen and J. Rogers, *On Democracy: Toward a Transformation of American Society* (New York: Penguin Books, 1983).
[16] W. Ryan, *Equality* (New York: Vintage Books, 1982).
[17] R.A. Brosio, "*Pro Bono Publico*: Educational Reform and the Historical Actor(s)," unpublished manuscript, 1984.
[18] A brief sampling of the theoretical and empirical work in this area includes J. Anyon, "Social Class and School Knowledge," *Curriculum Inquiry* (Spring 1981): 3-42; J. Anyon, "Ideology and United States History Textbooks," *Harvard Educational Review* 49, 3 (August 1979): 361-386; T. Sieber, "The Politics of Middle-Class Success in an Inner City School," *Journal of Education* (Winter 1982): 30-47; Bowles and Gintis, *Schooling in Capitalist America*; R. Rist, "Student Social Class and Teacher Expectations: The Self-Fulfilling Prophecy in Ghetto Education," *Harvard Educational Review* 40, 3 (August 1970): 416-451; M. Apple, *Ideology and Curriculum* (London: Routledge and Kegan Paul, 1979); M. Apple and N. King, "What Do Schools Teach?" in H. Giroux and D. Purpel, eds., *The Hidden Curriculum and Moral Education: Deception or Discovery* (Berkeley, Cal.: McCutchan Publishing Corp., 1983); H. Giroux, *Ideology, Culture, and the Process of Schooling* (Philadelphia: Temple University Press, 1981).
[19] M. Apple, *Cultural and Economic Reproduction in Education* (London: Routledge and Kegan Paul, 1982). See also the recent work of K. Sirotnik, "What You See Is What You Get: Consistency, Persistency, and Mediocrity in Classroom," *Harvard Educational Review* 53, 1 (February 1983): 16-31; and J.I. Goodlad, *A Place Called School* (New York: McGraw-Hill, 1983).
[20] See B. Bernstein, *Class, Codes, and Control: Towards a Theory of Educational Transmission* (London: Routledge and Kegan

Paul, 1977); J.C. Baratz, "Language and Cognitive Assessment of Negro Children: Assumptions and Research Needs," *American Speech and Hearing Association Journal* (Summer 1969): 72-88; R. Shuy, "Detroit Speech: Careless, Awkward, and Inconsistent, or Systematic, Graceful, and Regular?" *Elementary English* (May 1968): 565-569.

[21] H. Giroux, *Theory and Resistance in Education: A Pedagogy for the Opposition* (South Hadley, Mass.: Bergin and Garvey, 1983).

[22] R.C. Remy, *Handbook of Citizen Competencies* (Washington, D.C.: Association for Supervision and Curriculum Development, 1980). Similar critiques could be made of J.P. Shaver, ed., *Building Rationales for Citizenship Education* (Arlington, Va.: National Council for the Social Studies, 1977).

[23] T. Popkewitz, "The Latent Values of the Discipline-Centered Curriculum," *Theory and Research in Social Education* 5, 1 (1977).

[24] This enduring rationale statement is taken from the National Education Association's 1938 statement, "Purposes of Education in American Democracy."

[25] National Commission on Excellence in Education, *A Nation at Risk* (Washington, D.C.: U.S. Department of Education, 1983), 5.

[26] A similar program advocating "new basics" is offered in M. Adler, *The Paideia Proposal: An Educational Manifesto* (New York: MacMillan, 1982). National Commission on Excellence in Education, *A Nation at Risk*, 24-25.

[27] I am indebted to my colleague Dr. Crystal Gips, herself a former school principal, for pointing out how passivity in general pervades these recommendations. Note how students are to be "introduced" to, and thus learn, science rather than be active producers or expressors—exactly the role they are expected to play politically.

[28] See T. Kuhn, *The Structure of Scientific Revolutions* (Chicago: The University of Chicago Press, 1970); and P. Feyerbrand, *Science in A Free Society* (London: New Left Books, 1978).

[29] R. Johnson, "Socialism and Popular Education," *Socialism and Education* (Winter 1981).

[30] Giroux, *Theory and Resistance in Education: A Pedagogy for the Opposition*, 201.

[31] Giroux, "Theories of Reproduction and Resistance in the New Sociology of Education: A Critical Analysis" and *Ideology, Culture, and the Process of Schooling*; G.H. Wood, "Beyond Radical Educational Cynicism," *Educational Theory* 32, 2

(Spring 1982) and "Schools, Social Change and the Politics of Paralysis" (Unpublished doctoral dissertation, University of Illinois, 1981); D. Kellner, "Ideology, Marxism, and Advanced Capitalism," *Socialist Review* 8, 6 (1978): 37-65; M. Erben and D. Gleeson, "Education as Reproduction: A Critical Examination of Some Aspects of the Work of Louis Althusser," in Young and Whitty, eds., *Society, State and Schooling: Readings on the Possibilities for Radical Education* (Philadelphia: Fulmer Press, 1977).

[32] See, for example, P. Willis, *Learning to Labour: How Working Class Kids Get Working Class Jobs* (London: Saxon House, 1977); "Cultural Production and Theories of Reproduction," in *Race, Class and Education*, L. Barton and S. Walker, eds., (London: Croom-Helm, 1983); Women's Study Group, Center for Contemporary Cultural Studies, eds., *Women Take Issue* (London: Hutchinson, 1978); D. Robins and P. Cohen, *Knuckle Sandwich: Growing Up in a Working-Class City* (London: Pelican Books, 1978); P. Corrigan, *Schooling and the Smash Street Kids* (London: MacMillan, 1979); A. McRobbie and R. McCabe, *Feminism for Girls* (London: Routledge and Kegan Paul, 1981); T. Popkewitz, B.R. Tabachnick, and G. Wehlage, *The Myth of Educational Reform* (Madison, Wisc.: University of Wisconsin Press, 1982); P. Olson, "Inequality Remade: The Theory of Correspondence and the Context of French Immersion in Northern Ontario," *Journal of Education* (Winter 1983): 75-78.

[33] J. Dewey, *Democracy and Education* (New York: MacMillan, 1916) and *Experience and Education* (New York: Kappa Delta Pi, 1938.)

[34] A. Gramsci, *The Prison Notebooks*, Q. Hoare and G.N. Smith, trans., (New York: International Publishers, 1971). For further discussion, see H. Entwistle, *Antonio Gramsci: Conservative Schooling for Radical Politics* (London: Routledge and Kegan Paul, 1979); and R.A. Brosio, essay on Antonio Gramsci in *Twentieth Century Thinkers*, St. James Press, in press.

[35] P. Freire, *Pedagogy of the Oppressed*, M.B. Ramos, trans., (New York: The Seabury Press, 1970).

[36] H. Kohl, "Can the School Build a New Social Order?" *Journal of Education* 162, 3 (Summer 1980): 62.

[37] This example is drawn from the work of myself and my colleagues in attempting to assist teachers with infusing local history, that of Appalachia, into the daily school culture. See George H. Wood, "Schooling in Appalachia: Power, Powerlessness, and

the School Curriculum," *Journal of Curriculum Theorizing*, forthcoming.

[38] R. Darnton in "Poland Rewrites the History," *New York Review of Books*, 16 July 1981, discusses a recent example of precisely such a use of cultural capital in his discussion of Poland. The Polish labor movement "Solidarity" has begun to reclaim the history of people's liberation movements in Poland from Soviet censors. The revolutionary potential of this knowledge, which comes from filling in the "blank spaces" of Polish history, is demonstrated in the inspiration such history lends to the "Solidarity" movement. Darnton sees it as follows:

> Try telling a Pole that events don't matter, that diplomacy and politics are epiphenomena, that one can neglect dates in order to study structure. He will reply that the difference between 1940 and 1941 (the disputed dates of the Katya massacre) is a matter of life and death; that nothing could be more important than the secret provisions of the Ribbentrop-Molotov pact; that the whole meaning of Poland can be strung out on dates, 1772, 1793, 1795, 1830, 1919-20, 1939, 1944-45, 1956, 1968, 1970 and 1980. The events of August transfomed the world for him. For the rest it can go back to work at its old task, teaching lessons and shaping a national consciousness (p. 10).

[39] See, for example, D. Clustor, *They Should Have Served That Cup of Coffee: Seven Radicals Remember the 1960s* (Boston: South End Press, 1979); R. Conney and H. Michalowski, *The Power of the People: Active Nonviolence in the United States* (Culver City, Penn.: Peace Press, 1977); and H. Zinn, *A People's History of the United States* (New York: Harper and Row, 1980).

[40] F. Adams, "Highlander Folk School: Getting Information, Going Back and Teaching It," *Harvard Educational Review* 42, 4 (Fall 1972): 497-520. In addition, it has yielded a wide heritage of artistic forms which celebrate resistance, see G. Carawan, *Voices From the Mountains* (Urbana, Ill.: University of Illinois Press, 1982). Drawing again from our work in Appalachia, the Highland Center provides an excellent example of creating such cultural capital. Programs designed to empower the poor and minorities in the region focus on drawing from shared, lived experiences their understandings of oppressive forces at operation. Additionally, work focuses on reclaiming the culture of opposition in the region through both political and cultural action. This work has brought forth the leaders and the

black civil rights movement (including Rosa Parks and Martin Luther King), the Southern labor movement, and the current struggles for economic and political justice.

[41] Kohl, "Can the Schools Build a New Social Order?" 64.

[42] P. Dreier, "Socialism and Cynicism: An Essay on Politics, Scholarship, and Teaching," *Socialist Review* 10, 5 (September-October 1980): 105-131.

[43] Carnoy and Shearer, *Workplace Democracy*.

[44] R.F. Butts, "The Revival of Civic Learning Requires a Prescribed Curriculum," *Liberal Education* 68, 4 (Winter 1982): 377-401

[45] T. Gitlin, "Seizing History," *Mother Jones* (November 1983): 32-38, 48; J. Herbers, "Grass-Roots Groups Go National," *The New York Times Magazine* (September 4, 1983); H. Boyte, *The Backyard Revolution*.

[46] For example, see T. Good, "Teacher Expectations and Student Perceptions: A Decade of Research," *Educational Leadership* 38, 5 (February 1981): 415-422; J. Anyon, "Social Class and School Knowledge," 3-42; and Jeanne Oakes, *Keeping Track* (New Haven, Conn.: Yale University Press, 1985).

[47] See R. DeLone's discussion of this in *Small Futures: Children, Inequality, and the Limits of Liberal Reform* (New York: Harcourt Brace Jovanovich, Inc., 1979).

[48] R.W. Connell, P.J. Ashenden, S. Kessler, and G.W. Dowsett, *Making the Difference* (Sydney, Australia: George Allen and Unwin, 1982).

[49] For an excellent discussion of blue collar workplace reality, see B. Sexton and P. Sexton, *Blue Collars and Hard Hats: The Working Class and the Future of American Politics* (New York: Random House, 1971).

[50] J.I. Goodlad, *A Place Called School* (New York: McGraw-Hill, 1983); and E. Boyer, *High School: A Report on Secondary Education in America* (New York: Harper and Row, 1983).

[51] Immediately, I must disclaim any allegiance to the current "merit pay" proposals being floated by leading politicians. What I am proposing is adoption of a system similar to that in Great Britain. In this system, the teacher has the possibility of moving through five career tracks within which pay is equal by seniority but differentiated between tracks. In addition, responsibility for curriculum development, supervision of new teachers, etc., increases with each step. To move up a track, the teacher must meet, to the satisfaction of a committee of his/her colleagues, a series of performance and educational standards. The top track in this system is that of Head-Teacher, thus

encouraging the best teachers to become the building leader. I anxiously await either the NEA or AFT to embrace such a plan.

[52] S. Arons, *Compelling Belief: The Culture of American Schooling* (New York: McGraw-Hill, 1982); I. Illich, *De-Schooling Society* (Cuernavaca, Mexico: CIDOC, 1970); E. Reimer, *School is Dead: Alternatives in Education* (Garden City, N.Y.: Doubleday and Company, 1979); and J. Spring, *The Sorting Machine* (New York: David McKay, Co., 1976) and *Educating the Worker-Citizen: The Social, Economic, and Political Foundations of Education* (New York: Longman and Co., 1980). For a more detailed critique of this position, see G. Wood, "The Theoretical and Political Limitations of Deschooling," *Journal of Education* (Fall 1982): 360-377.

[53] G. Wood, "School Boards and School Governance: A Case Study" (Paper presented at the annual meeting of the American Educational Research Association, Montreal, Canada, 1983) and "Who's in Charge Here: The Image and Reality of Local School Control" (Paper presented at the annual meeting of the American Educational Research Association, New Orleans, 1984); L.H. Ziegler and M.K. Jennings, *Governing American Schools: Political Interaction in Local School Districts* (North Scituate, Mass.: Duxbury Press, 1974).

Part Two

Civic Education in a Pluralistic Society

Chapter Five

African-American social theory and history have the potential to provide critical and reflective insights for a civic education appropriate to a society committed to equity and justice.

5

The Use of Cultural Knowledge in the Civic Education of Teachers

By Beverly M. Gordon

THE United States is a pluralistic society and, like any civilization, is concerned with reproducing and perpetuating itself. It accomplishes this task, in part, by educating its youth in the values and philosophical foundations upon which the nation is based. Social institutions, especially the public schools, play an important role in attaining this goal. In the process, they maintain the normative structure—the values and social views of the dominant Anglo-Saxon and other ethnic European majority cultures.

American minority professoriate groups such as African-Americans, Native Americans, Hispanics, and Asians, along with the minority communities themselves, have a special interest in the philosophy, values, and beliefs that are legitimized and disseminated in teacher preparation programs that ultimately affect minority children's images of themselves as future citizens. Conventionally accepted assumptions and models used to explain the nature and behavior of minority children, and paradigms and methodologies employed to educate these children, for example, have taught teachers to form negative rather than positive images of minority students and to dismiss their cultural history as marginal to mainstream participation in civic life. This is largely because the treatment of minority cultures in the teacher education curriculum fails to acknowledge the extent to which the historical experience, the history, if you will, of minorities in school is tied to the socio-cultural, political, and economic order and produces hierarchy, exclusion, and inequality among social classes and ethnic groups.[1]

The civic education of our teachers must help them realize that the values and beliefs of the majority are embodied in the linguistic and cultural information taught in school and negate any other information which deviates from the school's normative structuring of reality. Ultimately, schools contribute to society's ability to propagate the existing power structure by reproducing specific social relationships and forms of consciousness.[2] That is, the entire system of values, attitudes, beliefs, social practices, and norms that in one way or another function to universalize the ideological and social relations within the established order is perpetuated, in part, by schools as formal agents of socialization. Within this context, if students are ever to acknowledge and understand our cultural pluralism, educators must begin to analyze the knowledge they impart and the attitudes they foster.

Civic education, or citizenship education, as it is incorporated in teacher preparation as well as in the school classroom, illustrates how schools affect the reproduction of social relations and forms of consciousness that characterize our cultural makeup. R. Freeman Butts, for example, argues that civic learning in schools should transmit the fundamental ideals of our polity.

> The fundamental ideas and values upon which our constitutional order is built should be the core of sustained and explicit study... I think that the educational profession should be trying much more rigorously and vigorously to become knowledgeable and explicit about the substantive concepts and ideas that form the common core of American citizenship...

careful and scholarly and deliberate study of the ideas and values that pervade a democratic polity and should pervade the schools that profess to prepare for a common citizenship in that polity.[3]

Butts' point is well founded. In an important sense, civic learning already does transmit a fundamental ideal for our polity. But, the problem with universalizing a "common" mode of citizenship in the school curriculum is that it ignores the social conflicts and contradictions which permeate our culturally plural society. Thus, the citizenship of those groups within the polity that have expressed their citizenship by questioning, critiquing, and challenging the inequities and injustices within the system is undervalued or treated as deviant. Further, the current theoretical approaches to prejudice in schools, which we teach our nation's teachers, do not effectively reveal the social hegemony that controls minority group status. As Faustine Wilson-Jones points out, teacher education itself does not allow for the study of the prejudice in institutional structures which foster the cultural and cognitive deviancy theories, pathological and deficiency models, rationales, and attitudes that have been historically and systematically utilized to suppress minorities.[4] That is, while there are research studies illuminating the subtleties of elitism and racism in social institutions such as schools, this literature has not influenced teacher preparation in any significant way.[5] The majority of teachers are still taught that minority cultures and their histories are in some way peripheral, deviant, or deficient and that these historical political struggles fall outside a "common" mode of citizenship.

In this paper I argue that the civic learning of teachers as well as the students they teach can promote an emancipatory rationality which can be used to critique the conflicts of interest and the contradictions between minority and majority social thought and philosophies of civic participation. I contend that in a critical democratic civic education, teachers as well as students can explore the phenomena of mediation between the dominant culture and minority groups. Specifically, I want to demonstrate that African-American social theory and thought in education, drawn from philosophy and sociology, has the potential to provide critical and reflective insights for a civic education appropriate to a society committed to equity and justice.

The Rationality of Civic Learning

What is needed in teacher education is a sense of how cultural knowledge, which is part of the historical context, flows from the natural and practical world and evolves into an emancipatory rationality with implications for social theory. Missing are the real links of practical experiences generated from the life-world of the community culture—those experiences or lessons that scholars have identified as part of the cultural knowledge base of a particular community. These "currents of thought," pervasive within the history and current daily activities of a community, are what scholars must incorporate in the philosophical and social theory of their constituency.[6]

A crucial starting point in this approach is the examination of traditional concepts of citizenship education as well as the relationship between schools and the larger society. This examination not only makes citizenship education problematic but also makes problematic the role that schools play as social and economic institutions. The relationship between society and schools as agents of social and cultural reproduction is marked by enormous inequities in wealth and power. Consequently, any notion of education for citizenship has to be measured against its function as a mode of ideological domination. Is the goal to be to adapt people to an existing society, or to help students and others become critical thinkers and active participants capable of redefining the nature of their own lives? Our first task, then, is to determine the critical categories we can evoke to unravel the way in which citizenship education can function either to reproduce the social conditions that are tied to a class-stratified society or to increase the opportunity for social justice and economic opportunity.

Drawing on the Frankfurt School's notion of rationality, Henry Giroux, in "Critical Theory and Rationality in Citizenship Education," identifies three specific modes of rationality—the technical, the hermeneutic, and the emancipatory—which are used as approaches to teaching citizenship education.[7] According to Giroux, modes of rationality must be judged to the degree that they illuminate for educators and students ways in which meanings and values are constructed in schools, and identify those whose interests they serve. Giroux believes that a given rationality provides the possibility for personal development, critique, and social action if that rationality and its notion of citizenship raise questions concerning the knowledge taught, the interests served, and the relationship between specific forms of knowledge and a people's access to modes of power.

Giroux finds technical rationality flawed because it ignores the contradictions and conflicts that exist in the social order. Lost are the "normative, historical, political landscapes" that give them meaning. The hermeneutic rationality, while concerned with problem solving and the decision-making process, is also weak because it fails to understand how such societal meanings are maintained or how they interpret and/or distort reality. As a result, "the basic nature of existing social arrangements in the wider society go unquestioned or are questioned in relatively narrow terms."[8] As an alternative to these, Giroux articulates a theory of citizenship education grounded in an emancipatory rationality based on critique and action. He perceives the function of an emancipatory rationality as:

> Aimed at criticizing that which is restrictive and oppressive, while at the same time supporting action in the service of individual freedom and well-being. This mode of rationality is construed as the capacity of critical thought to reflect on and reconstruct its own historical genesis, i.e., to think about the process of thinking itself. More specifically, the capacity to think about thinking points to a mode of reasoning aimed at breaking through the "frozen" ideology that prevents a critique of the life and world on which rationalizations of the dominant society are based. Similarly, emancipatory rationality augments its interest in self-reflection with social action designed to create the ideological and material conditions in which nonalienating and nonexploitative relationships exist. This suggests a view of citizenship education based on a different view of sociability and social relationships than those that presently exist.[9]

Giroux identifies two modes of citizenship education that fit within an emancipatory rationality: the political economist and the culturalist. For purposes of the present discussion, however, I will focus on the culturalist position and the implications regarding its concentration on, and use of, cultural knowledge.

As Giroux explains, the cultural reproduction literature focused on how "consciousness, ideology, and power enter into the way human beings constitute their day-to-day realities" and "how actions within the grip of structures such as schools escape, resist, and transform the effects of the latter."[10] Thus, a critical imperative for an emancipatory theory of citizenship education is the politicalization of culture. For too long educators have "bought" the mainstream, social science definition of culture as simply a people's way of life. The definition is much too narrow, however, and limits discussions of concepts such as class, conflict, and power. Giroux argues that society produces specific forms of culture and specific ways of looking at the world, and that a dominant culture represents the ruling political, economic, and social interest. Based on this position, he suggests that culture be defined "in terms of its functional relationship to the dominant social formation and power relations in a given society."[11] By defining culture in this way, we come to realize that we no longer merely say that there are many cultures. The real issue is the way in which the dominant culture mediates between itself and secondary cultures. To what degree, we can now ask, does it impose on these cultures images of themselves that are, in fact, perscriptive and oppressive? And, to what degree are the schools as cultural institutions inextricably concerned with the production and definition of meaning that supports, sustains, and reproduces that culture?

Giroux presents the emancipatory form of citizenship education as a heuristic tool for teachers to use in reformulating the concept of power. He strongly believes that the politicalization of culture will raise teacher consciousness when analyzing school knowledge and student cultural wealth. In return, he predicts that the passions, intellect, and imaginations of both teachers and students will be stimulated—a phenomenon which will move them toward action for change.

Giroux's proposition is not without its difficulties, however. One of its weaknesses, as George Wood has pointed out, is in its application. Wood places Giroux's work in the genre of "resistance theory" and is correctly apprehensive about its transferability.[12] While Giroux provides a litany of assumptions and practices, such as allowing students to speak in their own voices to authenticate experiences, he does not address the fundamental concern of most educators—the form and function of this pedagogy in the classroom on a daily basis.[13] However, examples of this kind of pedagogy do exist: for example, Ashton-Warner's work with Maori children in New Zealand; Searle's work with poor working-class children in England; Freire's work with Brazilian peasants; Brown's work with minority and poor children in Oakland, California; and Shor's work with minority working-class poor at a community college in the City University of New York system.[14] These teachers have incorporated the authentic language of their students, and the methods they employ seem to be generated from a theoretical base connected to the historical conditions within which they were developed and within which they serve as guides to practice.[15]

Citizenship education must then have as its imperative the development of a critically thinking and active citizenry capable of redefining the nature of their own lives. This necessity is grounded in the relationship between knowledge and human activity in which Jurgen Habermas, among other critical theorists, argues that "history, social reality, and nature (as known) are all a product of the constituting labour of the human species." As Held noted of Habermas,

> [Habermas] argues, from an understanding of humans as both toolmaking and language-using animals: they must produce from nature what is needed for material existence through the manipulation and control of objects and communicate with others through the use of intersubjectively understood symbols within the context of rule-governed institutions. Thus, . . . humankind has an interest in the creation of knowledge which would enable it to control objectified processes and maintain communication. There is however, on [Habermas'] account, a third interest: an interest in the reflective appropriation of human life, without which the interest-bound character of knowledge could not itself be grasped. This is an interest in reason, in the human capacity to be self-reflective and self-determining, to act rationally. As a result of it, knowledge is generated which enhances autonomy and responsibility (*Mündigkeit*): hence, it is an emancipatory interest.[16]

Conceptualized in this manner, citizenship education necessitates incorporating "pedagogical models for new forms of living and social relations."[17]

Such a model can be found in the study of the educational history and scholarship of African-Americans as an example of social criticism and resistance to racism and capitalism. African-American history, placed in the context of American society, provides emancipatory insights. It affirms cultural sovereignty and documents continuous self-reflection allowing for new discourse and an active democratic citizenship.

In particular, my ongoing study of African-American education history reveals several currents of thought in African-American philosophical, sociological, and educational scholarship which have potential emancipatory power in the classroom. These include civic traditions of self-help, service, nationalism, economic autonomy, and political power. In the following two sections, I examine the genesis of these traditions and argue that they can assist us in reconstructing the content and pedagogy of civic education.

History as Cultural Knowledge

During the early 1900s, the use of educational science in curriculum studies played an unfortunate role in the perpetuation of cognitive inferiority theory and, as its consequence, second-class status for African-Americans. Educational science was employed to differentiate cognitive ability in children. While such psychological and scientific management principles were introduced as administrative conveniences in the cities for handling the influx of children of immigrants and former slaves, they became an anathema to Blacks struggling for social, political, and economic advancement through education. Historians have carefully documented Edward Thorndike's educational psychological theories, most notably the principles of intelligence testing, as a rationale for paradigms of social efficiency and the "differentiated" curriculum introduced by David Snedden, the social engineer, and curricularists John Franklin Bobbitt and W.W. Charters to prepare various groups of children for different roles and functions in adult society. Unfortunately for African-Americans, their position within this hierarchical framework was considered inferior to Whites, a belief that was "verified" by empirical scientific methods which became a legitimate part of the quoted research and literature.[18]

From 1890 to 1920, however, early Black scholars, such as Booker T. Washington, W.E.B. DuBois, and Kelly Miller, generated their own historical perspectives on the place of African-Americans in a newly developing industrial arena in United States history. Several points can be made concerning the thought of these men, especially regarding the role of education in the development of the African-Americans as a national community. They were very nationalistic and dogmatically believed that Blacks needed to take charge of every aspect of African-American life and culture. In their writings, a collective self-knowledge and the need for understanding formed the basis for a cultural mode of rationality grounded in the ideology of emancipation, self-reliance, economic automony, and political power. Both Washington and DuBois articulated a body of cultural knowledge upon which subsequent political, economic, social, and philosophical thought and African-American scholarship would be derived.

Washington and DuBois were instrumental in the production and dissemination of knowledge in the interest of African-Americans.

Both formulated paradigms and conceptual frameworks and organized and, in Washington's case, built institutions into knowledge-producing systems which sought to study and explain, on an institutional level, the condition of Blacks in American society. They were also pragmatists, especially Washington, who applied knowledge to build an industrial foundation and economic autonomy. While Washington argued for an agricultural, scientific base to serve the needs of Blacks still in the South in the 1890s and early 1900s, DuBois adamantly defended the need to provide a more classical, theoretical education for the best and the brightest of the race. However, though DuBois clashed with Washington about the means of uplifting and developing the Black nation, their goals of economic autonomy, political power, self-reliance, and community service were consistent. While it is not the intention of this present discussion to examine in detail the Washington-DuBois debate, it should be noted that elsewhere I have called for a re-examination of Washington, based on a reassessment of his writings and political influence in Alabama.[19]

We can posit that this tension, or, if you will, "dialectic," between the theoretical and the practical paradigms illustrated by DuBois and Washington, was indicative of the emergence of "cultural" knowledge and social theorizing which was called for, and subsequently generated, from the real needs of the African-American community. Furthermore, such knowledge and theorizing assisted in the further development of African-American scholarship which argued for collective effort on the part of the entire community towards economic autonomy, self-reliance, and unity. The work of Kelly Miller of Howard University, for example, reflected the nationalistic character of early twentieth century Black scholarship. Writing in 1908, Miller was concerned about the progress and the development of African-Americans and argued for economic independence and self-reliance. Like DuBois, he also rejected the social Darwinist theories which dominated English and American sociological thought. While he explicitly blamed White racism for attempting to thwart Black progress, he also addressed the problems within the African-American community itself. Miller reasoned that the "Negro's Part in the Negro Problem" was the schism between the educated Blacks and the masses. Miller's realization that the Black bourgeoisie accepted White paradigms and learned to hate themselves and the masses is a precursor to what Carter G. Woodson would say 25 years later.

Moreover, Miller recognized the necessity for both the theoretical and practical in the struggle to advance the Black race. As a result, he stressed the need to evaluate the "kind" of education Blacks received.

On the one hand, he proposed training in the intellectual classical fields which he termed "higher education" and, echoing DuBois, stated that "a most significant indication of progress is the emergence of a superior class. The talented tenth constitutes the controlling factor in the life of any people." On the other hand, he supported agricultural and industrial science education. His two-pronged approach represented acknowledgment of the potential symbiotic relationship between higher education and industrial activities.[20]

This early nationalist sentiment was seriously challenged by alternative influences on many young Black scholars from 1910 to the 1930s.[21] The sociological influence of Robert Park and Ernest Burgess, of the Chicago School of Sociology, grounded in social Darwinist theory, shifted young Black scholars away from the very independent paradigms of nationalism, economic autonomy, self-reliance, and service to the assimilationist and integrationist perspectives that reinforced a dependency ideology which even today haunts African-Americans.[22] In a very provocative way, the Chicago School introduced a technocratic rationality paradigm that labeled Blacks as inferior, based on evolutionary theory, and reinforced the broader capitalist and racist sources of oppression—namely ideological and intellectual hegemony.

While the assimilationist and integrationist paradigms embraced by the Chicago School of Sociology had a profound influence on the sociological conceptual frameworks which allegedly depicted and explained the circumstances, condition, and plight of African-Americans; scholars from the African-American community vigorously rejected these conceptual frameworks, pointing out the problematics of an uncritical acceptance of assimilation and democratic liberalism. Moreover, these African-American scholars realized the far-reaching and more damaging implications of the schism within the African-American community between the "educated" and the masses as a direct result of the negative impact of the deficit theory paradigms on those impressionable young Black scholars who studied them.

Through the critiques and criticisms produced by these scholars, a more clearly delineated emancipatory paradigm seems to have emerged. Of the many Black scholars virtually unknown in the dominant educational literature, I will briefly discuss only two who reconceptualized the emancipatory potential of education in the interest of African-Americans and pointed out a methodology and an ideology which revitalized the civic traditions of self-help, service, nationalism, economic autonomy, and political power from the works of their fathers whose voices had been drowned out and long forgotten. It is in such scholarship, written by those who are the oppressed, that we find "thick meaning" which could provide teachers with some foundational guidelines for reconceptualizing curriculum and pedagogy in the interests of groups outside the dominant society. Such reconceptualizing might also help us to ask how the commonsense daily curriculum of public schooling, as well as teacher preparation programs, is selected, packaged (interpreted), and then disseminated as legitimate knowledge. It might also be asked to whom is this knowledge given and to whom is it not given, whose interest does it serve, how does this knowledge continue to be perpetuated, and how might it be changed?

Social Theorists and the Challenge of Education

The decade of 1926 to 1936 produced a record percentage of Black college graduates, both in the South and in the North, more, in fact, than those of the entire previous century. In 1933, at the height of this thrust to provide Blacks with higher education at both the undergraduate and graduate levels, Carter G. Woodson critiqued the education of Blacks and set forth a philosophical and ideological road map to guide the Black community in its economic, social, and political development. *The Mis-Education of the Negro* spoke to the crisis Woodson saw in the "kind" of education that Blacks were receiving. The training African-Americans had access to was debilitating, crippling, and greatly prohibited the social development and economic advancement of the community as a whole. Woodson's thesis that Blacks had been miseducated by being given knowledge that systematically taught them self-hate and inferiority was an indictment of the status of Black education in America. Woodson realized that the education of Black students was built on ecological paradigms and assumptions which, by their very nature, promoted White racism and rationalized the colonial existence of Blacks in American society. He was deeply worried about this kind of education and argued that because of such academic training, Black students would never become a constructive force in the development of the race. But, Woodson also realized that it was difficult for Blacks to break with these theories, which were presented as commonsense knowledge, because few had been taught to question and to challenge the assumptions shaping social reality. As he explained, "when you control a man's thinking, you do not have to worry about his actions. He will find his proper place and will stay in it."[23]

What we learn from Woodson has implications for civic education. Knowledge in and of itself is not enough to ensure a politically cognizant and socially active polity. In retrospect, it was naive to assume that access to high-status knowledge and academic training alone guaranteed better opportunity and overall advancements for African-Americans. Racism will not yield to knowledge acquisition alone. Through Woodson's discussion, we realize that theoretical paradigms scientists use to interpret and employ knowledge are inherently political. Woodson realized that by accepting the paradigms they studied as normative, the educated Blacks could not easily escape the "logical" conclusion of simultaneously accepting Black inferiority. Thus was the kind of contradiction which alienated the educated Blacks, particularly from the masses of their less fortunate brethren. He concluded that educated Blacks were filled with self-hate and contempt for themselves and the masses and legitimized this self-hatred by rationalizing that the masses were incapable of building an economic power base. As a consequence of this miseducation, instead of joining with the masses in a collective effort, the "educated Negro" (here Woodson referred to the intelligentsia, theorists, and scientists) rejected and deserted the masses. Only the Black businessmen and businesswomen, he believed, truly helped and were most influential in promoting the development of African-American people.

For Woodson, the most important contribution an individual was obligated to make would be to serve the race in its development. He called for Blacks to gain control over their institutions, realizing that Washington was the only Black who built and retained control over an educational institution.[24] He believed that in White schools African-Americans did not receive adequate preparation in either industrial or classical education. In industrial education, for example, he observed that African-Americans did not have sufficient opportunities to practice their craft and upon graduation were barred from trade unions. In classical education, African-Americans did not fare much better, he reasoned, because such training had not produced a meaningful supply of thinkers and philosophers to help in the advancement of the community: "They have not risen to heights of Black men farther removed from influences of slavery and segregation."[25]

The emphasis which emerges from Woodson's thoughts necessitates a resolution of the Washington-DuBois debate. Implicit in Woodson's view is a call for the community's foundation to be built on the reconciliation between theory (that is, educational preparation) and practice (the application of theory to real world situations); and, just as importantly, a reconciliation between the scholars and the intellectuals and their constituency (the masses and the business community). Woodson believed in "self-reliance" to spiritually and economically uplift the African-American nation. Using the development of social collective enterprises as an example of the kinds of activities he believed that Blacks should have been engaging in, Woodson argued that Blacks had to serve each other and pull together as a community. Interpersonal cooperation was essential: the sense of community had to permeate through and forgo individual strife and conflict.

Collectively, Woodson's efforts and those of his predecessors were component parts of a broader African-American cultural mode of rationality wrought out of the history of the Black experience in America. When speaking about Black history and about viewing one's self from a historical context situated within the racist and capitalistic structure of American society, Woodson rekindles our sensibilities to our physical beings and to our own social experiences, through personal history, aesthetics, and oral tradition.

The philosophy Woodson promoted was based on service to and the development of the African-American community, and it worked toward the realization that imitating Whites was an admission of self-hate and rejection. In his new program, Woodson's reconceptualization and reconstruction of higher education as a mechanism of service is nationalistic and carries overtones of Washington. His call for "radical reconstruction" of the analytical framework and paradigms used to view African-America is as current as Giroux's call for the same. Woodson realized how social science paradigms and assumptions shaped reality and influenced societal policy. Understanding that theoretical paradigms were socially constructed, he suggested that Blacks critique these paradigms and generate their own.

Building upon the idea of Black scientists generating their own paradigms, Woodson's idea of creating new pedagogy to teach Black people about themselves, their neighbors, and their heroes, which he described as the mark of a "real teacher," precedes by 30 years Freire's concept of education for critical consciousness, as does the research methodology he suggested as a preliminary step in establishing a curriculum for the people.[26] Woodson was well aware of the necessity for generating philosophy, social theory, and ideology which assumed that Blacks would have to save themselves.

Ultimately, Woodson's articulation of a cultural mode of rationality furnishes us with the understanding that studying the historical struggles of people provides teachers and students with a civic and political awareness of how society functions from another perspective. This politicalization of culture makes cogent Giroux's argument that a critical study of culture is essential for an emancipatory pedagogy—in this case, one which teaches about those who oppress and demystifies domination and colonial rule. Culture, as Woodson uses it, is also self-instructive to the community in that it points out weaknesses and areas in which the community as a whole needs to improve. It would follow then that, interestingly enough, Woodson did not embrace Marxist theory because he viewed the Marxist influence as an outside force coming into the Black community with a European ethnocentric tradition not germane to the situation of Blacks in America. Woodson believed that radicalism had to come from within the African-American community if it was going to succeed. Blacks, Woodson held, could not depend on or wait for liberal White support—they had to act for themselves.

Seven years after Woodson's examination of Black education, William T. Fontaine took up Woodson's challenge to critique the dominant social science paradigms and generate new ones. In his essay "An Interpretation of Contemporary Negro Thought from the Standpoint of the Sociology of Knowledge," Fontaine confronted Blacks' naive and uncritical acceptance of democracy as the heavenly antithesis to their servile state. The concept of democracy for African-Americans, Fontaine argued, was bankrupt because it was "powerless to prevent the simultaneous existence of poverty and wealth, intelligence and ignorance, dead end kids and prep school Buster Browns . . . " For Fontaine, democracy was incapable of bringing equity and equality to descendents of slaves who occupied a caste status in American society.[27]

Fontaine argued that Black scholars should reject the "democratic liberal science *Weltanschauung*" and adopt a "defensive psychology" posture. This would be generated, in part, by a reconceptualization of history which incorporated the Black perspective in interpreting and reconstructing the African-American experience. The knowledge which was generated within this defense psychology, as Fontaine characterized it, was "socially determined" as the result of the ascribed caste status.[28] Social determination meant, as Fontaine explained, "that there was a correlation between the knowledge propounded by Negro scholars and the social situations confronting the Negro group."[29]

For example, he applauded scholars such as Carter G. Woodson, who unmasked the "sins of omission and commission in writers like Hegel, Dunning, J.W. Burgess, J. F. Rhodes, A. D. White, etc.," and Charles Wesley, who made methodological contributions in historiography by realizing the importance of subjectivity and point of view:

Wesley not only contends that "history is an

expanding concept embracing the ways in which ALL people have lived throughout the ages," but in addition to the inclusion of facts about the Negro he believes that the Negro's perspective could be used in the interpretation of these facts.[30]

Reminiscent of Woodson's call for a "new" educational program to counter the miseducation of Black people, Fontaine's philosophy for Black teachers was one of counterindoctrination which he described as a "toughminded" approach. Fontaine's contribution to African-American cultural knowledge was the ability to go beyond "reform": breaking with the democratic liberal scientific *Weltanschauung* and stating that such opposition was a psychologically healthy position for the African-American community.

Cultural Knowledge as a Basis for Pedagogy

Elsewhere I have argued that while research and writings on Black educational history have provided for the past 45 years much material on the topics of integration, desegregation, boycotts, liberalism, and responses to these issues from the Black and White communities, a major shortcoming in this literature was, and is, the absence of a synthesis of this body of cultural knowledge into a cultural mode of rationality, a social theoretical base that would give leadership and direction to the Black community.[31] My concern is that, while there has been a tendency for American majority scholars to apply a critical theory paradigm to view minorities and the poor, there is little discussion about the differences between the European and American cultural, social and political, and racial fibers.[32] Conversely, even less has been stated about alternative paradigms generated by the minority group scholars themselves.

The hegemonic impact of European radical theory on Black cultural, political, and ideological thought is not new. Theorists such as Marable, Jones, and Aronowitz are now beginning to articulate the differences in American and European social, cultural, and political contexts and the implications of these on neo-Marxist thought and the possibilities and criticisms of applying this paradigm to other cultural settings or racial groups. Contemporary Black scholars realize that socialism alone does not insure the abolition of racism. In fact, "there is not ... a body of knowledge which could be described as a Marxian theory of racism which can be directly applied to our understanding of American society."[33] What African-American educational scholars must do now, in the tradition of Woodson, DuBois,

Bond, etc., is articulate their own unique cultural mode of rationality and accompanying pedagogy. In this context, it is fortunate that there has been a resurgence of interest in the concept of African-American culture.[34]

Within contemporary African-American literature, there appears to be an acknowledgment of the existence of a cultural mode of rationality, although at the present time there is little formal writing on the topic particularly in educational literature and research. Awareness of such a mode of rationality comes as the result of the persistent emergence of African-American scholars who are conceptualizing alternative scientific and philosophical paradigms that are designed to systematically analyze African-American culture. African-American scholars in various disciplines—such as Berry and Blassingame in American history, Boykin and Jones in educational psychology, Franklin and Anderson in educational history, Outlaw in philosophy, Gordon in curriculum theory, Ladner in sociology, and Marable and Childs in political science, among many others—are now grappling with current issues and concerns in their systematic study of African-American cultural tradition and knowledge.[35]

Beyond the concerns of Black theorists, which I have discussed at length elsewhere,[36] this truncated piece of African-American educational history has several implications for a participatory citizenship and a new civic education for teachers. Furthermore, this essay asks that teachers "look anew," as Maxine Green[37] would have them do, and critically evaluate the curriculum and evolve an emancipatory pedagogy for the civic education of students.

One implication of this essay is that the objective (neutral) knowledge given in schools is in fact socially constructed and disseminated. That is, the knowledge given in textbooks—story and pictures in literature, math, science, history, art texts, and other curricular and extracurricular activities—represents an, not the, interpretation of the world.

Secondly, viewing the history and social context of a minority group from their perspective, not through the dominant social science paradigms, helps to clarify facts and values and explain how different and competing paradigms and interpretations of the phenomena emerge. By unpacking the conflicting views and alternative paradigms, we are better able to understand how dominant views persist and are perpetuated through institutional legitimation, such as in teacher preparation based on the nineteenth century educational, psychological, managerial paradigm grounded in social Darwinist thought.

This essay also implies that the oppressed, those with the least, must struggle the most for an improved society; that a more just and equitable society is in their vested interest; and, in order to go beyond the current status quo, the community will respond by generating new paradigms to transform and transcend the conflict or crisis. Moreover, the paradigms and social theory generated from the community are more precise tools for research and analysis because they provide a sharper understanding of the group beliefs, opinions, and values.

Finally, this essay demonstrates how emancipatory categories respond to the daily lives and events of a people as a result of an experience, situation, or need for certain action.

From these lessons of history, we can begin to talk about classroom pedagogy that is emancipatory in nature. A citizenship education which employs critical and reflective thinking holds much promise for a more responsive, socially active citizenry concerned about all in the polity and willing to work to improve society in a way that promotes justice and equity for all citizens. I use the term *emancipatory pedagogy* to try to capture the essence of a process that is complicated, complex, and involves many intricacies that go beyond the scope of this paper. Giroux's "Critical Writing and Thinking in the Social Studies" or his "Episodes in American History" are excellent examples of an emancipatory learning for American high school classrooms.[38] Giroux teaches that the same facts viewed from different perspectives can result in different interpretations of historical events. He clearly demonstrates that there is a relationship between the facts of an event and the values brought to the task of interpretation by the writer. Again, the realization that knowledge is socially constructed mandates that all people have the potential and ability to make culture, and, even more importantly, they have the ability as citizens to change it.

Emancipatory Pedagogy: Challenges and Implications

Emancipatory pedagogy is the reconceptualization of knowledge into new forms of ideology and paradigms that help illuminate and clarify the cultural realities of all groups. Emancipatory pedagogy is also a counterindoctrination against the blind acceptance of the concepts of the dominant culture as demonstrated in Fontaine's discussion of the meaning of democracy. Emancipatory pedagogy is the freeing of one's mind to explore the essence and influence of one's primary culture throughout the world and the ability to pass on that information to the next generation as a foundation on which to build models for democratic civic participation.

This critical awareness can most certainly be taught in teacher education courses. Teachers and students can learn to examine critically the descriptive language and information in school texts and materials that are given as objective and factual. In an inteview with Cynthia Brown over a decade ago, Herbert Kohl discusses using this kind of emancipatory model with children. Kohl attempted to adapt some of Freire's ideas to his own pedagogical work with minority and poor children. His comments on the realization and validity of one's own culture and how this might be applied in classrooms, are worth quoting at length.

> [T]o realize that one's everyday actions have to do with culture, and that it is possible through a strong sense of one's own creative input into the world to take increasing power over oppressive conditions . . . can be dealt with in a lot of different ways. I take this to be one of [Paulo Freire's] central theses . . . in terms of a very, very strong sense of everyday culture, the very, very strong sense of images not of the oppressor but of images of oneself. It is just a whole way of transferring the material, the style, context, the very definition of what is worth learning. That becomes one important way of dealing with some of [Freire's] more general ideas—the whole question of what is of value is what the majority culture says is of value. So even though you learn things, and as . . . things are being transferred to you, you don't value them. Or you have an ambiguous relationship towards the valuing of them. When that is shifted . . . you have a transvaluation, a real change of values, in which some of the materials of the oppressor can be incorporated into your system as opposed to incorporating yourself into the system of the oppressor.
>
> That can be done in a lot of different ways, and literacy is not the only vehicle necessary for that. Music, theatre, dance, games, just language, even oral language, the validity of one's own oral language, and the retranslation . . . I've noticed, for example, a lot of black kids beginning to understand how they

read history books, how to translate history books written for the validation of white capitalist culture into terms of oppressing other people rather than trying to help other people in liberal society. They have to re-translate words like progress and discovery and therefore understand that language, certainly the language of history and language of self-justification, is moral and not an objective description of the world. A lot of that has to do with understanding notions like justice, notions like equality. When people come to an awareness that language is being used to confound them and can be re-translated into language which is both their own and much clearer-headed, you have a form of liberation. You have a real form of pedagogy, I mean, that is teaching and learning.[39]

"Teaching" and "learning" history or social studies can become, for both teachers and students, an exercise in using classroom materials to learn how to re-translate words (and facts) intended to present an objective description of the world. Consider, for example, the following passages dealing with another minority group, the Native Americans, taken from "Highlights of Ohio History," an Ohio Bell Telephone publication for Ohio elementary school children. These passages provide an excellent opportunity to apply the emancipatory principles which make problematic what appears to be objective or neutral.

> In 1669, the famous French explorer LaSalle wrote his name in Ohio history by his discovery of the Ohio River... Told about the river by the missionaries, he was warned of the fierce Iroquois who guarded it.
>
> Ohio pioneers not only had to conquer a vast wilderness; they had come to terms with the many Indian tribes that inhabited the territory. Many of these Indian chiefs and their tribes have left their mark on the pages of Ohio's history. Among them are ... Chief Tecumseh ... Many others, such as the Delawares ... gave up their struggles against the settlers in the Greenville Treaty. In 1842, the Wyandot tribe was the last tribe to leave the

Ohio country and open the entire territory for peaceful settlement.[40]

By making problematic (studying) the meaning and assumptions of words such as *discovery, fierce, missionaries, conquer, hostile, struggles, treaty,* and *peaceful,* students and teachers can discern what is and is not being taught. They may also come to understand that facts and values are interrelated and, most importantly, that the interpretations of events, conditions, etc., will have also been decided if the paradigms and assumptions are predetermined. This type of critical analysis through the reconceptualization of knowledge assists in unpacking colonialism and racism in textbooks which talk of the "hostile" Indians threatening the settlers but say nothing about the righteous indignation on the part of the Native American nations for whom genocide and displacement became facts of life.

The success of an emancipatory pedagogy, however, rests on the following dictum: the pedagogy must shift away from colonialism in order to emphasize emancipation of the mind and spirit. Such a thrust can be actualized in several ways. First, instead of teaching future teachers and students with negative imagery, we can allow students to speak with their own authentic voices as Sylvia Ashton-Warner demonstrated, and then engage them in formal classroom work using their own cultural resources as a bridge between them.[41] In this effort, instructors can turn to reading materials such as the autobiographies, for example, of Chief Joseph, Tecumseh, Geronimo, Zora Neale Hurston, Susan B. Anthony, Marcus Garvey, Toussaint L'Ouverture, Reies Tijerina, Malcolm X, and W.E.B. DuBois. This approach is what Woodson had in mind when he argued that the best teacher was the one who taught people using their own folk heroes and heroines.

A second suggestion to further the use of emancipatory pedagogy would be for preservice and in-service teachers to study the accounts of the classroom teachers mentioned in the beginning of this essay who incorporated this pedagogical style into their own curriculum. Sylvia Ashton-Warner, Chris Searle, Cynthia Brown, Ira Shor, and Paulo Freire are all master teachers, whose style, pedagogical ability, and political awareness merits serious study. The contribution they made to the field was in providing real situations and examples of what an emancipatory style could or would look like on a daily basis in classroom settings. Such examples are very useful to practicing teachers because they assist them in studying the nature of classroom relations, the nature of cultural capital that students bring with them to the learning situation, and finally they assist teachers in teaching and learning the dialectical process.

Before implementing any of these suggestions, however, teachers and teacher educators must realize that this is merely a starting point which can—and must—be modified and expanded as we challenge ideological hegemony. It is also important that teacher educators understand how other cultural traditions, such as an African-American rationality which emphasizes self-help, service, economic autonomy, political power, and nationalism, can contribute to a reconstruction of civic education and provide a mode for citizenship which values cultural pluralism, questioning, challenging, and criticism and goes beyond and is more authentically democratic than current notions of "common citizenship."[42]

If our goal is to educate thinking, active citizens in this society, we can begin by exploring the historical resistance of minority and other oppressed groups in dominant society as a basis for pedagogy and the emancipatory modes of rationality that emerged from their struggles. Through this action, citizenship education will evolve into political awareness and critical analysis of reality, leaving far behind the stifling trappings of a mindless indoctrination process.

Notes

[1] Michael Apple, *Ideology and Curriculum* (London: Routledge and Kegan Paul, 1979); Pierre Bourdieu, "Cultural Reproduction and Social Reproduction," in Jerome Karabel and A. H. Halsey, *Power and Ideology in Education* (New York: Oxford University Press, 1977); Paul Willis, *Learning to Labour* (Farnborough, Hants, England: Saxon House, Teakfield Limited, 1978); Beverly M. Gordon, "Towards a Theory of Knowledge Acquisition for Black Children," *Journal of Education* 164, 1 (Winter 1982); Beverly M. Gordon, "The Educational History of Nine High School Dropouts," University of Wisconsin-Madison, Unpublished Dissertation, 1979.

[2] For an in-depth discussion, see Beverly Gordon, "Towards a Theory of Knowledge Acquisition for Black Children."

[3] R. Freeman Butts, "Teacher Education and the Revival of Civic Learning: A Reprise of Yesteryear's Theme," *Journal of Teacher Education* 34, 6 (1983): 48-49.

[4] Antonio Gramsci (1971), and Raymond Williams (1976), among others, have referred to this mode of control as ideological hegemony. They have argued that society can reproduce itself in part through the permeation of a general worldview. By this I mean the entire system of values, attitudes, beliefs, social practices, and norms that in one way or another function to univer-

salize the ideology and social practices of the established order of the class interest that it dominates. Furthermore, it can be argued that this dominant worldview is perpetuated, in part, by schools, families, and other agencies of socialization. Though such a worldview is far from monolithic, it does exercise a powerful influence in shaping the social structure and social relationships for the larger society.

[5] In explanation, a myriad of reasons can, no doubt, be given, the least of which is that undergraduate students, upon entering higher education, come laden with their own ideological baggage which is difficult to unpack and analyze critically. It might also be that while pathological deficiency models are condemned in certain areas of the scholarly community, these theories are still embraced and, in fact, were never really discredited or discarded by other segments of that same community.

[6] As Lucius Outlaw argues, "The turn must be made to the life-world of African-American people, in all of its ambiguities, complexities, contradictions, and clarities; to our concrete life-praxis, in search of our distinct orientation with regard to the matters to be addressed in a revolutionary transformation of the American order. Such orientations are given, for example, in the mediated folk tales; in religious practices; in political language and practices prevalent during various times under various conditions; in forms of music, poetry, language of common currency, etc. As these forms of expression, in their concreteness as life-praxis, are constitutive elements of the life-world of African-American people, then the meanings they hold, in symbolic and/or explicit form, contain fundamental orientations. Reclaiming them through acts of reflection will provide understandings of the historically conditioned concerns of black people. Such acts of reclamation or interpretive understanding constitute the practice of philosophical hermeneutics. As such, they are fundamental, for they must provide the clarified historical grounds for the orientation of present and future philosophical and practical activities in the interest of African-American people" [Lucius Outlaw, "Philosophy, Hermeneutics, Social-Political Theory: Critical Thought in the Interest of African-Americans," in Leornard Harris, ed., *Philosophy Born of Struggle: Anthology of Afro-American Philosophy from 1917* (Dubuque, Iowa: Kendall/Hunt, 1983), 66].

[7] Giroux defines rationality as " . . . a specific set of assumptions and social practices that mediate how an individual or group relates

to the wider society. Underlying any one mode or rationality is a set of interests that defines and qualifies how one reflects on the world. This is an important epistemological point. The knowledge, beliefs, expectations and biases that define a given rationality both condition, and are conditioned by, the experiences into which we enter. Of critical importance is the notion that such experiences only become meaningful within a mode of rationality that confers intelligibility on them" [Henry A. Giroux, *Ideology, Culture, and the Process of Schooling* (Philadelphia: Temple University, 1981)].

[8] Henry Giroux, "Critical Theory and Rationality in Citizenship Education," *Curriculum Inquiry* 10, 4 (Winter 1980): 343.

[9] Giroux, "Critical Theory," 347.

[10] Giroux, "Critical Theory," 348. The cultural reproduction literature is best exemplified by Pierre Bourdieu and Jean-Claude Passeron, *Reproduction in Education, Society and Culture* (London and Beverly Hills: Sage, 1977); and Richard J. Bernstein, *The Restructuring of Social and Political Theory* (Philadelphia: University of Pennsylvania Press, 1978). The new sociology of education literature is promulgated by Nel Keddie, "Classroom Knowledge," in *Knowledge and Control*, Michael F. D. Young, ed., (London: Collier Macmillan, 1971); and Rachael Sharp and A. G. Greene, *Education and Social Control* (London: Routledge and Kegan Paul, 1975).

[11] Giroux, "Critical Theory," 352.

[12] George Wood, "Beyond Radical Educational Cynicism," *Educational Theory* 32, 2 (1982).

[13] These recommendations also include allowing active student participation in the learning process, teaching students to think critically and to juxtapose different worldviews, and making sure that classroom pedagogy draws upon the cultural resources that students bring with them to the learning situation.

[14] Cynthia Brown, *Literacy in Thirty Hours* (Chicago: Alternative Schools Network, 1978); Paulo Freire, *Education for Critical Consciousness* (New York: The Seabury Press, 1973); Chris Searle, *Classrooms of Resistance* (London: Writers and Readers Publishing Corp., 1975); Ira Shor, *Critical Teaching and Everyday Life* (Boston: Southend Press, 1980); and Sylvia Ashton-Warner, *Teacher* (New York: Basic Books, 1964).

[15] Beverly M. Gordon, "Teaching Teachers: 'A Nation at Risk' and the Issue of Knowledge in Teacher Education," *Urban Review* 17,1 (1985): 33-46.

[16] David Held, *Introduction to Critical Theory* (Berkeley: University

of California Press, 1980).

[17] Henry Giroux, "Theories of Reproduction and Resistance in the New Sociology of Education: A Critical Analysis," *Harvard Educational Review* 53, 3 (1983): 257-293.

[18] Gordon, "Towards a Theory of Knowledge Aquisition for Black Children," 90-108.

[19] Beverly M. Gordon, "The Invisibility of African-American Thought and Scholarship in Educational History: 1890 to 1940," Unpublished Essay, 1984.

[20] Kelly Miller, *Race Adjustment: Essays on the Negro in America. 1908.* (Miami, Florida: Mnemosyne Publishing Co., Inc., 1969).

[21] James Anderson, "Northern Philanthropy and the Training of the Black Leadership: Fisk University, A Case Study, 1915-1930," in *New Perspectives on Black Educational History*, Vincent P. Franklin and James D. Anderson, eds., (Boston: G. K. Hall and Company, 1978), 97-111.

[22] Benjamin P. Bowser, "The Contribution of Blacks to Sociological Knowledge: A Problem of Theory and Role to 1950," *Phylon* 42 (1981): 180-193.

[23] Carter G. Woodson, *The Mis-Education of the Negro* (1933; second edition, Washington, D.C.: AMS Press, Inc., 1977), xiii and 103. In the course of this cultural instruction, Woodson even takes religions to task: " . . . If Negroes got their conception to religion from slaveholders, libertines, and murderers, there may be something wrong with it, and it would not hurt to investigate it. It has been said that the Negroes do not correct morals with religion. The historian would like to know what race or nation does such a thing. Certainly the whites with whom the Negroes have come into contact have not done so" (p. 73).

[24] Woodson, *Mis-Education*, 57.

[25] Woodson, *Mis-Education*, 14.

[26] Woodson, *Mis-Education*, 151.

[27] William Thomas Fontaine, "An Interpretation of Contemporary Negro Thought from the Standpoint of the Sociology of Knowledge," *Journal of Negro History* 25, 1 (1940).

[28] William Thomas Fontaine, "Social Determination in the Writings of Negro Scholars (1944)," in Leonard Harris, ed., *Philosophy Born of Struggle: Anthology of Afro-American Philosophy from 1917* (Dubuque, Iowa: Kendall/Hunt, 1983).

[29] Fontaine, "An Interpretation."

[30] Fontaine, "An Interpretation."

[31] Beverly M. Gordon, "Toward Emancipation in Citizenship Education: The Case of African-American Cultural Knowledge," *Theory and Research in Social Education* 12, 4 (Winter 1985): 1-23.

[32] Stanley Aronowitz, *The Crisis in Historical Materialism* (New York: Praeger Special Studies - J. F. Bergin Publishers, 1981).

[33] Manning Marable, "The Third Reconstruction: Black Nationalism and Race in a Revolutionary America," *Social Text—Theory/Culture/Ideology* 2, 1 (1981).

[34] John Brown Childs, "Concepts of Culture in Afro-American Political Thought," *Social Text—Theory/Culture/Ideology* 2, 1 (1981); and Horace Mann Bond, *Negro Education in Alabama—A Study in Cotton and Steel*, A Susan Colver Rosenberger Prize Essay for 1937, (New York: Octagon Books, 1969).

[35] Mary Frances Berry and John W. Blassingame, *Long Memory: The Black Experience in America* (New York and London: Oxford Press, 1982); A. Wade Boykin, "Psychological/Behavioral Verve: Some Theoretical Explorations and Empirical Manifestations," in *Research Directions of Black Psychologists*, A. Wade Boykin, A. J. Franklin, and J. F. Yates, eds., (New York: Russell Sage Foundation, 1979); Childs, "Concepts of Culture"; Vincent P. Franklin and James Anderson, eds., *New Perspectives in Black Educational History* (Boston: G. K. Hall and Co., 1978); Gordon, "Toward Emancipation"; Gordon, "Teaching Teachers"; Gordon, "Invisibility of African-American Thought"; Gordon, "Towards a Theory"; Beverly M. Gordon, "An Investigation into the Nature and Dimensions of Afro-American Epistemology and Its Implications for Educational Theory and Practice," Unpublished Essay (Columbus: The Ohio State University, 1983); James M. Jones, "Conceptual and Strategic Issues in the Relationship of Black Psychology to American Social Science," in Boykin, Franklin, and Yates, eds., *Research Directions*; Joyce Ladner, ed., *The Death of White Sociology* (New York: Vantage Books - Random, 1973); and Outlaw, "Philosophy, Hermeneutics, Social-Political Theory." In African philosophical thought, Cesaire (1972) and Mbiti (1970) both talk about the relationship between theory and practice. African philosophy and culture constitute a continual merging of theory and praxis.

[36] Gordon, "Toward Emancipation."

[37] Maxine Green, *Landscapes of Learning* (New York: Teachers College Press, 1979).

[38] Henry Giroux, Charles Capazano, and Ray W. Karras, *The Proc-*

ess of Writing History: Episodes in American History* (Providence, R.I.: Center for Research in Writing, 1977). Also see, Henry Giroux, "Critical Writing and Thinking in the Social Studies," *Curriculum Inquiry* 8, 4 (1978): 291-310.

[39] Brown, *Literacy in Thirty Hours*, 35-36.

[40] *Highlights of Ohio History: The Ohio Sesquicentennial, 1803-1953* (Columbus: Ohio Bell Telephone Co., 1953), 5.

[41] Ashton-Warner, *Teacher*.

[42] Butts, "Teacher Education," 48-49.

Chapter Six

Civic education provides a conscience collective which justifies present inequalities in the name of future equality by rationalizing a class differentiated school system.

6

Will the Schools Rebuild an Old Social Order?

By Andrew R. Trusz and Sandra L. Parks-Trusz

THE past three decades have been a time of national turmoil with respect to the issue of actualizing equality of opportunity for all our citizens. Both foreign and American journalists, politicians, and social activists have called our attention to discriminatory practices and barriers to opportunity in the land which dared to proclaim that "all men are created equal." This phrase is commonly understood to mean that merit rather than heredity is the basis for one's rung on the social ladder. Obviously, a meritocracy cannot exist where some citizens are held back at the starting gate.

Three factors have put public education in the forefront of the struggle for equal opportunity. The first centers on the relationship between an educated citizenry and the survival of democracy,

> but the fundamental historic reason why the founders of this Republic called for public schooling was that the education of all the people was essential for the achievement and maintenance of a republican form of government. This purpose has been paramount in much of the subsequent efforts to establish a truly universal, free, common system of public schools.[1]

As second-class citizenship was eliminated by the extension of civil rights, the question of second-class education also had to be faced.

The second reason for the visibility of the public schools in the struggle for equality of opportunity centers on the perceived role of the public school as the nurturer of talent. The public schools theoretically provide the common ground where each child should have the same opportunity to display his or her talent and character. Hence, neither class nor race nor sex represents a handicap which cannot be overcome through diligent effort. Public schools are, in the best sense, seen as being perfectly neutral social instruments which recognize, nurture, and reward talent with the possibility of upward mobility.

The third reason for the focus on the public schools relates to the amenability of the public schools to legislative mandate. While we likely would not forcibly relocate people into race and class integrated neighborhoods, the public schools as public property can be forced to equalize educational resources and to accept an integrated population. Such a population offers the best long-term prospects for an integrated society by demonstrating through individual achievement and intergroup contact the bankruptcy of stereotypes and the waste of talent engendered by discrimination.

Hence, from the 1954 judgment that separate inherently meant unequal, to the uncovering of racism and sexism in textbooks and language, and the discovery of class, race, and sex bias in standardized tests (the supposedly objective mediators of merit), the public schools have exemplified the national dilemma. It is a public dilemma precisely because increasing opportunity for the disenfranchised necessarily decreases the favored advantage held by other classes.

However, the "progressive" criticisms, revisions, and restructuring of public education over the past 30 years seem to have compounded the problem. In urban areas, an integrated school system seems no closer than it was 30 years ago. The loss of white students to a burgeoning private school system has turned the end of *de jure* segregation into *de facto* segregation. The loss of middle-class support for public schools has been expressed with a variety of complaints: academic standards are too low; discipline and respect for authority are not enforced; teachers are unfit both academically and as role models; God has been expelled; teachers elicit information from students about their homelife and their private belief systems; "nice" kids constantly have to worry about having their coats, wallets, and other property stolen and are enticed into participating in sex and using drugs; in short, the culture of the public schools is bankrupt. Public education has become fragmented and many argue that more attention is paid to the rights and needs of racial and ethnic minorities, women, gays, drug pushers and abusers, pregnant students, etc., than to those who come to school to learn how to read, write, compute, and become responsible, productive citizens. Public education is in trouble. The public schools face the prospect of class as well as racial isolation. What can be done to restore confidence in the public schools and stem the tide of privatism?

Civic Education

Among a growing number of educators, civic education is seen as the means by which confidence in public education can be restored and the rising tide of privatism reversed. This is to be accomplished by returning public education to its fundamental purpose of "developing informed, thinking citizens"[2] who are steeped in the theory and practice of democratic principles. Students are to be provided with the skills, attitudes, and knowledge that will allow them to participate in the resolution of the pressing socio-political issues of the technologically sophisticated twenty-first century society. Similarly, teachers are to be prepared to serve as repositories of knowledge, tolerance, and democratic behaviors—role models who will enable their students to become committed to basic public virtue in their role as citizens.

It is not surprising that when the legitimacy of public schooling is being questioned educators would return to the arguments which were initially made to establish public schools. Hence, civic education proponents cite the Jeffersonian notion that democracy cannot exist without an educated citizenry, as well as the value of the common public school in tying together a society composed of diverse groups. R. Freeman Butts, a leading proponent of civic education, for example, has asserted the leading role of the public schools in providing the sense of common republican values which allowed America to absorb the massive influx of immigrants in the nineteenth and early twentieth centuries without the social fabric being torn apart.[3] It is the fear that the social fabric may currently be similarly threatened by divergent publics which prompts Butts' call for civic education. He thus "heartily endorse(s)" John W. Gardner's assessment of the current state of civic affairs:

> I am a strong defender of our pluralism, meaning by pluralism a philosophy and set of social arrangements that permit the existence of many competing ideas, many belief systems, many competing economic units . . .
>
> But a society in which pluralism is not undergirded by *some* shared values simply cannot survive. Pluralism that reflects no commitments whatever to the common good is pluralism gone berserk. . . .
>
> At this moment we are a nation in disarray. No point in mincing words. This is a moment when the innumerable interests, organizations, and groups that make up our national life must keep their part of the bargain with the society that gives them freedom by working toward the common good. Right now. In this time of trouble. Their chance for long-term enjoyment of pluralism will be enhanced by a commitment to the common good as we go through this difficult passage. At least for now, a little less *pluribus*, and a lot more *unum*.[4]

Civic education, then, is to provide that set of undergirding shared values. Those values are explicated in Butts' "A Decalogue of Democratic Civic Values for the Schools."[5] The value concepts of the "Decalogue" are divided into two subgroups:

> those that primarily promote desirable cohesive and unifying elements in a democratic political community and those that primarily promote desirable pluralistic and individualistic elements in a democratic political community.[6]

The unifying values constitute the *unum* which

> promotes a Cosmopolitan Civism in which our sense of civic duty should embrace the

best of our historically generous, open, and tolerant approach to difference rather than our narrow, bigoted, provincial demands for conformity.[7]

The *pluribus* stresses

a "stable pluralism" in which the freedoms, diversities, privacies, due process, and human rights that we should honor, respect and encourage must be based upon a strong underpinning of political and psychological legitimacy which in turn arises from the cohesive elements of civism.[8]

These values are further defined by comparing their "True Forms" with their "Corrupted Forms":

True Forms of Unum		Corrupted Forms
Justice	vs.	"Law and Order"
Equality	vs.	Enforced sameness and conformity
Authority	vs.	Authoritarianism
Participation	vs.	"Majoritarianism"
Personal obligation for the common good	vs.	Chauvinism

True Forms of Pluribus		Corrupted Forms
Freedom	vs.	Anarchy
Diversity	vs.	Unstable Pluralism
Privacy	vs.	Privatism
Due Process	vs.	"Soft on Criminals"
International Human Rights	vs.	"Cultural Imperialism"[9]

These then are the values which are to be restored to a central place in public education. By committing the public schools to these eternal verities of democracy, civic education reasserts the necessity of free, universal, common public schools. As Butts states in his discussion of the danger posed by educational privatism:

I am convinced that in the long run the academic community and the educational professoriate must reaffirm the public purposes of teacher education and the civic goals

of universal education as the foundation of a
free and flourishing democratic society. They
must convince the public that education is
primarily a public good rather than primarily
a means to private fulfillment or personal
preferment.[10]

Clearly, the extension of private schooling through tuition tax waivers, educational vouchers, and educational savings accounts presents, in Butts' view, a danger to the long-term public good by depleting the resources of our common schools. Civic values are the mortar which hold together the diverse private interests in our democracy.

A Sociological Critique

As an ideal, Butts' proposal is unexceptional. The values propounded are virtually unequivocal within the Western tradition. It is also the case that Butts' discussion of the role of education in society is reminiscent of Durkheim's. In Durkheim's schema, education is crucial to the preservation of the social order because it provides the means by which children are transformed into useful social beings by being exposed to the essential ideas and beliefs of their society:

Education must assure, among the citizens, a
sufficient community of ideas and sentiment,
without which any society is impossible; and
in order that it may be able to produce this
result, it is also necessary that education not
be completely abandoned to the arbitrariness
of private individuals.[11]

Education is thus a state concern inasmuch as it provides future citizens with a sense of community and concomitant reciprocal obligations. The *unum*, as Durkheim's "conscience collective," makes possible a common identity; the *pluribus* a personal identity. Butts' "Decalogue" thus provides the core ideas through which individuation is possible within a system of sacrifice for the common good.

Important to Durkheim's social vision was the rise of public education as the objective instrument for eliminating inherited social advantages. Durkheim's division of labor rests on the assumption that there are natural dispositions among people which must be identified. Schools are the instrument for nurturing these natural propensities in a rational, scientific manner. A good society according to Durkheim would be one in which "social inequalities exactly express natural inequalities."[12] Thus, schools have a dual role. While inculcating the conscience collective they must also provide the means for the rational ordering of society. The meritocratic ideal is therefore realized through a common school in which all citizens have equal opportunity to display their talents.

Durkheim's principal sociological problem was the impossibility of finding an unbiased set of values and selection criteria for creating the perfect social order. Some means of preferment inevitably biased the selection process. Hence, for Durkheim society was perpetually in the process of approaching a true division of labor. Civic education, we will argue, faces the same problem. While the ideal is unimpeachable, in reality civic education leaves the attainment of a fully informed citizenry at some future point while justifying present inequalities as a necessary step in the attainment of the ideal. In other words, we believe civic education provides a conscience collective ("a lot more *unum*") which justifies present inequalities ("a lot less *pluribus*") in the name of future equality. It does so by rationalizing a class-differentiated school system and, paradoxically, halting the democratic process of realizing equal opportunity.

It is not the lack of civic education which has caused a lack of confidence in public schools and the flight of students to private institutions. Rather, it is the attempted extension of equality of opportunity which has led to middle-class disfavor with public education. Specifically, the growth of private school enrollment can be historically situated with the judicial demise of neighborhood schools. As social policy, busing is intended to remedy the effects of segregation. It is intended, in other words, to promote equality of opportunity. It is to do so by mixing both races and classes. The white flight and occasional extreme violence, as in Boston's "Southie," which greeted busing plans indicates that for many equality and quality cannot coexist; that busing represents special privilege not equality.

This suggests that it is fear of loss of preferment which prompted opposition to busing and subsequent white flight. As radical critics such as Jencks, Bowles and Gintis, Karier, Spring, Bane, Carnoy, and others have demonstrated, public education is a source of preferment based on class factors. The single most reliable predictor of school success remains social class background. Attempts to actualize equality of opportunity threaten this function. Hence, resistance to mixing members of the growing underclass with middle- and even working-class children is to be expected. When that underclass is primarily black, racism serves to compound and in some ways confuse the resentment.

The locus of that preferment, as these critics have demonstrated, lies in the textbooks, sorting techniques, and "objective" tests employed in the schools. Equal opportunity requires that the role of minorities, including women and working-class members, be re-evaluated in textbooks, for example. Ability grouping, however labeled, has also been called into question because ability, in the manner in which it is presently evaluated, seems to follow class background. This is a particularly acute issue in terms of standardized tests and the whole logic of test construction and validity. Indeed, the controversy over tests has prompted many institutions of higher education to de-emphasize them even as grade schools and high schools are beginning to make more extensive use of such devices. If equality is to be achieved, questions of content and evaluation must be seriously addressed.

Ironically, civic education would allow the educational community to avoid these issues. It will do so by helping to revive the positivistic, ameliorative function of public schooling. As educational practice, civism has stressed an idealized middle-class vision of America. It has, as Butts himself argues elsewhere, trivialized contemporary issues while exaggerating the degree to which democratization has taken place in America.

In the nineteenth century, Butts argues,

> the political curriculums of the emerging public schools were largely oriented toward a civic program that initiated the poor, the foreign, and the working-class children into the political community by literacy in English; by didactic moral injunctions; by patriotic readers and histories; and by lessons that stressed memory and recitation of the structural forms of the constitutional order.[13]

The state of civism in the early twentieth century is, for Butts, summarized in Tyack's discussion of "conservative persuasion":

> In an urban and industrial society, whose agriculture was fast being mechanized and aimed at a world market, the school books painted a sentimental picture of rural bliss. In a period of great stress on the family, they drew a cloying picture of home sweet home. In times of industrial violence they ignored the condition of labor and described unions as the evil plots of foreigners, anarchists, and Communists. In the midst of unparalleled political corruption they portrayed statesmen of stainless steel. The Negro appeared infre-

quently in the texts, and then usually in the guise of Sambo. People of other nations often appeared as foils to illustrate the superior virtue of Americans. A pervasive Protestantism colored the readers and downgraded other religions either openly or by implication. A pluralistic, expansive society undergoing great intellectual, social, economic, and political change, was reduced in the textbooks, as Ruth Elson has observed, to a "fantasy made up by adults as a guide for their children, but inhabited by no one outside the pages of schoolbooks."[14]

Just 20 years ago, Litt found that class-based definitions of citizenship were common in the schools. For lower-class students, civic education stressed duties while middle-class students were informed of their rights.[15] In a study of history textbooks in connection with the Bicentennial, one of the authors found that the roles of working-class Americans, women, and other minorities were constantly overlooked or at best glossed over in such texts.[16] American history was portrayed in a messianic vein with contemporary problems such as racism, sexism, and class bias being remnants of once serious problems which the mere passage of time would fully resolve with little or no conscious effort.

Certainly one expects that Butts does not wish to repeat these excesses. While he wishes to establish the serious scholarly study of democratic principles and practices as the core of the curriculum for both students and teachers-in-training, he also admits that the values in his "Decalogue" are "normative concepts, each with extensive histories of scholarly analysis, controversial interpretation, and conflicting practice."[17] It is the definitions of these values that will determine the final meaning of civic education. Not only are the past formulations of civism (used at a time when civism was a fundamental purpose of the curriculum) not encouraging, but contemporary proposals offer little more. While Finkelstein writes of the need for a curriculum which empowers the language of students,[18] and Jones-Wilson offers minority teachers as potential exemplars of true civism, a special issue of the *Journal of Teacher Education* devoted to the theme of civic education contains little discussion of how to and what to study with regard to constitutionalism. The articles instead argue for the inclusion of various studies as part of civic education ranging from Adler's "great books," to scientific literacy as a fundamental form of civism, to the need to examine the content of mass media, to studying the effects of technology on citizenship, to an expression of concern that without empirical modes of inquiry "civic education will degenerate even further into passive nostalgia or active separatism."[19]

When civic education is discussed as the basis for curriculum, it is in the positivistic, ameliorative vein of its historical formulation. Oldenquist argues:

> Citizenship education must begin with information about our nation, government, and ideals, taught so as to provide grounds for developing pride and affection; it should also include field exercises in public service and political participation. If instead we start nine-year-olds with a litany of evils and injustices, they will be likely to learn cynicism and alienation. A teacher may say, "But I teach about problems and injustices because I want to make my country better; if I did not have concern and affection for it I would not care about reforming it." Precisely. The teacher did not acquire affection for our country by being told that we exterminated Indians, lynched Blacks, and slaughtered Vietnamese. The teacher's concern and affection *survived* this knowledge because of prior training and experience, and the pupils, like the teacher, need to acquire a basis for good citizenship before they are plunged into what is ugly.[20]

The sad truth is that we did exterminate, lynch, and slaughter and for many students knowledge of those events is a part of their everyday experience. It has been the failure of schools to come to grips not just with these actions but their causes which has made schooling appear absurd for many students. At minimum it leaves students to perpetually rediscover that social reality is rooted in the narrow bigotry of the ugly side of the *unum*. Arguing as Oldenquist does that slum kids especially need to be taught the virtues of "basic civility, honesty, a work ethic, and the postponement of gratifications"[21] is to re-engage in mobilization of bias and blaming the victim. That is to say, underclass culture is portrayed as flawed, creating a social dead end; moreover, people who do not break out of their underclass culture have only themselves to blame. Social inequality is not recognized, only personal failure. Citizenship education, then, at one and the same time puts the final solution to social problems into the next generation while rationalizing the present as the best we can do.

That civic education is likely to again take the form of a Durkheimian positivistic ameliorism is enhanced by the current concern over the decline in academic performance. While the problem of academic decline predates legislative and judicial efforts at equality of opportunity, and is thus in a sense a separate issue, the solutions being implemented enhance the likelihood that civic education will be given a positivistic cant.

In relying so extensively on testing for assessment and teacher selection, such proposals are necessarily committing schools to grouping based on selection mechanisms which we find to be class biased. The grouping derives logically from the assessment tests. As we have argued elsewhere,[22] fairness dictates that when students fail the second-grade assessment, for example, they must be remediated. While this may result in their passing on the second attempt, it also means they have fallen behind their age cohorts. Should a student fail the test a second time or fail the fifth-grade exam, the student will fall further behind. By high school this will result in a performance gap which will necessitate grouping in order to prepare students for the final graduation exam.

There is as well the question of where to set the passing grade. Should it be set based upon the knowledge of those students who pass each test the first time through? If so, is it reasonable to expect those who have been remediated at some point to pass an exam on material they have perhaps not seen and certainly are not as well prepared for? Or, is the typical ninth-grade level more appropriate since more students would have adequate preparation and familiarity with the material?

While these issues are in themselves serious, they beg the more fundamental question of the class bias in test and curricular materials. As Jane Mercer has observed, tests "screen in those persons whose behavior fits their expectations and ... screen out those whose behavior does not fit their expectations."[23] Kagan further informs us that these expectations are those of the "white, middle-class community" which "like any other moderately isolated social group, has created over the years a specialized vocabulary, reservoir of information, and style of problem solving summarized under the concept of 'intelligence.' "[24] By their nature, then, the tests are class biased and the grouping they lead to is also based on class. Without access to the middle-class culture underlying such a selection mechanism, education becomes a process for many students for being selected out because of their background.

Indeed, the logic of test construction requires a certain failure rate.

While a failure rate of 80 percent on a ninth-grade English assessment, as was recently the case in Memphis, is unacceptable, there will come a point when the failure rate is acceptable. That is to say, standards of performance will have reached a point at which it is unreasonable to expect all students to pass a test because of presumed differences in ability. A sufficient number of students will have been selected out.

All of which is not to say that academic standards won't improve. The extra homework, greater emphasis on literacy, and improved physical environment will almost certainly improve overall academic performance. But, it will also contribute to the performance gap. While the performance of all students may well improve, the gap between the best and the worst will widen and this will be seen as "proof" that the decline has been reversed. In addition, as students are selected out, performance on such measures of quality as the SAT will likely continue their recent upward turn because the less qualified will not take such exams. Indeed, new tests such as the "Student Achievement and Advisement Test (SAAT)" as proposed by Boyer in *High School* may be developed based on the core curriculum the student studied "to provide <u>advisement</u>, helping students made decisions more intelligently about their futures"—of course—"not to screen students out of options, but to help them move on with confidence to college and to jobs."[25] Students will be able to select themselves out based on a Durkheimian rational, scientific basis.

Proposals for academic improvement, then, with their reliance upon testing will prepare students for their "special milieux." However, as we have seen, that place in fact will not be determined by scientific means but by class factors.

In addition to asserting a probable connection between the demise of civic education and the rise of the private school movement, Butts attempts to construct a similar relationship between the fortunes of public education and public attitudes toward schools of education and the teachers they produce:

> Now, I think that it is no accident that the rise of privatism in educational discourse comes at a time when attitudes towards schools of education are also at a low ebb.... Decline in faith in public universal education can easily be traced in the public mind to the low estate of schools of education, their faculties, and their students.[26]

While there may be a link between public opinion regarding the quality of the public schools and the quality of the teaching profession, the relationship between this and a decline in the civic education of teachers is not documented. Indeed, we think that any attempt to historically document a high status for the teaching profession at any time since the creation of public schools in this country would be difficult to accomplish. The teaching profession has historically been occupied by low-status persons, i.e., women, students from the lower quartile of their college class, and lower-class members. (The exception here is the greater status of teachers in the minority community.) The traditional connection between status and income has been consistently lacking in the case of teachers. Certainly, colleges of education and their faculty have never enjoyed the status accorded to their colleagues in arts, sciences, medicine, etc. Hence, civic education proposals are not strengthened by the attempt to connect civic education, teacher education, and public regard for schools.

Conclusion

The public schools are being revived. The erosion of confidence is ending. Academic performance is improving. Legislative mandates are returning the public schools to basics. Teacher education is achieving more credibility through increased emphasis on subject matter and competence testing. The legislative battle over prayer in the schools continues, thus giving hope to some. But, as we have seen, this strengthening of public education rests on revitalized particularistic values and behaviors rooted in middle-class culture.

As Durkheim's work suggests, any social order needs a legitimizing ideology. Civic education offers such an ideology for public schooling. However, this is only a legitimate ideology if we wish to postpone the democratic imperative of equal opportunity in favor of a system of race- and class-based preferments. Will the schools rebuild an old social order?

Notes

[1] R. Freeman Butts, "Curriculum for the Educated Citizen," *Educational Leadership* 38 (October 1980): 7.
[2] *Ibid.*, 6.
[3] R. Freeman Butts, *Public Education in the United States: From Revolution to Reform,* part II and part III (New York, NY: Holt, Rinehart and Winston, 1978).
[4] Butts, "Curriculum," 8.
[5] *Ibid.*
[6] *Ibid.*

[7] *Ibid.*
[8] *Ibid.*
[9] *Ibid.*
[10] Butts, "Teacher Education and the Revival of Civic Learning: A Reprise of Yesteryear's Theme," *Journal of Teacher Education* 34, 6 (November-December 1983): 49.
[11] Emile Durkheim, *Education and Sociology* (New York, NY: The Free Press, 1956), 80.
[12] Emile Durkheim, *The Division of Labor* (New York, NY: The Free Press, 1956), 378.
[13] Butts, *Public Education*, 95.
[14] *Ibid.*, 185.
[15] Edgar Litt, "Civic Education, Community Norms, and Political Indoctrination," *American Sociological Review* 28, 1 (February 1963): 69-75.
[16] Maxine Seller and Andrew R. Trusz, "High School Textbooks and the American Revolution," *The History Teacher* IX, 4 (August 1976): 535-554.
[17] Butts, "Curriculum," 8.
[18] Barbara Finkelstein, "Thinking Publicly About Civic Learning: An Agenda for Education Reform in the 80s," in *Civic Learning for Teachers: Capstone for Educational Reform* (Ann Arbor, MI: Prakken Publications, 1985), 13-24.
[19] See Faustine C. Jones-Wilson, "The Effect Upon Minorities of the Civic Education of Teachers"; Mortimer J. Adler, "Understanding the U.S.A."; Kenneth Prewitt, "Civic Education and Scientific Literacy"; Carlos E. Cortes, "The Mass Media: Civic Education's Public Curriculum"; Bernard Murchland, "Citizenship in a Technological Society: Problems and Possibilities"; and Manfred Stanley, "How to Think Anew About Civic Education"; *Journal of Teacher Education* 34, 6 (November-December 1983).
[20] Andrew Oldenquist, "On the Nature of Citizenship," *Educational Leadership* 38 (October 1980): 33.
[21] *Ibid.*, 34.
[22] Andrew R. Trusz and Sandra L. Parks-Trusz, "The Social Consequences of Minimum Competence Testing," *Educational Studies* 12, 3 (Fall 1981): 231-241.
[23] Jane Mercer, "Test 'Validity,' 'Bias,' and 'Fairness': An Analysis from the Perspective of the Sociology of Knowledge," *Interchange* 9 (1978-79): 3.
[24] Jerome Kagan, "The Case Against I.Q. Tests: the Concept of Intelligence," in Robert J. Antonio and George Ritzer, eds., *Social Problems* (Boston, MA: Allyn and Bacon), 242.

[25] Ernest Boyer, *High School* (New York, NY: Harper and Row, 1983), 134.
[26] Butts, "Teacher Education," 49.

Chapter Seven

The norms for the male's civic membership and participation have been derived from his relationship to political entitlement, while the norms for the female's civic membership and particiption have been derived from her role in the family and location within the economy.

7

The Education of the Citizeness

By Susan Douglas Franzosa

> Free schools are for citizenship, and good citizenship demands the fullness of manhood. Therefore, to culture youths in the fullness of manhood is the express object of free schools.
> —*NEA Proceedings*, 1873*

IN 1792, in the very first sentence of *The Vindication of the Rights of Women*, Mary Wollstonecraft asserted, "In the present state of society it appears necessary to go back to first principles in search of the most simple truths, and dispute with some prevailing prejudice every inch of ground."[1] What Wollstonecraft was arguing for in the *Vindication*, of course, was the extension of the political rights of man to woman. Her intent was to show that women could, if given equal opportunities within the social and political order, exercise the rights and fulfill the responsibilities of the citizen just as capably as men. But what Wollstonecraft realized, and what she asserted in this first sentence, was that in order to enfranchise women as citizens worthy of social and political rights, it would be necessary to rework many of the fundamental assumptions of classical political philosophy. She understood that women's full citizenship in the state depended on her full citizenship as a subject within the rational constructs that explain and justify the state's existence.

While women have made considerable social and political progress since the publication of the *Vindication*, it has nevertheless taken almost two centuries for scholars to begin to recognize that if they are to explain the experiences of women as well as men, the first principles, or in some cases "every inch of ground," within their disciplines must be reconceptualized. For, as feminist scholars have found along with Wollstonecraft, once one begins to ask relatively simple questions about women and their experience, the explanatory power of time-honored theoretic constructs and methodologies is often found to be inadequate. Thus, the disciplinary paradigm begins to come under critical scrutiny and itself becomes an object of reconstruction.

Recent feminist scholarship in the traditional disciplines testifies to the effects of searching for the most "simple truths" about women and their experiences.[2] In the case of history, for example, the research questions asked during the last 15 years have not only made it possible to reconstruct a more inclusive account of the social along with the military and political past, it has also led to a re-periodization in historical scholarship. In literature, the parameters and rationale of the traditional literary canon have been questioned and reworked and more attention has been paid to literature falling outside conventionally accepted genres. In psychology, feminist scholars have successfully urged a rethinking of models of normalcy based solely on the study of male experience and have begun to develop more integrated heuristic tools. In the biological sciences, female growth and development is increasingly being treated as something more than an inferior version of male growth and development. And, as Darlene L. Boroviak writes, feminist work in the social sciences has led to:

> the formulation of new theoretical models to replace old ones that do not fit women's

experience, to a crossing of disciplinary boundaries and increasing pressure to legitimize inter-disciplinary work, [and] to a questioning of traditional social science methodologies based upon positivist notions of scientific objectivity.[3]

In educational studies the need to account for the experiences of women is no less acute than it is in other more traditional disciplines. And, as Jane Roland Martin's recent work has so ably demonstrated, such an accounting will affect the way the central issues within the field are understood and explained.[4] In the history of educational thought, for example, classical personifications of the ideally educated citizen can be shown to encode normative generalizations appropriate to males, but not females, within particular societal contexts and, further, to avoid any consideration of what social structural changes would be necessary to enable females to achieve an ideal citizenship. Plato's "philosopher king," John Locke's "cultured gentleman," and Jean Jacques Rousseau's "Emile," or, in the American context, Thomas Jefferson's "republican man," Horace Mann's "sober, wise and industrious man," or G. Stanley Hall's "fully realized social aristocrat," are not gender neutral.[5] Rather, they are ideals based on the assumption of male normalcy.

The assumption of male normalcy has had an effect not only on the way classical models for the ideally educated citizen have been constructed and evaluated, however, it has also biased the construction of explanatory frameworks and emphases in contemporary educational research studies. As Dale Spender has contended, women and their experiences have either remained invisible or, alternatively, have been dismissed as anomalous unreliable data in historical, sociological, and psychological treatments of education. Spender quotes Sandra Acker's survey of studies published between 1960 and 1980:

> One would conclude that numerous boys but few girls go to secondary modern schools; that there are almost no adult women influentials of any sort; that most students in higher education study science and engineering; that women rarely make a ritual transition called "from school to work" and never go into further education colleges.[6]

When girls and women are included as subjects, Acker finds considerable confusion about how to "fit them in":

> Witkin is puzzled as "the findings for girls . . . were not anticipated." For Synge, the high

> educational aspirations of rural girls were "contrary to expectations." Robinson and Rackstraw admit "at present we have no supportable explanation to offer for these occasional sex differences in performance." Liversidge is surprised that working class girls' occupational aspirations don't differ much between those in grammar schools and in modern schools, unlike those of boys. And Robertson and Kapur go so far as to say that their results for women students are bizarre.[7]

The invisibility of women and the inability to satisfactorily account for their educational experiences have been particularly apparent in recent discussions of the development and role of civic education in the United States. Within the current debate, there has been virtually no attention given to the way gender distinctions affect the reception of the curriculum or govern adult modes of civic participation, and no attempt has been made to evaluate the gender biases of models for good citizenship. The "simple truth" of the female's historic social and political disenfranchisement has either been ignored or hurriedly discounted in assessing the civic curriculums of the past or in building rationales for the civic curriculums of the future.

As contemporary educational scholars continue their debates on civic education and deliberate on the appropriate curriculum for a modern citizenship, it is imperative that women's educational experience be made visible. In the American context, after all, women's educational experience is hardly an anomaly. It is, in fact, absurd to assume that the experience of at least 50 percent of those who attend schools can be dismissed as irrelevant, or acknowledged only as an exception that proves the rules. Rather than proving the rules of interpretation, women's educational experience serves to reveal the tacitly held and hidden norms affecting all students. It proves that the rules which govern an understanding of civic education need to be reconceptualized.

In what follows, I will argue that women's educational experience clearly demonstrates that civic education has a broader purpose than training for good citizenship. By reviewing historic rationales for civic education and evaluting their implications for the modes of "citizenship" expected of women, I intend to show that civic education in the United States has had as much to do with socializing students to accept existing social relations that inhibit full adult participation in civic society as it has had to do with training them to assume the role of the fully entitled citizen. That is, civic education has functioned not only to produce citizens, it has reproduced and legitimated the terms of exclusion that make citizenship itself a meaningful category. Attention to these issues, clearly facilitated by recovering the educational experience of women, it seems to me, will be necessary if those concerned with civic education are to satisfactorily explain and ultimately reconstruct the goals and practices which should govern the education of all people within a modern democratic society.

The Aims of Civic Education

The question "What are the aims of civic education?" traditionally evokes the response that civic education produces the good citizen. The conventional approach to a description of what civic education can accomplish, then, is to advance a model of the good citizen. Yet models of the citizen and the educational aims they personify are necessarily exclusionary, for formal legal citizenship is an exclusive rather than an inclusive political right awarded on the basis of place of birth, age, ownership, sex, and other requirements of entitlement. And, even in contexts in which legal citizenship is universally granted to all adult members, the opportunities to exercise the citizen's rights and duties have not been socially guaranteed. Actual modes of civic participation have been and continue to be differentially coded according to such variables as race, religion, class, and gender. Further, since models for good citizenship are politically derived, they are ideologically partisan. The characteristics of citizenship they esteem, however worthy they might seem as individualized personal goals, are neither appropriate to all nor can they be attained by all. Models of the good citizen, then, when taken as educational goals, represent not what all students can hope to achieve in civil society but what legitimates the full civic participation of a select group: the citizens in that society

What, then, does the definition of civic education as education for citizenship actually mean? If the aim of civic education is understood as education for citizenship in the formal sense, the fully entitled future citizen appears to be its only true student. Clearly, this has not been the case in the American context, in which all students within the state public schooling system, including those who will be disenfranchised as adults, have been understood as the recipients of a civic education. The aims of civic education, then, must encompass more than training for full legal citizenship. And, civic education must include differentiated levels of expectation for its students even when a single model of the citizen is advanced as the personification of the state's educational ideal.

Within the American public school, for example, preparation for full citizenship was clearly irrelevant to the education of the female student prior to August 26, 1920. In the terms of English common law, prior to that date, women could be considered to be "civilly dead."[8] They were not entitled to own property, hold political office, independently manage their own financial affairs, or vote. But it would be incorrect to assume that girls were not given a civic education. The civic utility of education for girls was not deemed irrelevant to the roles they would play as adults and, in fact, was continually invoked as an argument for the taxes that would support the common schools. Further, in the American school, the civic education of girls was not conducted separately in sex-segregated institutions and classes. Traditionally, from the beginning of American public education, girls as well as boys attended the same elementary schools, and, after the 1830s, the same secondary schools. They were present in the same classrooms and were subject to the same formal curriculum. While not destined to become legal citizens, they were given, and were expected to receive, a civic education long before the final adoption of the Nineteenth Amendment.

This suggests that the future "citizenship" expected of girls was understood quite differently from the future citizenship expected of boys: that the seemingly singular goal of the civic curriculum actually entailed a series of alternative goals for citizenship which were differentiated according to existing genderized social relationships. Within this context, then, the use of the term *citizenship* is highly problematic. It tends to mystify rather than clarify the purposes of civic education.

As I will argue in the following sections of this chapter, civic education cannot be defined merely as education for citizenship. Rather, the aim of civic education has been to inculcate societal norms which legitimate a hierarchical system of membership and participation. Within the American public school system, the norms for male membership and participation have been derived from the male's relation to political entitlement in the state, while the norms for female membership and participation have been derived from the female's relation to the family and location within the economy.

Thomas Jefferson and Schooling for Statecraft

Although the term *citizenship* began to be invoked in arguments for the education of both sexes as early as the eighteenth century,

American educational history reveals serious ambiguities on the question of citizenship and gender. In 1779, as governor of Virginia, Thomas Jefferson proposed a free and universal state school system in which the free white children of all classes would have the opportunity to receive the rudiments of a liberal education. Although Jefferson's proposal was not enacted, it serves to illustrate the more advanced republican sentiments concerning the state's role in education during his era. According to Jefferson, the state had a responsibility as well as a need to provide an education that would prevent political tyranny by "illuminating the minds of the people at large." Further, state elementary schools would discover virtuous and talented political leaders of state. Jefferson contended:

> Those persons, whom nature hath endowed with genius and virtue, should be rendered by liberal education worthy to receive, and able to guard the sacred deposit of the rights and liberties of their fellow citizen . . . without regard to wealth, birth or other accidental conditions or circumstances.[9]

The larger public school system, as Jefferson envisioned its development, would be meritocratic. Those with natural genius and virtue who distinguished themselves in elementary school would be given the opportunity to master ever higher levels of intellectual achievement at publicly supported secondary schools and the state college. A talented few would emerge having earned the right to lead and govern. There was, however, one circumstance, or accident of birth, that would prohibit a free white child's continued educational and political opportunities. The public education of girls was not to be supported beyond the first three years.

> There were to be, in the wards into which it was planned to divide Virginia for the purpose of elementary education, local schools open free for three years to all white children, male and female. Each year an overseer was to choose from the approximately ten schools under his charge the boy of greatest promise from among those whose parents were unable to provide further instruction. These chosen boys were to be sent to secondary schools in larger areas.[10]

A conventional understanding of Jefferson's philosophy of civic education is that he, like other Enlightenment thinkers of his day, believed that intellectual achievement rather than hereditary right was an ideal way of determining the individual's status within the political order. Within this interpretative context, citizenship for Jefferson can be described as a series of hierarchical levels of informed public participation ranging from the nominal role of "the people at large" to those whose education has proven them fit to "guard the sacred deposit of the rights and liberties of their fellow citizen."

But, this explanation of Jefferson's position only works when one is describing his educational provisions for free white males. Blacks, of course, were totally excluded because as slaves they fell outside the social parameters of membership in the state. Women's status was less clear. They would be given three years of education as members of "the people at large," but, however talented, they were not to be allowed to compete for positions within the state meritocracy. Since they were not destined for legal citizenship at any level and were certainly not considered naturally suited to its highest expression in the practice of statecraft, further public support of their education was deemed unnecessary.

Jefferson, unlike many of his contemporaries, however, did advocate at least a minimum state schooling for female children. While he believed that women should not participate in public life equally with men, he nevertheless saw their early education as integral to civic well-being. Women, he contended, had at least an indirect "influence over government" because they had a direct influence over their sons. After a visit with Jefferson at Monticello in 1820, the Scottish activist Frances Wright reported:

> In other countries it may seem of little consequence to inculcate upon the female mind "the principles of government and the obligations of patriotism," but it was wisely foreseen by that venerable apostle of liberty that in a country where a mother is charged with the formation of an infant mind that is to be called in future to judge the laws and support the liberties of a republic, the mother herself should well understand those laws and estimate those liberties.[11]

Clearly, Jefferson understood the civic utility of providing a state system of education that would not only maximize the opportunities for all white males to compete for the academic credentials he wanted to associate with legitimate leadership, but would also school the nation's future mothers in the foundational principles of republicanism. However, for Jefferson, the extent of the female's relation to civic duty, unlike the male's, could not be determined through her success at school. Rather, her sex and location within the family prescribed that she fulfill her responsibilities to the state only within the domestic sphere. Her formal civic education, while it was to teach her about citizenship, was not intended to prepare her for her own citizenship but for the mothering of citizens. Thus, Jefferson's call for a public system of education that would be conducted "without regard to wealth, birth or other accidental conditions or circumstances" and his prescriptions for a rational social meritocracy held only as they applied to free white males.

In the years following Jefferson's *Bill for the More General Diffusion of Knowledge*, advocates of public education advanced similar justifications for the education of the female. In 1787, Benjamin Rush asserted:

> The equal share that every citizen has in the liberty and the equal share he may have in government of our country, make it necessary that our ladies should be qualified . . . by education to concur in instructing their sons in the principles of liberty and government.[12]

Rush, like Jefferson, excluded the possibility of women citizens but saw female education as important to the state. Sixty years later, Horace Mann argued in the same vein that although "the rulers of our country need knowledge . . . mothers need it more; for they determine, to a great extent, the very capacity of the ruler's mind to acquire knowledge and apply it."[13]

The Common Schoolers and Schooling the Electorate

Mann and his contemporaries in the common school movement went beyond Jefferson's proposals for a meritocratic public school system by advocating that both sexes be equally educated through the eighth grade and, in some cases, beyond. And, unlike Jefferson's plan, the plans of the common schoolers placed emphasis on the schooling of a general electorate rather than on the production of intellectually accomplished leaders of state. Common schooling for all, Mann argued, would enable "each citizen to participate in the power of governing others."[14]

Again, women's actual political entitlements and location in the family made them exceptions to the rhetorical rules. While their educational opportunities may have been extended, their part in "governing others" remained largely confined to the domestic sphere and was extended only so far as the classrooms in which they were now beginning to teach in greater numbers. As a result, while the need to commonly educate the citizenry operated as the rationale for educating the male, the female's potential influence over her husband, sons, or students remained the chief rationale for her civic education.

Despite these differences, however, in the nineteenth-century common school the female's instruction in citizenship was not explicitly distinguished from that of the male's. Elizabeth Peabody, in her defense of the need to teach history to girls as well as boys, wrote:

> It is not necessary for every man to be an astronomer, chemist, linguist: but it is inevitable for every man to be a citizen. . . . Every American has in some degree the function of a statesman; and should have something of a statesman's education.[15]

Girls, along with their brothers, were expected to learn the citizen's rights and duties as well as the skills and attitudes associated with their exercise. In the schools, girls and boys learned to revere and support the laws that provided for women's disenfranchisement and prohibition from speaking in public, owning property, holding political office, and voting. As an adult, a woman who had been properly educated would be expected to act in accord with her exclusion from the public sphere and fulfill her duties to the state by teaching or nurturing others. Girls would not become more competent citizens as a result of their educations. Instead, they would use their "something of a statesman's education" to become "civilizing influences."

The pervasiveness of views about woman's natural role is evident in justifications that were advanced for the re-education of "wayward" girls during the mid-nineteenth century. In 1857, in a report to the Massachusetts legislature, the first superintendent of the Lancaster Reform School for Girls argued:

> It is sublime work to save a woman, for in her bosom generations are embodied, and in her hands, if perverted the fate of innumerable men is held. The whole community, gentlemen, personally interested as they are in our success because the children of the virtuous must breathe the atmosphere exhaled by the vicious, will feel a lively sympathy for you, in your generous endeavors to redeem the erring mothers of the next generation.[16]

The establishment of Lancaster, it was believed, would "affect the material interest of every citizen; and its beneficial operation [would] as certainly return a manifold recompense, purifying in its nature, into the bosom of society."[17]

The woman's role was increasingly sentimentalized in the popular literature and widely read "ladies magazines" that began to come to prominence during the era. One author outlined the distinctions being drawn between the male and female that were supposed to suit them to their separate roles.

> Woman has not the vigor and depth of thought, the accuracy of analysis and the fidelity of judgment which are characteristic of man, and which seem to indicate his peculiar fitness to direct the helm of society. . . . Woman is not a lower creation. . . . She hath in an eminent degree intenser affections, loftier sentiments, a deeper love of the pure and gentle and the virtuous.[18]

These attempts to genderize intellectual traits and capabilities were not confined to the popular press. Many of those who championed women's entry into teaching and higher education during the period claimed that what were widely accepted as the "womanly virtues" should be trained more thoroughly so that they could be put to efficient social use. Some, like Catherine Beecher, maintained that this could best be done by training girls in subjects which were specifically related to their conventional roles and obligations within the household. For girls Beecher advocated instruction in "domestic," rather than political, economy.[19] But, the common schoolers disagreed and continued to argue for, and ultimately win, a uniform civic curriculum for both sexes. Interestingly, they saw no contradiction in expecting that a uniform education for all should result in genderized forms of civic participation.

When one considers the sources of the differences in the rationales advanced for the civic education of women and men, participation in the economy rather than participation in the political state becomes central. As Ann Douglas has argued, in the nineteenth century the civic participation expected of the adult female was simply an elaboration of her increasingly separate and well-defined role in the private and domestic sphere.[20] In the early decades of the century, industrialization, urbanization, and increased immigration had occasioned drastic economic and social reorganization. From an agricultural nation in which the household was the center of productive activity for both sexes, the United States moved toward a system in which productive wage labor took place away from the home. Men now left home for work and, with the rise of the common school, children left home for the school. Domestic labor, the keeping of the home, and the training and nurturance of young children increasingly became the sole province of women. The romanticization of the private home as the cradle of the state and the sentimentalizing of the woman as naturally capable of nurturant motherly activities served to solidify the gender distinctions appropriate to the growth of a capitalist economy. Thus, woman's relation to her work, rather than her relation to political citizenship, determined her need for "something of a statesman's education." The male's civic education prepared him for the practice of citizenship and statecraft, but it was not intended to train him for his work in the factory or office. In contrast, the woman's civic education supplied her with the material she was to transmit to others in her work in the home and school.

The civic education of the period, although uniformly given, served dual purposes and maintained and rationalized the gender roles prescribed by the economy. Teacher attitudes towards their students, reflected in their accounts of "rough house boys" and "sensitive girls," affirmed the societal consensus that the girl's natural disposition was an appropriate counterbalance to the boy's.[21] If cultivated, it would serve to civilize and tame the potentially violent and unruly male and make him fit for full citizenship. Readings in history during the period provided the appropriate texts. They not only included glorifications of great men like George Washington, who had been brave but naughty in his youth, but *biographical sketches of his mother* as well.[22] Presumably, without the moral training and advice young George received from his mother, his career as first citizen would have been quite different. Thus, girls learned in their classrooms that their position in the social order, their centrality in the home and exclusion from public life, was essential to civic continuity, morality, and manners.

As the history of nineteenth-century American education shows, then, the civic utility of public education has not been confined to the training of citizens. Civic education was designed to train both male citizens and female civilizers. Within the academic curriculum, this was accomplished through the study of state history, daily practice in classroom manners, and the reading of didactic stories. Models of the good citizen and models of his mother helped legitimate the distinctions that kept women in the home and men "at the helm." Civic education thus functioned to support genderized modes of adult participation by protecting the boundaries associated with citizenship.

Turn of the Century Redefinitions

By the end of the nineteenth century, as the common schools began to serve the children of an increasingly diverse public of first generation European immigrants, the relationship between citizenship and gender within the school context became more complex. Girls could now be included along with boys in training for a citizenship that had come to mean getting along with one's coworkers and neighbors rather than the intelligent practice of statecraft or the informed exercise of political rights and privileges. Within this context, the gender distinctions of previous generations' rationales for civic education were barely distinguishable. What seemed most necessary according to an educator of the period, was that

> education develop a feeling of social like-mindedness which binds the members of a group together in such a way as to make them a unit. The individual student will then come to regard himself as a real part of the group in which he identifies his interest with group interests and looks upon common motives, purposes and activities as *ours* rather than mine.[23]

At first, educators at the turn of the century proposed that intelligent citizenship could be accomplished through an academic curriculum which emphasized the study of history, American government, geography, economics, and political science. In 1893, for example, the Committee of Ten's recommendations emphasized training in college-level skills that could enhance the future citizen's abilities to "think like historians and political scientists."[24] But, the academic rigor they proposed was criticized as inappropriate for the great majority of students who would not attend college or grow up to become public leaders. "Social like-mindedness," which remained the acknowledged goal for most of the public school's students, was not necessarily compatible with thinking like historians and political scientists and would have to be taught by some other means.

By 1916, the American Political Science Association began to recommend that a distinction be made between academic training in the arts of government and training in what was called "basic civics."[25] In order to accommodate the needs of those who would not go on to higher secondary or college education, they proposed a hierarchy of studies. It would begin by focusing on "community civics" and work towards the study of principles of state, federal, and world government in the upper years of high school. The school's major responsibility was now articulated as the socialization of "the average citizen" rather than the production of leaders of state or an educated citizenry. In 1919, the National Education Association, for example, advocated that "citizenship" be taught through the social studies.[26] Yet, citizenship within this context had little to do with political entitlements. The social studies would concentrate on the promotion of "good health, profitable use of leisure time, family, vocation, good character, and cognitive skills." Another document of the time urged:

> The old civics, almost exclusively a study of government machinery, must give way to the new civics, a study of all manner of social efforts to improve mankind. It is not so important that the pupil know how the President is elected as that he shall understand the duties of the health officer in his community. The time formerly spent in the effort to understand the process of passing a law over the President's veto is now to be more profitably used in the observation of the vocational resources of the community.[27]

Provisions for the new civics during the era thus placed major emphasis on the average student's achievement of competency in social skills within the local community while reserving the study of concepts in the social and political sciences for the minority who would go beyond the first two years of high school.

Ironically, the specialization of the civics curriculum that occurred during this period was an unacknowledged concession to some of the arguments that proponents of women's higher education had advanced during the previous century. Emma Willard, Mary Lyon, Catherine Beecher, and the influential editor Sarah Hale had all proposed that the school's curriculum should incorporate the study of family, leisure, character, community service, and health within the curriculum.[28] But, they had proposed these studies for women. By the 1920s, studies that had originally been thought particularly relevant to the preparation of women for motherhood and domestic labor had found their way into the general civics curriculum. But, it wasn't a victory. They were now officially given inferior institutional status. And, they were used to more effectively accommodate lower-class students to social and vocational roles in which it was assumed that they would have no need of the knowledge and skills associated with the arts of government. The citizenship thought appropriate for all but the more advanced students pointedly avoided the study of politics in favor of informational units on vocational opportunities and community social services. In a sense, what had happened was that lower-class students of both sexes were now being treated as if they were, like the women of previous generations, simply not destined to participate in the higher realms of public life. They were, in fact, being treated like women.

It is striking to note that at the point that women were about to become legal citizens, the character of civic education changed. It changed, however, not in a way that was designed to maximize the opportunities for women's participation in public life, but in ways that defined the economically disadvantaged in terms of the gender distinctions that had been so thoroughly romanticized in the previous century. Within this context, the realities of entitlement and disenfranchisement seemed irrelevant to training in "modern citizenship." Modern citizenship meant social like-mindedness and cooperation. It did not require a detailed knowledge of political rights and duties. It could not only be taught to all, it could be practiced by all. Thus, by the early twentieth century, the civics curriculum moved from the inculcation of values, beliefs, and behaviors appropriate to mere membership, or civilian status, in the early years of the student's schooling, to the intellectual cultivation of talents associated with full citizenship and what is conventionally termed statesmanship in the later school years.

As revisionist historians of the era have convincingly argued, this organizational framework disempowered the economically disadvantaged of both sexes.[29] One is thus tempted to identify socioeconomic class as the primary curricular bias affecting the student's civic education. But, the factors affecting the civic education of women are more complex. By 1920, increasing percentages of young women remained in high school beyond the first two years, took college preparatory courses in which they learned about the principles of government and politics, earned diplomas, and went on to colleges and universities.[30] Women were thus being admitted to the upper levels of training in citizenship.

Admission to what Virginia Woolfe called "the procession of educated men,"[31] however, did little to affect the power of the civics curriculum to inculcate traditional attitudes about women's unsuitability for a place in public life. This was accomplished not by explicitly limiting women's educational opportunities, but by providing curricular content that excluded women or made their contributions to society and the state invisible. While nineteenth-century students had studied the significance of women's work in nurturing the future citizen, and early twentieth-century social studies had begun to address social issues thought relevant to woman's traditional sphere of activity, the courses of the higher civics now avoided treating women altogether. Advanced students of both sexes were given instruction in political science, history, and economics that emphasized the activity and contributions of men in government, war, and industry. Consistent with the civic education of previous eras, then, advanced male and female students were instructed in a uniform civic education but received, and could be expected to act upon, this education differently.

Citizenship and Gender in the Contemporary Context

Contemporary educational understandings of citizenship are no less ambiguous on the question of gender than these early twentieth-century models. In fact, they may be more so. For, as women have achieved the legal, if not the social, guarantee to full citizenship, it has been tacitly assumed that the school's civic curriculum reflects truly gender neutral models for citizenship.

Fred Newmann, in his review of the problems of present day civic education, argues that while citizenship remains an explicit curricular goal, there is no real clarity on what it means or how it can be taught. Newmann finds that there is "a lack of consensus on goals, no thorough conceptual base," and no "systematic rationales" in contemporary programs claiming to promote citizenship. Thus, while he identifies eight distinguishable approaches to instruction in civic education, he contends that they are without the comprehensive justifications that would allow educators to choose between them. As a result of the ambiguities, Newmann finds that the term *citizenship*, by default, has come to mean "a general conformity to prevailing social norms." He concludes, "for many adults, the goal of civic education is to produce youth who, male or female, embody virtues such as those listed in the Boy Scout Law." As Newmann correctly observes, citizenship has come to mean a common network of social responses and behaviors that, while derived from traditional expectations for a normal American boy, are thought appropriate goals for the cooperative social conduct of both sexes.[32] For both male and female students, these expectations foster social conformity rather than a critical political consciousness. They substitute manners for active engagement in the political process. However, once again, the case is more complex for female students.

Recent feminist critiques of the American public schools have thoroughly explored the way the tacit assumption of male normalcy pervades the informal and formal curriculum and disempowers women today. In the late 1960s, Gerda Lerner's study of the school's formal history curriculum, for example, revealed that accounts of women's lives and experiences were routinely excluded from course outlines and texts.[33] More recent studies confirm that this remains true of core courses in the higher civics curriculum—political science, history, and economics—as well as in the social studies.[34] Although women's underrepresentation has been corrected somewhat by the curriculum integration projects that were facilitated by Lerner's and others' work, women are still routinely portrayed in roles associated with the private sphere of domestic labor while emphasis is placed on public sphere activities and contributions of male leaders. Women's social activism and political struggles are rarely if ever mentioned. Thus, female students remain unable to recognize themselves in the models the curriculum provides for exemplary civic participation.

As Dale Spender contends, teachers often collaborate with the gender bias of traditional courses of study.[35] Not only have women's contributions, experiences, and activism been "kept off the record," teacher attitude affects the way female students visualize their futures in public and private life. Spender writes:

> Every teacher who assumes that women will be preoccupied by child care, who cannot visualize women in paid employment or living satisfactorily without men, who does not recognize that women in general work harder and that they receive less money, plays an active role in perpetuating patriarchy. Teachers who do *not* make it their business to find and present the facts of women's lives to boys as well as girls in their classes, are engaged in political acts, practicing indoctrination, and presenting only one side of the story.[36]

The content of the civics curriculum, as Spender and others have recognized, includes more than the historical figures and topics represented in the formal course of study. Thus, it is not sufficient to address the gender biases involved in conventional expectations for public political participation by merely integrating the study of women within the curriculum. While this is an important first step, the informal or hidden curriculum also teaches students to distinguish between the citizen and the citizeness. For, as recent studies of classroom life indicate, the way students are treated and encouraged to act continues to foster gender distinctions favoring male leadership and female acquiescence.[37] Sex-role stereotyping pervades curricular materials, classroom interaction patterns, and school authority relations at all levels of schooling in the United States. Thus, the total organizational framework, selection, and delivery of content functions to define the student's relation to adult roles that remain coded according to gender. The results of the female's education in citizenship can be seen in the recently documented evidence of her continued ambivalence towards participating in the traditionally understood public sphere activities of men and her acceptance of the naturalness of her domestic labor.[38]

Conclusion

R. Freeman Butts has contended that a nation's provisions for civic education derive from a "citizenship principle," a society's collective understanding of what constitutes the principles of good citizenship.[39] What this has meant is that the school's interpretation of citizenship has not been soley governed by legal and political precedent. That is, while the Declaration of Independence, Bill of Rights, and Constitution may define the limits and conditions of full legal citizenship in the United States, within the educational context an understanding of the term *citizenship* has been dependent on societal norms and conventions. While these norms and conventions reflect gender as well as racial and class biases, American educators have seemed to do their best to ignore or minimize this fact.

As we have seen, citizenship as taught in the schools has been a highly malleable term. What has been constant, however, is that the schools' interpretation of citizenship has been consistently at odds with the political realities of disenfranchisement and unequal access that students face as adults within civil society. During each period, educational reformers and theorists concerned with civic education have typically skirted the question of who the fully entitled citizen is and have assumed that during the years of their civic educations, all students can and should be treated "as if" they would become fully entitled citizens modeling their behavior according to the ideal characteristics of a political leader, a statesman, a cooperative member, or a Boy Scout. Unfortunately, many writers in educational studies have tacitly accepted the omission of a consideration of gender in their discussions of civic education and citizenship. What becomes obvious when one considers the educational experience of women, however, is that the school's formal rationales for schooling in citizenship only work when one is describing the aims for men's civic education. Rationales for women's education, whether explicitly expressed or simply implicitly understood, have been more directly tied to the part women have been expected to play in maintaining the domestic economy.

It makes little sense, then, to continue to uncritically accept conventional readings of the goals and functions of civic education. As the experience of female students within the American public schools illustrates, without some clarity on who the fully entitled citizen is, or can be, a curricular imperative to teach citizenship comes to mean no more than a directive to teach conventional morals and manners that reflect the biases of the culture rather than to teach the knowledge and skills that would allow students to evaluate the social and political terms of entitlement and to empower them to change them. It is essential, then, that educators and students ask what is meant by *citizenship* and critically recover the historical ambiguities and contradictions encoded in the term. Only then will they be able to demystify the school's models for citizenship and begin to reconstruct the school's civic curriculum.

A feminist critique of the history of civic education necessarily initiates that process of demystification by asking that the "anomaly" of women's civic education be explained. The explanation of the "problem" of women has far-reaching implications. As Johnella E. Butler has claimed in the case of the humanities, "fitting women in" involves a reconsideration of the central questions bearing on the education of all persons. She writes:

> Taking women and gender seriously is part of an all encompassing move to redefine our fundamental definition in education of who is human, what do and can humans do, and of the recognition of and incorporation of cultural variations on the human theme.[40]

Butler contends that a discipline that does not deny human reality will

> recognize the maiming function of the cultural hegemony that informs our artistic criticism, our methods of philosophical and historical inquiry and description, and will replace that hegemony with a mentality and approach that does not cancel out opposites and differences, but that allows them to coexist.[41]

For the feminist scholar who has chosen to take women and gender seriously, the invisibility of women's experience, the remarkable oversight of her disenfranchisement, and the curricular dependence on gender-based models of citizenship are forceful indications of the need to reconceptualize our understanding of civic education. By rejecting the idea that male experience be taken as the norm and by insisting on an account of the citizeness as well as the citizen, a feminist perspective points the way to a reconceptualization that, first, makes citizenship itself a central problematic within the curriculum; and, second, establishes the ground for a more thorough scholarly examination of civic education's broader role in reproducing the social values and relationships that constitute civil society.

Notes

[*] Harry F. Harrington, "What Should Be the Leading Object of American Free Schools?" in *NEA Proceedings, 1873* (Peoria, IL: NEA, 1873), 222.

[1] Mary Wollstonecraft, *Vindication of the Rights of Woman*, Miriam Brody Kramnick, ed., (New York, NY: Penguin Books, 1982), 91.

[2] See Bonnie Spanier, Alexander Bloom, and Darlene Boroviak, *Toward a Balanced Curriculum* (Cambridge, MA: Schenkman Publishing Co., 1984); Dale Spender, ed., *Men's Studies Modified: The Impact of Feminism on the Disciplines* (New York, NY: Pergamon Press, 1981); Allison Jagger, ed., *Feminist Frameworks* (New York, NY: McGraw-Hill, 1978); and Susan Douglas Franzosa and Karen Mazza, *Integrating Women's Studies into the Curriculum* (Westport, CT: Greenwood Press, 1984).

[3] Spanier et al., *Toward a Balanced Curriculum*, 42.

[4] Jane Roland Martin, *Reclaiming A Conversation: The Idea of the Educated Woman* (New Haven, CT: Yale University Press, 1985).

[5] Jane Roland Martin discusses the effects of traditional male models on curriculum in "The Ideal of the Educated Person," *Educational Theory* 31 (Spring 1981): 97-110.

[6] Spender, *Men's Studies Modified*, 163.

[7] Spender, *Men's Studies Modified*, 164.

[8] For further discussion of the impact of this on the writing of educational history, see Patricia B. Campbell and Susan E. Katrin, "Present But Not Accounted For: Women in Educational History," WEEA, US Department of HEW: Office of Education, 1980.

[9] Thomas Jefferson, *Bill for the More General Diffusion of Knowledge*, 1779, quoted in Merle Curti, *The Social Ideas of American Educators* (Totowa, NJ: Littlefield Adams, 1968), 3.

[10] Jefferson, in Curti, *Social Ideas of American Educators*, 41.

[11] Frances Wright, *Views of Society and Manners in America—in a Series of Letters from That Country to a Friend in England*, Letters XXIII, in *The Feminist Papers*, Alice S. Rossi, ed., (New York: Bantam Books, 1981), 102.
[12] Benjamin Rush, "Thoughts Upon Female Education," in *Essays Literary, Moral and Philosophical* (Philadelphia, PA: Thomas and Samuel Bradford, 1787), 75.
[13] Horace Mann, "A Few Thoughts on the Powers and Duties of Woman, 1853," in *Lectures on Various Subjects* (New York, NY: 1859), 65.
[14] Elizabeth Peabody, in Curti, *Social Ideas of American Educators*, 132.
[15] "The Importance of Historical Study in the Education of Woman," *The Una* III, 2 (February 1855): 28.
[16] Quoted in Barbara Brenzel, "Domestication As Reform: A Study of the Socialization of Wayward Girls, 1856-1905," *Harvard Educational Review* 50, 2 (May, 1980): 17.
[17] Quoted in Brenzel, "Domestication as Reform," 22.
[18] "Letters," *Ladies' Companion* IX, 7 (September 1838): 232.
[19] Catherine Beecher, *A Treatise on Domestic Economy, 1841* (New York, NY: Schocken Books, 1977).
[20] Ann Douglas, *The Feminization of American Culture* (New York, NY: Avon Books, 1978).
[21] See Eleanor Wolfe Thompson, *Education for the Ladies 1830-1860* (New York, NY: Kings Crown Press, 1947).
[22] Thompson, *Education for the Ladies*, 3(e).
[23] Charles L. Robbins, *The Socialized Recitation* (New York, NY: 1920), 13.
[24] "Report of Committee of Ten," in *Educational Ideas in America: A Documentary History* (New York, NY: McKay, 1969).
[25] R. Freeman Butts, *Public Education in the United States* (New York, NY: Holt, Rinehart and Winston, 1978), 192-93.
[26] Butts, *Public Education in the United States*, 194-96.
[27] Quoted in Butts, *Public Education in the United States*, 195.
[28] Merle Curti, "The Education of Women," in *The Social Ideas of American Educators*, 169-93.
[29] Colin Greer, *The Great School Legend* (New York, NY: Basic Books, 1972); Joel Spring, *The Sorting Machine* (New York, NY: McKay, 1976); and David Tyack, *The One Best System* (Cambridge, MA: Harvard University Press, 1974).
[30] Patricia Albjerg Graham, "Expansion and Exclusion: A History of Women in American Higher Education," *Signs* 3, 4 (1978): 759-73.

[31] Virginia Woolfe, *Three Guineas* (New York, NY: Harcourt Brace, 1966), 62-3.
[32] Fred Newmann, "Building a Rationale for Civic Education," in *Building Rationales for Citizenship Education* (Arlington, VA: National Council for the Social Studies, 1977), 1-31.
[33] Gerda Lerner, *The Majority Finds Its Past: Placing Women in History* (New York, NY: Oxford University Press, 1979).
[34] Myra Sadker and David Sadker, *Sex Equity Handbook for Schools* (New York, NY: Longman, 1981).
[35] See Dale Spender and Elizabeth Sarah, eds., *Learning to Lose: Sexism and Education* (London: The Women's Press, 1980); and Dale Spender, *Invisible Women: The Schooling Scandal* (London: Writers and Readers Publishing Coop., 1982).
[36] Spender, *Invisible Women*, 115.
[37] Sadker and Sadker, *Sex Equity Handbook for Schools*.
[38] Elizabeth Fennema and M. Jane Ayer, eds., *Women and Education: Equity or Quality* (Berkeley, CA: McCutchan Publishing, 1984).
[39] Butts, *Public Education in the United States*, 395. See also, R. Freeman Butts, *The Revival of Civic Learning* (Bloomington, IN: Phi Delta Kappa, 1980).
[40] Johnella E. Butler, "The Humanities: Redefining the Canon," in Spanier et al., *Toward a Balanced Curriculum*, 38.
[41] Butler, "The Humanities," 38.

Part Three

Global Thematics and Modern Citizenship

Chapter Eight

It is imperative that those concerned with renewing a civic curriculum in America's public schools begin to take account of national and international contexts in which changes in educational policy are enacted.

8

Rethinking the Progressive Nature of Civic Education in the Modern World

By Ronald K. Goodenow

"Popular education had its origins in a social philosophy of civilizing the masses just sufficiently to teach them their place, whilst taking care not to give them ideas above their station in life."

—*Harold Entwistle*

THERE can be little doubt that the contemporary world is beset by problems of fragmentation, nationalism, and alienation and that the conceptions of "progress" nurtured throughout this century by liberal reformers have come under siege on many fronts and in many nations. This has had a profound effect on educational policy and practice. Indeed, Harold Silver, a distinguished British historian of education, has written that educational conditions in Britain and the United States have deteriorated to the point where it is hard to know what is either progressive or conservative. "We must endure," he writes, "a climate clouded and confused by competing claims of all sorts."[1]

Similarly, Robert Cowen, a comparativist at the University of London Institute of Education, summed up his recent research into the state of contemporary American education by observing he could find in America

> no theory of curriculum. Instead there were available (a) piecemeal statements, by representatives of sub-fields of education, of what curriculum provision ought to be on the criteria of their sub-field; (b) powerful critiques [which] indicated what had been wrong with curriculum theory in the twentieth century; (c) visionary accounts of what curriculum might be in some socially indeterminate future. None of these kinds of statements were able to combine psychological, sociological and epistemological assumptions into a coherent theory of educational transmission.[2]

Recent literature from such well-known American scholars as David B. Tyack and Diane Ravitch asserts that American education is not only adrift, but bereft of social consensus about its ends and wallowing in a sea of political crosscurrents, mediocrity, and lack of purpose. Tyack found far more unity, creativity, and energy in the Great Depression.[3] Ravitch has become identified closely with many of the goals of the Reagan Administration, which on the heels of the government's *A Nation at Risk* and many studies from foundations, is promoting an agenda which includes values training, voucher plans, greater emphasis on Western civilization, discipline, English language instruction, prayers in the schools, and a dramatic reduction of federal funding.

It is hard to find a concrete, liberal response to these conditions that has much prominence, let alone public support. There seems to be little theoretical or philosophical literature which engages attention. Teachers, professional associations, and administrators are struggling with shifting demographics, changes in funding patterns, and the many "reforms" being introduced at the state level. Schools of education, often exhausted by budget cuts, are trying to adjust to new credentialing modes and the need suddenly to train a new generation of teachers. Educators, like many other Americans, find that they must adjust to a dramatic shift in America's economic base as the nation loses millions of jobs to foreign competition, many old industries die, and the issue of "post-industrialism" poses perplexing questions to policymakers and those who ponder relations between the schools and "the enterprise culture" advocated by government and corporate officials.

This said, some groups of educators who have deep roots in twentieth-century progressive education and represent a liberal establishment at least momentarily in political and intellectual disarray have been calling for a renewed attention to civic education and have advocated the creation of a unifying *civism* within the public schools' curriculum, locating themselves between the extremes of radical and reactionary prescription, utilizing organizations such as the Jennings Randolph Forum and even the right-wing Hoover Institution either to disseminate or discuss their views.[4] Singling out such conservative challenges to public schooling as voucher plans, R. Freeman Butts, one of the most ardent defenders of public schooling and foremost advocates of a new civism, echoes Cowen's point when he claims that:

> In none of these movements do I find a well-formulated conception of the common public good or of the obligation of schooling to try to promote a sense of civic community. Today, even the *rhetoric* of "good citizenship" as the prime purpose of education is all but missing from the educators' and the public's lexicon. We need to remind ourselves of the historic meaning of the idea of citizenship and the historical efforts of public schools to make it a reality.

Operating within the progressive liberal tradition, Butts argues that "the prime contribution of the schools . . . is to enhance as far as possible the political capabilities of students to think and act as citizens who will support and improve the liberal political community."[5]

Consistent with the liberal position on the purposes of public schooling, Butts and other contemporary educators who advocate a new civism hope to promote a view of the future inclusive of what seems to be missing now: political community and unity. While preserving, protecting, and reinvigorating the major features of the existing system and leaving to parliamentary and judicial means the larger questions of social change, common schooling in a core of democratic values, they argue, will overcome the present divisive nature of cultural pluralism and the competing claims of special interest groups, who now constitute a major "problem" for educators. In Butts' view, as in Dewey's earlier in the century, public schooling will build the consensus necessary to hold our diverse society together. Clearly, the success of these efforts is dependent on the individual's willingness to participate with others to "support and improve the liberal political community." The spirit of citizenship—the acceptance of beliefs and even myths regarding the nature of the American democratic community—engendered by the schools, it is believed, will go a long way to guarantee the requisite national unity upon which any meaningful change can be built. Fundamental to this philosophy is a pedagogy respectful of legal tradition and due process, a proper appreciation for the democratic roots of the American ideal, and a faith in the school's ability to assimilate diverse groups of students and revive an interest in heightened political participation and expression: goals which find far more expression here than in the neo-conservative agenda and separate many civic educators from other advocates of "reform." Reminiscent of the progressive reform era, then, the reconstruction of individual attitudes through schooling is thought paramount to the restoration of a healthy democratic society. Civic education—education for citizenship—is thus a logical focus for the contemporary liberal reformer and the problematic character of contemporary pluralism. A new civic education will prepare people to play intelligent roles in a modern society and render irrelevant or devisive the bonds of kinship and identification which detract from the whole. It will protect students from irrational claims and forms of self-interest, including those of the private business sector, that divert attention from consensual democracy.

The purpose of this essay is not to critique in any definitive way the content, character, or motivations of a movement as diverse and complex as the contemporary one for civic education—one that intersects with "moral education," "social education," "values education," and, in some parts of the world, "religious education." It does, afterall, encompass and include many organizations, publications, professors, teachers, and administrators, as diverse as progressive education itself.[6] Nor will this essay question the motives of its advocates, many of whom are justifiably frightened by the current political climate.

Rather, taking some of the movement's ideas on modern pluralism and diversity, which seem characteristically "progressive" in nature, I will question whether they provide an intellectual foundation adequate enough to build a truly democratic community, offering as much a critique of progressivism as of civic education. My first assumption is that this is a time of important industrial, technological, and demographic transformations perhaps as fundamental as those which, in the late nineteenth and early twentieth century, gave rise to the revolution in educational thought and practice which many civic educators represent. My second assumption is that an international perspective is required. It is imperative that those concerned with renewing a civic curriculum in America's public schools begin to take account of national and international contexts in which changes in educational policy are enacted. We all must learn more about the international impact and place of American education and incorporate a global perspective in the schools, where research continues to suggest a frightening lack of knowledge about foreign affairs and responsibilities. Only in these ways can we avoid a citizenship of self-centered national isolationism and foster awareness of a common humanity in a fragmented world that is challenging many of our most precious liberal values on many political and intellectual fronts.

For reasons which will become apparent further along in this essay, I do not necessarily agree with Butts' views on "interdependence," but I am otherwise sympathetic to Butts, who played a key role in the development of post-World War II third world programs at Teachers College, Columbia University, when he writes that:

> Looking beyond our national boundaries, the most appalling feature of [contemporary American life] is the massive public ignorance and indifference concerning the relation of the American community to the emerging but inchoate world community. The issue of world interdependence is plain enough to the academic profession as well as to the public, if we but think a moment of the facts of energy, population, food, trade, oil, war, finance and space. But few, even in academia, translated the facts, the dangers, and the possibilities of interdependence into a primary educational purpose.[7]

In what follows, then, I will put some of the goals of civic education into a broad perspective, which includes the insights of non-Americans, to argue that those who support the liberal movement toward the reconstruction of a "primary educational purpose" for

American public schools must take into account two issues related to my basic assumptions. First, we need to examine whether the quest for political community necessitates the rejection of permanent manifestations of cultural diversity. That is, must future American citizens be taught that claims derived from ethnic, religious, class, gender, or other group experiences are illegitimate and dangerous responses of special or local interests which have to be blunted if America is to hold together? Are they to be recognized as temporarily legitimate or are they, in some form, to become a permanent part of the political landscape? If they are to be permanent, can democracy and an allegiance to the American "nation" be sustained? And, are these the kinds of interests about which civic educators should worry, or do they represent diversions from important changes in the political economy which enhance the power of corporations and other forces which serve class and other possibly exploitive interests more powerful than those represented by Hispanics, Blacks, women, or those who defend the handicapped? Second, reflecting the concerns expressed by Butts, it is imperative that we all understand the degree to which many of our concerns and practices have a global context and impact. Such a recognition could help us to grapple with aspects of cultural and political legitimacy that, in their domestic and international settings, are not entirely dissimilar and through comparative analysis could be highly instructive.

In Search of Unity

It ought to be said at the outset that the educator's search for unity, common beliefs, and good citizenship is not, needless to say, unique to the United States, nor is it confined to progressive educators. The use of schools to produce a unifying citizenship has become a hallmark of "progress" in most societies. Writing of the emergent nations of the third world, for example, John Bock observes that:

> The fundamental question is the extent to which individuals and groups living within the boundaries of the new states consider themselves to be members of those states. In most plural societies, parochial levels of identity, ranging from family and tribe to ethnic or linguistic groups, rival the nation as a primary source of identification.[8]

Regardless of political orientation or the degree to which individual, as opposed to collective, endeavor is emphasized, there can be little question that all pluralistic societies strive for "nation building" and "development" and that the "old ways" of the tribe, the priest, or the village are often given short shrift on the road to social "modernization." The resulting educational policies are major features of modern mass education and are used to justify vast expenditures on system building. It is held that nations which succeed in socializing their youth in school have a better chance at prosperity and international respectability. Educational resource development is seen as a form of investment in human capital that will also help create jobs, build responsible elites, aid the creation of democracy, and assure the nation a place in global economic and political networks.

As an integral part of America's own "development," the educational system has had a primary responsibility for building national identification and enhancing the country's power and prestige in the world. This has been a constant motif and is perhaps most readily recognized in the early twentieth-century Americanization movement and the enormous interest in education which followed the launching of the Soviet Sputnik. As historians have pointed out recently, this concern has helped shape the structure of educational endeavor in an urbanizing nation, or what David Tyack has called "the one best system." The abiding theme, evident in contemporary opposition to bilingualism, debates on immigration, and the current drive for "excellence," is that national unity must take precedence over the neighborhood, ties to family and religion, and, of course, many forms of ethnic and group expression. More than their conservative counterparts, who would rely on authoritative teaching in the disciplines, progressives would utilize a more child- and community-centered pedagogy which draws on modern psychological research and cross-disciplinary perspectives to reach these ends.[9]

As a prime ingredient of American educational history, then, the mere presence of impoverished foreign and other ethnic populations has contributed significantly to the evolution of the American school system in its current bureaucratic and "professionalized" forms, and it continues to do so. This, along with a desire to defend the nation and compete with the Soviet Union, has framed the structure and content of knowledge transmission in both formal and informal curricula and has led to a dramatically expanded federal educational bureaucracy. How the American experience, the family, gender relations, the readiness of some cultures for democratic participation, the role of religion, and the nature of "community" have been portrayed in instructional materials and programs illustrates much of this structure. As a number of historical studies have found, they reflect an interest in promoting assimilation, social order, productive labor, and the protection of the national interest. Moreover, education for citizenship has often stressed an illiberal and perhaps self-defeating training for orderly and law-abiding behavior accountable more to authority than to the democratic process. For some groups, including blacks, the schooling of "responsibility" has been imposed at the expense of education for constitutional rights and privileges. For others, e.g., women, inferior social roles have been reinforced and rationalized.[10]

To be sure, citizenship training stressing uniform values and responsibilities rather than freedoms and rights results from the social and economic features of a rapidly industrializing nation that required cheap and compliant labor. However, stress on uniform values and responsibilities has also been accompanied by a condescending concern to control those thought to be culturally inferior. This has been most evident in the education of blacks and Native Americans. But, within particular regional contexts, other groups have been subject to caste discrimination and the kind of stereotyping which has portrayed some, such as the Italians and East Europeans, as not quite "ready" for participatory democracy because of religious and other allegiances. This latter stereotyping found currency even among progressive educators who did not always accept cruder forms of economic exploitation, blatant racism, or the melting pot ideology.[11]

In this context, and in view of the white Anglo-Saxon Protestant middle-class interests served by the school through much of the nineteenth and early twentieth centuries, many groups developed alternative political, economic, and educational institutions. These, in turn, often became the subject of urban "reform" efforts. Parochial schools, for example, were portrayed as divisive reflections of shopworn traditional values or corrupt impulses, as reflections of powerlessness, or as parts of viable economic and political substructures. And so, aside from the conclusions of some radical scholars, it has occurred to very few educators that the public school's efforts to socialize in a uniform citizenship may have contributed historically to the very problems it is now called upon to cure.

Current advocates of civic education have, then, inherited patterns of institution building and reform that complicate their work. There can be no denying that Dewey and others associated with the progressive education movement showed a pioneering interest in cultural pluralism. Yet, at the level of the schools, much of this interest was, and continues to be, subsumed in a broader concern for cultural assimilation to core values, developing national character, and seeing the school itself as far more important than the family, the neighborhood, the church, or the ethnic group. At its worst, progressivism has fostered centralized control, standardized "scientific" testing, and even an anti-intellectualism which disturbed the likes of Dewey and led the school away from a tough and critical analysis of the structure and diversity of social life in America. Arguably, a price for this condition is an inability to grapple with the enormous class and ethnic differences which seem to be creating divergent and, to many, threatening voices in American life.

Exclusion and the persistence of unequal wealth and power have led to contradictory but marked responses. Political outcomes have included the Ethnic Heritage Studies Act and considerable mention during the Nixon years of the "white ethnic" factor. Further to the left, the rise of feminism, black assertiveness, and other manifestations of group identity over the past few years became furtively visible in Democratic Party politics in the 1984 elections. As the 1980s draw to a close, the protests of Protestant fundamentalists who feel isolated by the secular culture and, in many instances, poverty and economic change, loom large on the national agenda. Recent census data on structural unemployment among blacks and other inner-city dwellers raises the spectre of a permanent European-style "underclass," a phenomenon with grave implications in cities and metropolitan areas otherwise blessed with the growth of the high-technology and service sectors which increasingly require advanced skills training. What's more, the population mix and class structure of the United States is affected increasingly by events beyond our borders. The international situation, including the war in Vietnam, the old and new cold war, and America's policies in the Caribbean and Central America have not only influenced what is taught, but added responsiblities and strains. They have contributed to a massive influx of newcomers from parts of the world heretofore subject to immigration quotas and the stigma of inferiority. That many recent immigrants have maintained strong ethnic identity, shown proclivity to hard work, and demanded political power and recognition poses interesting problems for an educational policy not so easily swept under the rug of assimilation as in years past—witness the controversies over bilingual education which pits Hispanic groups against the Reagan Administration. Nor, can the group activism of former anti-war protestors, environmentalists, feminists, and those critical of the education establishment be contained easily within the boundaries of new calls for national unity or individual political responsibility.

Competing demands of national, group, and individual identities therefore require civic educators and others to have a solid intellectual grasp of the texture of the problems they face: problems which may be far more rooted in fundamental political-economic conditions than their critique usually permits. Their critique must be reinforced by existing research on interest groups and democratic participation as well as upon a firm theoretical understanding of the interrelationship between democratic expression and the American political economy.

Beyond Special Interests and Liberalism

Criticism of the assimilationist assumptions which underlie the current civic education movement is mounting in many quarters. Fred M. Newmann, for example, goes right to the crux of the diversity issue when he writes that "in their zeal to advocate a particular approach to civic education, proponents often fail to explain how their approach responds to human diversity in interest, ability, age, sex, cultural affiliation, personality, and socio-economic status." But, the crucial point raised by Newmann is that "rationales must also confront demands by cultural, ethnic, political, and socio-economic groups to preserve a heritage or to serve group needs as defined by the group."[12]

Butts addresses the general problem, but comes to a slightly different conclusion. Tending to see a current emphasis on pluralism as a somewhat contemporary thing, he holds that:

> Attraction to pluralism resulted no doubt from the loss of credibility in governmental authority and from an emerging attitude that glorified "doing one's own thing." But as seen by serious scholars and analysts of the contemporary social and educational scene, the phenomenon was much more than that. It is nothing less than a new search for a legitimate authority upon which to base educational goals and practices. From a variety of sources, arguments have been propounded that the authority for education should rest primarily with the diverse pluralistic communities in American society rather than primarily in the common political or civic community.[13]

Implicit in this position is a suggestion that pluralistic group expression is at odds with crucially important civic values and that, further, governmental processes no longer seem to work for many groups. Setting aside the question of whether government has ever represented many groups now seeking legitimacy, examination of when and how government is effective in contemporary circumstances may suggest a set of conclusions slightly different, and even more optimistic, than those put forward by Butts. There is also a quintessentially progressive character to the comment. It is sympathetic to outbursts of temporary pluralistic expressions, but warns against their permanent expression, representing the foil of "interest groups" which have plagued progressive social scientists and educators for much of this century.

In a recent essay in *Teachers College Record*, political scientists Paul Peterson and Barry Rabe acknowledge that interest-group activity is

> among the most visible contributors to policy change in modern industrial societies. ... For many sympathetic analysts, interest groups serve not only as reservoirs of pertinent information but, even more, as critical intermediaries between the state and the public. Many critical scholars contend that group activities are so pervasive that they can hardly be distinguished from the activities of agencies, bureaus, legislative committees, and other bodies that exercise formal policy making authority. In short, whether groups are praised or blamed, their power is often assumed.[14]

Peterson and Rabe contend that the educational successes of most interest groups "can best be attributed to a distinct set of political circumstances that enabled the legislative and executive branches to take new policy steps." In the 1980s these circumstances include an increasingly fragmented quest for resources and influence, shifting federal policies and federal-state relations, and more judicial involvement in areas like affirmative action. Basically, changing circumstances and conditions mean that advocates of bilingual education, handicapped legislation, vocational education, and other issues have learned to make the system work in ways that are effective to them; and they often appear strident in the process. Hence, in the cases of special and bilingual education, which they see as examples of how interest groups can respond to openings offered by the judiciary, they write that:

> Innovations in special and bilingual education suggest greater interest-group activism during the past decade than in prior generations. Given the proliferation of federal programs and gradual expansion of funding for edu-

> cation, together with an explosion in the total number of active groups, this increased influence has been inevitable. Yet, the triumphs of groups representing the handicapped and language minorities remain in many ways anomalous. Their greatest successes were strongly predicated on judicial decisions, which afforded unusual opportunities for influencing anticipated legislative action. Unless comparable court decisions are made in other areas, one must guard against generalizing from their successes and considering their influence typical of groups interested in other federal categorical programs.[15]

According to this analysis, interest-group processes are an inevitable outcome of changes to the structure and responsibilities of the federal government: changes which are affected to some degree by the ideology and constituency of the political party in power. In this light, an important issue is the degree to which certain educational, ethnic, and other constituencies are located at either the center of Washington decision making, as when liberal administrations are in office, or at the periphery, as during the Reagan administration. Here, the character of ethnic and other needs are less significant as manifestations of divisiveness and pluralism than they are as reflections of complex political interactions.

The Peterson and Rabe interpretation is based on a mainstream functionalist analysis that should be given very close attention by civic educators because historically it is this intellectual tradition that has defined for many liberal progressives the character of group life. Now it suggests that increased citizen participation in electoral processes should not be confused with—and given less moral legitimacy than—citizen action through other more direct means. The current situation does not mean that consensual social values are necessarily being breeched. What is happening is that people are finding forms of representation as provided for and legitimized by a political system more alert to diversity and conflicting agendas. Indeed, if the past is any guide, it is possible to suggest that these new processes are themselves educative and capable ultimately of shaping electoral agendas around a new national consciousness which gives due recognition to many forms of pluralism. We may quibble about whether interpretations such as this make the system more effective in addressing fundamental structural problems, but it does suggest the origin of interest-group politics is not found within the groups themselves, but within a system that is itself undergoing change.

The role of political education in the face of these conditions is complicated because groups are now getting results through peaceful and legal means which would appear to transcend the "mere" process of voting or conventional political participation which the schools tend to emphasize. A close look suggests, however, that the new interest-group politics may reshape expectations so that *in toto* citizen use of electoral politics may actually increase. High participation in recent off-year and primary elections shows that, when politicians speak to issues raised initially by interest and single-issue groups, citizens will indeed register and vote. The problem facing educators may boil down to preparing young people to confront, in an open and confident way, the character of modern community life, its many constituencies, its power bases, and the choices people face as they try to meet their aspirations in an age of shifting access to resources. It also requires a new look at the role of the school.

In another essay in the same issue of the *Teachers College Record*, Frederick W. Wirt writes that the late twentieth century is witnessing "the diffusion of private resources out of the public schools ... the diffusion of public problems ... the diffusion of the public's policy expectations."[16] In an argument similar to that put forth by Newmann, Wirt turns the spotlight on professional educators. He sees the proliferation of local demands as a partial response to their insensitivity to local conditions, partly because many have accepted the mainstream liberal ideology on the concept of national community and the degree to which schooling is "apolitical." This aloofness, Wirt contends, gives many groups little choice but to express their demands nationally, to become more organized, and to be more visible. And so:

> Racial, professional, and lay school constituents became politicized. . . . All were alike in several respects. Each group found itself balked locally when it challenged the traditional authority of the professional to define the quality, quantity, and effectiveness of service—part of an international protest of clients against professionals. Then, each group appealed elsewhere for help, and each did so by rallying public opinion.[17]

Contributing to all of this, Wirt notes, has been the "diffusion of state capacities to govern education."

The basic issue to Wirt, though, is that of power. Contending that professional educators know that behind interest-group politics is a fundamental challenge to the power they have come to enjoy in American education, he writes that:

> They look today like the "big bang" cosmic theory in mid-flight. Elements float away from their once interlocking unity, their gravitational bonds of interest in education still there but weakening, yet all moved by the explosiveness of the challenge to professional autonomy.[18]

This crucially important point is often overlooked in professional literature. It suggests that educators, including education professors, must be considered by civic educators in much the same way as other "special interests." When civic educators ascribe to the schools the responsibility of advancing the interests of liberal community, they must be alert to the role of the professional educator as an "expert" who too often has been assimilationist, naive, or manipulative about power, politics, class, race, and other gut issues. They are part of the pluralist matrix of institutions and constituencies subject to fundamental forces of employment and social change.

The economic and political superstructure is linked inexorably to the ideological and mythic dimensions of educational policy and its relation to perceptions of choice and group legitimacy. The Canadian comparativist Vandra Lea Masemann writes of pluralism in liberal democracies, most of which have capitalist economies, and highlights a distinction often lost in the quest for national unity. In practice, she argues, perceptions and definitions of citizenship have been based on "notions of individual rights and responsibilities" rather than loyalty to groups or even the nation. *Choice* is very important and, indeed, an integral part of an individualistic public ideology.[19]

To illustrate this argument, Masemann identifies a somewhat complicated and paradoxical condition in which liberal democracies have striven for forms of national unity and identity derived from a political and economic set of myths reliant on beliefs which are failing the test of time. What they really teach is that *individual* effort in an environment blessed with *equality of opportunity* will overcome old constraints derived from outdated and outmoded cultures to produce mobility and success—precisely the progressive ideology. This requires that the old cultures be eliminated not only because they pose a threat to unity and even modernity, as also argued by progressives, but because they threaten individual opportunity. Yet, increasingly, minority groups realize that they must take the brunt of structural constraints against equality of opportunity. For many young people, myths on working hard and equal rights transmitted in school do not reflect reality. Can there be any doubt that they consequently end up being more alienated than assimilated? Masemann's analysis suggests that the inclinations of progressives and those who have considerable political and economic power are at the least quite similar, and at most deeply intertwined for reasons that are symbiotic. Fundamentally, she contends, it is in the interest of modern capitalism to go along with "progressive" forms of citizenship. She writes that:

> Liberal conceptions of citizenship render identity and loyalty much more malleable concepts than in pre-industrial, tribal, or strongly hierarchical or authoritarian societies.[20]

Masemann's interpretive model clarifies the inchoate and confused situation noted earlier in this essay. Pluralist alternatives to the "melting pot" ideology cannot offer fundamental relief to crude assimilationism unless they address issues of group legitimacy and power and do so in community settings which consider the nature of employment and political expression. This is because any pluralism which fails to recognize these issues is an illusive pluralism indeed.

Historically, many groups have fared only slightly better under avowedly progressive approaches that have stressed "cultural contributions," "tolerance," and "understanding" through intercultural and multicultural education. Although these pioneering efforts, going back to the 1930s, were supported by progressive educators like William Kilpatrick and John Dewey, they generally celebrated "diversity" as a means of assuring a degree of schooled order and consensus in the face of economic or international crises, the result being assimilationism of a rather subtle kind. Though some of their work critiqued capitalism, they virtually never addressed issues of power.[21]

The history of cultural pluralism in American education suggests that the goals of the new civics are not unusual, then. The United States, like all nations, seeks to use schooling to create national identity and a sense of individual responsibility and participation. Yet, in this country with its capitalist economy, diverse population, and traditions of open democratic participation and inquiry, there is a paradox of major significance. For, inherent in the intersection of schooling for unity and the liberal tradition of open and experimental inquiry are conditions which thwart the confrontation of issues of power and structure and thus inevitably increase the burdens placed upon the educator. Despite an occasional flirtation with Marxism by scholars on the left, or the romantic idealism to be found in some segments of the middle class, public schooling has remained a "great panacea"—its actual power to effect change is limited by economic, political, and cultural conditions well beyond its control.

Even progressive educators bent on social reform and occasionally tainted with the brush of radicalism by their critics have, then, shunned the direct expression of class or ethnic power in favor of attitude building and other "schooled" solutions. Moreover, for "practical" reasons inherent in the public responsibilities of schooling, as noted by Walter Feinberg in *Reason and Rhetoric*, some of the most ardent defenders of democracy and public education have damaged their democratic ideal through compromises, often of an intellectual kind. Some have opted for a faith in bureaucracy, commissions, planning, and other devices of an elite and aloof character. A peculiar and often condescending "child-centeredness" and "social-engineering" anti-intellectualism has crept into play. On this point, revisionists like Feinberg and those of less radical persuasion, such as Ravitch, would agree. Where they disagree is on the degree to which schooling as presently constituted and controlled can meet competing requirements for justice, unity, and equality.[22]

Towards an International Perspective

Civic educators must also gain a global outlook because good international relations are dependent in part on the degree to which diverse peoples and nations meet their social, economic, and political goals peacefully. A worldview also casts many American assumptions and influences in a new light. American education and its underlying theories and research have been transferred to other parts of the world to reinforce or build nationhood, order, and a responsible middle-class citizenry with Western values and allegiances. This influence, which has also represented cruder economic and geopolitical interests, reaches to Europe and beyond. It demonstrates the importance of probing the relationship of citizenship, diversity, social science, and schooling because it has been guided by many of the same liberal principles which are now seen as deficient in domestic context.

Britain, for example, has borrowed heavily from America to confront its growing racial and ethnic problems. America, which unlike Britain had addressed such issues for many years, gained attention a few years back because we had a liberal social science which was geared to developing practical solutions to "problems" defined often as cultural in character and therefore especially susceptible to education. American ideas served as a temporary respite from analyses which tended to ignore "urban" or "race" problems and in many cases, particularly in the case of Marxism, saw institutions like the school as having virtually no power to foster social change. The bloom is now off this rose. American social science has been more forthright in its incorporation of left scholarship and so, as much of the industrial order has gone into abject decline, the British came to recognize that the complex structural and demographic roots of their difficulties required more indigenous and integrated approaches. Though there is considerable interest in American education, especially as we approach postindustrial transformation issues and many British agencies look to Japan and elsewhere for importable ideas, there is a growing feeling that state-supported schooling will have to address more forthrightly problems of unemployment and multiculturalism.[23] This has led to enormous conflict between local and central government authorities, and it has profound implications for higher education and other sectors.

As Martin McLean has noted, the British learned that they were incapable of applying "American-style" solutions to an educational system with very different concepts of public responsibility and control.[24] This said, there is intense interest in a social education that is transcending an older emphasis on moral values and religion. British civic educators must now address industrial and urban decline as well as acrimonious national debates over what shape political socialization should take amidst varying interpretations of what it means to live in a "multicultural" society.[25] Needless to say, the issue of being properly "British" is setting off some of the same concerns about bilingualism, religion, interest groups, and other issues seen in the United States. What Americans do in civic education, then, is not without significance. Likewise, educators in this country should keep an eye on their British colleagues.[26]

Leslie Bash, a British comparativist, has looked at these developments and produced a valuable perspective for Americans. Civic educators, he warns, must be alert to three things: the covert culture which often eludes consideration in mainline educational thought, the degree to which the new political education movement itself constitutes a special interest "lobby," and the historical conditions which are giving rise to a revived interest in civic education. He writes that:

> With the relative failure of social democracy it was little wonder that classical liberalism/conservatism became legitimized once again, since it might be claimed that a return to a more established political ideology would

help to establish a sense of traditional values amidst social and economic uncertainty.[27]

Though Bash might be expected to disagree with the conventional American political science of Peterson, Rabe, and Wirt, his comment that "while national political cultures remain calcified in the past, societal infrastructures are undergoing radical change" is in line with their general observations.[28] Skeptical of any emphasis on liberal notions of "shared beliefs," Bash says it is far more important for schools to focus on conditions of everyday life in advanced capitalist countries. Structural and related changes, he contends, frustrate politics as usual—an issue not addresssed satisfactorily by many educators and political scientists. Most importantly, Bash asks that we be sensitive to "the widely accepted assumption of the correspondence between pedagogical theory and practice on the one hand—and educational outcomes on the other," something striven for by most educational theorists, though something that, as seen in earlier quotes from Silver and Cowen, has been especially hard to find amidst current conditions.

Bash and Masemann remind us, as well, that civic educators may have failed to recognize important transformations in the nature of modern life which require a paradigm shift in how political education is defined. Both are taken with the ideas of the Italian philosopher Gramsci, who would put at the core of all schooling a "vocational" view wholly cognizant of political economic conditions and giving the child a feeling of real power over the choices which determine his or her destiny. This, Bash contends, should be the foundation of all civic education for it offers the widest possible view of social, intellectual, scientific, and political life. It, he argues, combats the "myths of the covert political culture" through a critical analysis rooted in a very well disciplined and formal view of the world.[29] These ideas, I would argue, should not frighten American liberals for they are consistent in many respects with those of Dewey, who wrote in *The Public and Its Problems* that:

> Industry and inventions in technology . . . create means which alter the modes of associated behavior and which radically change the quality, character and place of impact of their indirect consequences. These changes are extrinsic to political forms which, once established, persist of their own momentum. The new public which is generated remains long inchoate, unorganized, because it cannot use inherited political agencies. . . . To form

belief, the public has to break existing political forms. This is hard to do because these forms are themselves the regular means of instituting change.[30]

Though problems of economic transformation, including the decline of industrialism and the growth of service- and technology-based societies, are becoming of increasing importance to all American educators and are accommodated nicely in the ideas of Bash, Masemann, Gramsci, and even Dewey, civic educators should also look in the direction of the third world. It provides a different example and a different insight into the relationship between progress and nationhood. It has significance both geo-political and local in character. We must work with and understand peoples in and from the third world who are confronting grim conditions linked inexorably to patterns of national development and urbanization affected deeply by the United States and other Western nations. The fact that we have striven for much of this century to impose concepts of nationhood, progress, and schooling on peoples who have little power over contextual political and economic conditions has led to simmering resentment and a search for alternatives not always to our liking. How we define in our own institutions a proper civic education is going to affect what is transferred abroad through the complex patterns of educational relations which we enjoy with many countries. The civic educator's responsibility is great indeed.

What also ought to be understood is that many countries introduced American-style research and institutions out of cultural and economic dependency, and as a theoretical proposition "dependency" has far more currency in many parts of the world than the "interdependency" which is often perceived as a liberal masking of exploitation and neo-imperialism.[31] Not surprisingly, some of the great American philanthropies, including the Rockefeller Foundation and the Carnegie Corporation, and the apex schools of education, including Teachers College, Columbia University, which have played an important role in defining how the school was to respond to diversity in America, took an active part in transferring to other nations progressive ideas on the role of education in building citizenship. This is a subject which begs for far more research. It is, though, reasonable to argue that enthusiasm for these ideas and the role of the modern school in national development led more than a few educators away from caring about the cultural and social implications of their work. Their zeal for institution building, elite formation, and importing prestigious Western ideas and practices has thereby contributed to an inability to deal with many current domestic conditions. The anticommunist context of much Western endeavor, moreover, did not help foster a hard look at underlying political-economic, social, and cultural issues. To do so made one appear to be sympathetic either to Soviet expansionism or the USSR's threat to the United States.[32]

Conclusion: Towards a New Agenda

This writer is of the opinion that America is in one of those watershed periods when national identity is undergoing a painful transition. This change, it may be argued, is to a large extent rooted in the ideals and culture of an American society that has given its educational system enormous and conflicting responsibilities. Though civic education draws attention to the seemingly fragmented quality of American life, it behooves us to ask if its vision and analysis may not obscure some essential cultural and structural features which have to be confronted lest the school be assigned obsolete and possibly irrelevant burdens. The foregoing observations by Dewey suggest that our public ideologies are quite capable of such masking, and one need not be a Marxist critical of "false consciousness" to agree. This essay has not attempted to pinpoint purposeful delusion. This is a possibility whenever social structural and political processes evidence changes that put our institutions and cherished beliefs on the defensive and whenever educators are poorly trained to understand them.

For scholars, this condition produces an obligation to refocus our work and have its conclusions discussed in the schools, among educators, and, of course, within the civic education movement. As we do so, some things should be "givens." There has to be more attention to the character of the various constituencies which contributed to the cacophony of voices and demands in a highly pluralistic society going through postindustrial transformation. We ought to study intergenerational consciousness about education and the ideals of this society. Much more must be known about how blacks, women, Native Americans, the handicapped, and the young—all of whom have been close to invisible in the historical record—have strategically confronted structural and other problems in their daily lives and which ideas on nationhood and common values *they* have taken seriously.[33] More must be known about the fundamental character of American economic life and how it affects the choices people make in light of opportunities for fulfillment and prosperity.

Ultimately, though, I would argue for far more research and general emphasis on the international character of nation building, economic conditions, and the educational transfers and relations which affect agendas. We will only learn what policies will break down barriers of class, race, gender, and ideology to offer greater human fulfillment and justice and guarantee peace if we can factor these "variables" into our own educational system far more forthrightly. How and why our progressive education and notions of "liberal community" have been exported must be known. Have they contributed to contemporary crises in third world nations as claimed by many revisionist scholars in the United States and abroad? What is our legacy as we have interacted historically with the rest of the world? Have we tried to build a "one best system" that is now coming back to haunt us and much of Western civilization? Is it possible to think about a global citizenship that does not wallow in cliches about "one world" or reflect naive applications of "intercultural understanding" and ideas of "interdependence"? Why do we know so little about the relationship between social science, education, and cultural relations as they become institutionalized in American government policies?[34] At the institutional level, why is so little known about how the transfer of ideas about education relates to the sociology of American universities and their curricula, when we know that the sociology of knowledge is a critically important prism through which to examine ideas of citizenship and other crucial issues?[35]

Finally, there should be a far more sophisticated international research base on civic education itself. Experimental cross-cultural demonstration projects should be established in diverse settings to produce a comparative scholarship that is far more geared to large policy questions than existing research, which often tends to be mired in large clusters of empirical data about attitudes and behavior and which says little about local conditions and the texture of the aspirations and experiences of young people and teachers in divergent national settings.[36] Once some of the major crises facing industrial and nonindustrialized nations are acknowledged by educators, the value of such study will be far more apparent. How the British, in a deprived and declining city like Liverpool, teach good citizenship to a truly hopeless generation of young people is not irrelevant to what is done in a city like Boston where, in the midst of enormous regional "postindustrial" prosperity, many youth are structurally unemployed because of race or location. We have to know far more about urban and rural comparisons, rural education being a vital concern in many parts of the world. We need to understand more about how we are locked into research traditions, sets of institutional interests, or even beliefs about the panacea of education that make it difficult to understand how the modern world is changing. Only then will it be possible to create a kind of coherence and understanding which is lacking now both within schools and in the larger societies that have placed so many burdens on them.

This agenda is not to deny the value of civic education, but to appreciate its importance and ask that it be truly sophisticated.

Notes

*I would like to acknowledge the assistance of Robert Cowen, Harold Silver, Barbara Finkelstein, Judith Torney-Purta, and Ralph Mosher in providing materials and some stimulating ideas. Grants from the Spencer Foundation and the John Dewey Foundation have made it possible for me to extend my research on progressive education to international topics. The Exxon Education Foundation has assisted my research in international educational relations.

[1] Harold Silver, *Education and the Social Condition* (London and New York: Methuen, 1980), 1.

[2] Robert Cowen, "Curriculum Issues, 1970-1990: Contents, Policies and Practices in the USA," *Compare* 11, 1 (1981): 8-9.

[3] David B. Tyack, Robert Lowe, and Elisabeth Hansot, *Public Schools in Hard Times: The Great Depression and Recent Years* (Cambridge, Mass.: Harvard University Press, 1984); and Diane Ravitch, *The Troubled Crusade: American Education, 1945-1980* (New York: Basic Books, 1983). See also, Diane Ravitch et al., "The Paideia Proposal: A Symposium," *Harvard Educational Review* 53 (November 1983): 377-411.

[4] For representative recent literature on the civic education movement, see Alan H. Jones, ed., *Civic Learning for Teachers: Capstone for Educational Reform*, Proceedings of the Seminar on Civic Learning in the Education of the Teaching Profession held November 11-13, 1984 at the Hoover Institution on War, Revolution and Peace, Stanford University, Stanford, California (Ann Arbor: Prakken Publications, 1985); Marc Landy and Wilson Carey McWilliams, "Civic Education in an Uncivil Culture," *Society* 22 (March-April 1985): 52-55; Peggy Ann Brown, "Promoting Civic Literacy," *Forum for Liberal Education* 7 (March 1985); Gordon R. Thomas, "Commitment and Action: New Directions in Citizenship Education Research," *History and Social Science Teacher* 19 (May 1984): 238-39; Joan N. Burstyn, "The Civic Purpose of Education: Process and Product," *Journal of Teacher Education* 34 (November-

December 1983): 2-5; and R. Freeman Butts, ed., *Journal of Teacher Education* 34 (November-December 1983)—a special issue on "The Civic Education of the American Teacher." For historical background, see Michael V. Belok, "The Instructed Citizen: Civic Education in the United States During the Nineteenth Century," *Pedagogica Historica* 18, 2 (1978): 257-74. For the place of civic education in international political socialization literature, see D. Heater and J. Gillespie, eds., *Political Education in Flux* (London: Sage Publicatons, 1981). Some civic educators have rather conservative intentions. See, for example, Morris Janowitz, "Toward a New Patriotism: Educating for Civic Consciousness," *Curriculum Review* 24 (March-April 1985): 14-18.

[5] R. Freeman Butts, *The Revival of Civic Learning: A Rationale for Citizenship Education in American Schools* (Bloomington, Ind.: Phi Delta Kappa Educational Foundation, 1980), 21. See also, R. Freeman Butts, "The Revival of Civic Learning Requires a Prescribed Curriculum," *Liberal Education* 68 (Winter 1982): 377-401.

[6] The definitive history of the progressive education movement is Lawrence A. Cremin, *The Transformation of the School: Progressivism in American Education, 1876-1957* (New York: Vintage Books, 1964).

[7] Butts, *The Revival of Civic Learning*, 118.

[8] John C. Bock, "Education and Development: A Conflict of Meaning," in Philip G. Altbach, Robert F. Arnove, and Gail P. Kelley, *Comparative Education* (New York: Macmillan, 1982), 80.

[9] See David B. Tyack, *The One Best System: A History of American Urban Education* (Cambridge, Mass.: Harvard University Press, 1974); and Ellen Condliffe Lagemann, *Private Power for the Public Good: A History of the Carnegie Foundation for the Advancement of Teaching* (Middletown, Conn.: Wesleyan University Press, 1983). I have addressed "exportation" of "the one best system," a subject which has received little attention from historians, in Ronald K. Goodenow, "Transcending the Legacy of Twentieth Century American Schooling: In Search of a Global Perspective," *Issues in Education* 2 (Summer 1984): 44-55, and "Beyond These Shores: Internationalizing the History of Education," *Teachers College Record* 84 (Spring 1983): 753-759.

[10] These topics have received considerable attention over the past few years. For introductions to the contemporary historiography

of American education, see John Hardin Best, ed., *Historical Inquiry in Education: A Research Agenda* (Washington: American Educational Research Association, 1983); and Ronald D. Cohen, "American Public Schooling," *Trends in History* 3 (Winter 1982): 1-14.

[11] See the various essays in Bernard J. Weiss, ed., *American Education and the European Immigrant: 1840-1940* (Urbana: University of Illinois Press, 1982); and William J. Reese, "Neither Victims Nor Masters: Ethnic and Minority Study," in Best, *Historical Inquiry*. See also, Ronald K. Goodenow, "The Progressive Educator, Race and Ethnicity in the Depression Years," *History of Education Quarterly* 15 (Winter 1975): 365-94, and "Multicultural Education: A Fifty Year Perspective on Policy Issues," in Wolfgang Mitter and James Swift, eds., *Education and the Diversity of Cultures* (Cologne: Bohlau Verlag, 1985), 205-18.

[12] Fred M. Newmann, "Building a Rationale for Civic Education," in James P. Shaver, ed., *Building Rationales for Citizenship Education*, Bulletin 52, National Council for the Social Studies (Arlington, Va.: NCSS, 1977), 28-29.

[13] Butts, *The Revival of Civic Learning*, 9

[14] Paul E. Peterson and Barry G. Rabe, "The Role of Interest Groups in the Formation of Educational Policy: Past Practices and Future Trends," *Teachers College Record* 84 (Spring 1983): 708. For another research perspective, see John J. Patrick, "The Implications of Political Socialization Research for the Reform of Civic Education," *Social Education* 33 (January 1969): 15-23.

[15] Peterson and Rabe, "The Role of Interest Groups," 720.

[16] Frederick M. Wirt, "Historical Givens, Alternative Futures, and Federal School Policy," *Teachers College Record* 84 (Spring 1983): 730-31.

[17] *Ibid.*, 731-32.

[18] *Ibid.*, 734.

[19] Vandra Lea Masemann, "Comparative Perspectives on Multicultural Education," in *Multicultural Education: Perspectives for the 1980s* (Occasional Paper, Department of Social Foundations and Comparative Education Center, SUNY/Buffalo, 1980), 28-29.

[20] *Ibid.*, 29.

[21] I have addressed this issue in numerous publications. See, for example, Ronald K. Goodenow, "The Progressive Educator"; "Multiculturalism and CBTE: A Historian's Reflection," *The*

Review of Education 2 (January-February 1976): 44-51; and *Intercultural Adaptation Through Education: Historical and Comparative Perspectives* (London Association of Comparative Educationists, Occasional Paper No. 6, July 1981). See also, Nicholas Montalto, "The Growth of Tolerance as a Form of Intolerance," in Weiss, *American Education and the European Immigrant.*

[22] See Walter Feinberg, *Reason and Rhetoric: The Intellectual Foundations of 20th Century Liberal Educational Policy* (New York: John Wiley and Sons, 1975).

[23] American influence in Britain, as well as in Australia and Canada, is discussed in Ronald K. Goodenow and William Marsden, eds., *Urban Educational History in Four Nations: The United States, the United Kingdom, Australia and Canada* (New York: Holmes and Meier Publishing Company, 1986). For an excellent overview and bibliography on the current state of British urban education, see Leslie Bash, David Coulby, and Crispin Jones, *Urban Schooling: Theory and Practice* (London: Holt, Rinehart and Winston, 1985).

[24] Martin McLean, "Education and Cultural Diversity in Britain: Recent Immigrant Groups," *Comparative Education* 18, 2 (1983): 179-81.

[25] For information on civic education in Britain, see Ray Derricott, "Social Studies in England: Perspectives, Problems and Reconsiderations," *International Journal of Political Education* 2 (August 1979): 213-33; F.F. Ridley, "Schools, Youth Programmes, Employment and Political Skills," *International Journal of Political Education* 4 (December 1981): 287-303; Alistair Ross, "Developing Political Concepts and Skills in the Primary School," *Educational Review* 36 (June 1984): 131-39; Clive Harber, "Politics and Political Education in 1984," *Educational Review* 36 (June 1984): 113-20; John Plumer, "Toward a Political Education. The English Experience," *Social Studies Teacher* 3 (September-October 1981): 9; Bernard Crick and Andrew Porter, *Political Education and Political Literacy* (London: Longman, 1978); and D. Heater, "A Burgeoning of Interest: Political Education in Britain," *International Journal of Political Education* 1 (November 1978): 325-45.

[26] See Ted Cohn, "Educational Knowledge Structures, Social/Political Education and the Legitimation Crisis: A Consideration of Recent Developments in Britain, West Germany and the United States," *International Journal of Political Education* 4 (August 1981): 181-94; and Judith V. Torney et al., *Civic Education in*

Ten Countries: An Empirical Study (New York: John Wiley and Sons, 1975) for comparative research.

[27] Leslie Bash, *The Poverty of Political Education* (London Association of Comparative Educationists, Occasional Paper No. 10 March 1984), 3.

[28] *Ibid.*, 7.

[29] *Ibid.*, 13.

[30] John Dewey, *The Public and Its Problems* (Denver: Allan Swallow, 1927), 30-31.

[31] There is enormous literature on dependency theory, its application to education, and its current status. For a useful introduction, see Martin McLean, "Educational Dependency: A Critique," *Compare* 13, 1 (1983): 25-42.

[32] There needs to be far more work on the global diffusion of liberal social science as applied to educational policy issues. For some interesting revisionist perspectives on this, see Edward H. Berman, *The Influence of the Carnegie, Ford, and Rockefeller Foundations on American Foreign Policy: The Ideology of Philanthropy* (Albany, N.Y.: State University of New York Press, 1983). I have looked at philanthropy and the role of modern schools of education and their ties to the international progressive education movement in transferring ideas on cultural adaptation and progress in Ronald K. Goodenow, "To Build a New World: Toward Two Case Studies on Transfer in the Twentieth Century," *Compare* 13 (Summer 1983): 43-59. See also, Ronald K. Goodenow and Robert Cowen, "Teachers College and the Third World, 1920-1955," *History of Education* (forthcoming); and Ronald K. Goodenow, "The American Foundation, National Interest and the World of Education," *Journal of Education* 166 (Fall 1984): 309-15.

[33] See Walter Feinberg, *Understanding Education* (New York: Cambridge University Press, 1983); and Barbara Finkelstein, "Exploring Community in Urban Educational History," in Ronald K. Goodenow and Diane Ravitch, eds., *Schools in Cities: Consensus and Conflict in American Educational History* (New York: Holmes and Meier, Inc., 1983), 305-319.

[34] There is scant scholarship on this very important question. For an excellent overview, see Frank A. Ninkovich, *The Diplomacy of Ideas: U.S. Foreign Policy and Cultural Relations, 1938-1950* (Cambridge: Cambridge University Press, 1984).

[35] For a fascinating analysis, the model of which should be applied to schools of education, see Roberta A. McCaughey, *International Studies and Academic Enterprise* (New York: Columbia

University Press, 1984).

[36]See Torney, "International Attitudes," in *Civic Education in Ten Countries*.

Chapter Nine

We are living through a radical transformation in our symbolic systems that is inevitably linked with social and civic evolution.

9

Civic Life and Civic Education: A Study of Changing Symbolic Systems

By Betty A. Sichel

In stable societies, institutions exert their claims upon the individual; traditions provide a sense of continuity and brotherhood. Transplanted as I was, I lacked a sense of loyalty to British or American institutions: I was not held in place by a national tradition. I had been uprooted; I was waiting to be reclaimed.
—*Michael Straight*[1]

IN the *Politics*, Aristotle asserts that the virtues and thus the judgments and behavior of a good citizen and a good person are frequently different.[2] Only in utopian societies or for rulers are the lives and decisions of good citizens and good persons identical. In actual societies, one often questions whether to be a good person or a good citizen. During the 1930s, a number of intelligent, talented young people were seduced by Soviet Russia. This was not a brief flirtation during an adolescent developmental crisis, but a lifetime marriage and one-way relationship requiring these youths to furnish state secrets to a foreign government. If asked to explain this disloyalty to their native countries, they might very well have cited the Aristotelian dichotomy: their overriding concerns were the principles and standards of good persons, and these concerns were at odds with their nation's political and social system and policies. Spys and traitors like Burgess, Philby, MacLean, and Blunt, it follows, were critical of good citizen virtues while they sustained good person virtues.

During the last few years, the Aristotelian dichotomy seems less relevant for explaining the behavior of those who sell national secrets to foreign powers. Agents no longer seem concerned about personal principles or their country's political and social system. They are rarely even cognizant of or worried about the social and political structure of those countries buying secrets. Rather than loyalty to one's own principles or those of one's native country, only the economic value of the secret is considered.[3] What is a secret worth? Which country will pay the highest price for a secret or a person's services? This present situation might be explained in number of ways.

First, someone might reject nation-states in general and argue that a world government can save us from nuclear destruction. Still following Aristotle, it might then be claimed that only with world government and community can people be both good citizens and good persons.[4] Thus, the widest dissemination of national secrets would destroy the present system of governments and national barriers. Whatever voids were created would be filled by a world government. Such an argument, however, cannot be used by those selling industrial and military secrets or services. For, instead of disseminating knowledge and skills to the widest possible audience, they are merely selling them to the highest bidder.

A second argument might be that the Aristotelian dichotomy is still tacitly accepted: these agents embrace the values of a good person and reject those of the good citizen. They might claim to be concerned with personal good, i.e., the virtues of the good person and not the virtues of the good citizen. By selling secrets to the highest bidder, these people advance their personal good and reject societal virtues. However, such reasons cannot be sustained. As they present themselves in biographical accounts, these agents do not possess self-consciously developed, personally warranted principles. They are not rejecting good citizen virtues by saying that there are higher principles than those accepted by their society. They are not looking to some higher good; saying that their society is immoral, does not accept the rights of all its citizens, does not consider the needs of the downtrodden, or advocates heinous policies and actions. Rather, these people merely gratify their own egotistical, selfish interests and desires.

It might still be argued that such egotism and selfishness are the basis of the principles accepted by those who presently sell secrets to the highest bidder. Again turning to Aristotle, one can understand why such an argument has no merit. For Aristotle concludes that virtues cannot be used for good or bad, only for good. The moral lives accepted by these agents are not rationally or consciously justified, but unthinkingly based on the profit motive no matter the action's morality or the consequences for the agent or society. There is no consideration of whether such deeds have negative effects on anyone—agent or country.

Third, a more viable reason is based on Michael Straight's biographical account of why he became a "mole." Straight was born to wealth, educated at progressive schools in New York and England, and then attended the London School of Economics and Cambridge University. He was intelligent, personable, and destined for success. Blunt, Straight's Cambridge don and respected mentor, explained that some "friends" had decided Straight's future. Blunt insisted that Straight was to return to the United States and become a mole. Why were the orders given by Blunt accepted so easily by Straight? Why were Blunt's orders hardly questioned? The problem here is not whether Straight eventually transmitted sensitive material, but why he originally accepted this role and maintained contacts with the agents of a foreign power. Straight himself proposes an answer: His childhood move from the United States to England and his progressive education did not prepare him or transmit those values necessary for loyal and active citizenship. He never developed the roots of a loyal citizen.

Whereas Straight's progressive schools stressed decision making and participatory democracy, little attention was paid to the standards used for making such judgments. Whereas community decisions and actions were decided by the group, these did not involve community welfare, but related to trivial matters such as whether a barber should come to the school or the boys should go to the village for haircuts. Whereas the young students had considerable freedom, this freedom was not grounded in a knowledge of democratic institutions and processes. Since classes did not include traditional content for comparison with present situations, realistic democratic values, symbols, and knowledge were not transmitted. Even if this line of reasoning is not valid for other defectors and spies during the 1930s, it might provide clues to explain the actions of more recent spies and traitors. Present-day vendors of national secrets may not have internalized the values, roots, or roles necessary for loyalty and citizenship. That is, they are uneducated in civic virtue and must be considered civic illiterates unless we want to accept a civic community based on selfishness.

Let's look at a revised scenario and how a different script might affect our evaluation of Straight's life and citizenship. If Straight had never met Blunt or Burgess, lived a quiet life, received a gentleman's education, joined an aristocratic riding club, returned to the United States, married, and lived an upper-class life, would he be judged a loyal citizen of the United States? Even if he knew nothing about politics or the basic principles of this country's democracy, even if he contributed nothing to the betterment of society and tacitly condoned social inequities, his loyalty would never have been questioned. In other words, by doing nothing, his loyalty and citizenship would have been assumed. But this hardly provides a satisfactory description of the good citizen or good member of a democratic community. Something more is needed, and that something more must be explored in order to understand the nature of good citizenship in a democracy, civic responsibilities, and civic education.

Particular periods have been singled out as times of radical, cataclysmic changes in the way people view civic life and citizenship. It will be argued in this essay that American democracy has reached such a point and that substantial changes must be made in the way we view citizenship and civic education. This reconstruction of the highways of civic education and civic life requires a number of phases. First, attention will be directed towards the idea that different historical periods require different conceptualizations of civic life and citizenship. Second, the cataclysmic changes occurring in American political and social life will be examined in relation to the necessity of reconceptualizing the nature of democratic citizenship and civic education.

Great Ideas in the Background

> A great idea in the background of dim consciousness is like a phantom ocean beating

> upon the shores of human life in successive waves of specialization. A whole succession of such waves are as dreams slowly doing their work of sapping the base of some cliff of habit: but the seventh wave is a revolution.
> —*Alfred North Whitehead*[5]

Where do we find that single wave which is destined to crash on the beach, cause a revolution, and change the contours of the land forever? Does one just look to the horizon for distant waves or is it necessary to journey to the far reaches of the ocean? Our quest for the first rumble, the beginnings of democratic society and citizenship, commences in the far distant past in the period between the feudal, familial society of Homer's *Iliad* and *Odyssey* and the classical Athenian participatory democracy of the Periclean Age. Athens quivered and simmered with the idea that human beings could control their own private lives, and political and social destinies, that human life was so precious that farmers no longer could use themselves or their families as security for debts,[6] and that membership on lawmaking forums and juries was chosen by lot and not based on wealth or inheritance. Democracy became participatory, and with this far-reaching change each citizen was required to take an active role in civic life.

Arguments abound that Athenian democracy was flawed, that it never reached perfection, that there was slavery, that foreigners and women were permanently disenfranchised, that oratory and wealth often swayed the mobs serving on judicial and legislative bodies, that decisions and laws were controlled by emotions not rationality, and that Athenian relationships with and policy toward other city-states were certainly not based on the democratic ideals Athens extolled. Even if we accept all these shortcomings and find that Athenian democracy was blemished, this does not diminish the importance of this democratic breakthrough in civic and political life, for an idealized Athens symbolizes the dreams of humanity. This democratic city-state is the first wave in the steady progression toward a fully democratic, just, and humane life.

This transformation of Athenian civic and political life is now viewed as the first in a series of wavelets which eventually crashed on foreign shores and created a radical transformation in human life. However, the classical Greeks saw this change from Homeric feudalism to Athenian democracy as a tidal wave. Scholars argue about why this change occurred. Did the transformation from an oral tradition to a written and literate culture;[7] travels to distant lands,[8] or Athenian internationalism; scientific revelations and mathematical discoveries; or the use of money and growth of a wealthy business class also cause a radical transformation in Athenian political and civil life?

Instead of searching for a single cause and effect and thus assuming that one of the above changes caused political and civic changes, I argue that changes in civic and political life went hand in hand with other intellectual and symbolic modifications. Though many factors seem to explain the evolution of Athenian political and social institutions, beliefs, and civic practice, another approach promises more fruitful results. This path searches for how changes in Athenian symbolic systems influenced civic life and education.

Plato's *Protagoras* provides an example of this transformation of Athenian symbolic systems. One way this radical transformation is revealed is by the different teaching methods used respectively by Sophists and by Socrates. After offering to show that virtue can be taught, Protagoras, the famous Sophist, prefaces his Great Speech by asking Socrates and a doting assemblage: "But what would you like? Shall I, as an elder, tell you, as younger men, a myth, or shall I argue the question?" (320C). After he is told to choose, Protagoras decides that "the myth will be more interesting." With this decision to use a traditional mythic presentation, Protagoras does not merely carefully camouflage his thoughts to avoid common hostility against Sophists (316D), but also points to a fundamental characteristic of his own era. That characteristic is revealed in the form of the Great Speech itself, not only by Protagoras's statement that a myth should be more interesting.

Though he begins the Great Speech with a myth, Protagoras concludes with a discursive form of presentation. Following this twofold form and after Socrates' speech, Socrates and Protagoras then engage in a dialectical argument. Why these three different modes of discourse, these different ways of presenting ideas? Protagoras and Socrates each actually point to the changing nature of the Athenian symbolic system, changes from the older Homeric heroic age values to those of the newer classical period. In addition, since the dialogue examines whether virtue, citizenship, and civic responsibility can be taught, the alteration in symbolic systems implies modifications in education.

Protagoras's use of the older mythic form represents Homeric heroic, manly virtues and earlier traditional civic life. Even though Athenians were already living in a different age, they longed for and continually dreamed about the lives and adventures of the mythic and heroic age. While surrounded by the symbols of a new period, they remembered, cherished, and verbally commended the symbols of a bygone age. The epic poetry of Homer, for example, was memorized and declaimed by students in the belief that the values and symbols of the *Iliad* and *Odyssey* were just as valid for fifth-century Athens as for the Homeric Age (*Prot.* 326A). Socrates questions whether Homeric values are still adequate for his own age. In the *Republic*, Socrates summarizes his young aristrocratic interlocutor Polemarchus's acceptance of traditional poets by saying:

> A kind of thief then the just man it seems has turned out to be, and it is likely that you acquired this idea from Homer. For he regards with complacency Autolycus, the maternal uncle of Odysseus, and says, "he was gifted beyond all men in thievery and perjury." So justice, according to you and Homer and Simonides, seems to be a kind of stealing, with the qualification that it is for the benefit of friends and the harm of enemies (*Rep.* 1, 334 A-B).

Plato's *Laches* similarly offers examples of the continuing vigor of Homeric symbols. During the classical age, Homeric manly virtues, e.g., courage, were thought to guarantee wealth and respect. Even during the later period depicted in *Laches*, people believed that success in private and public, in their civic roles, and personal lives was dependent on possession of these manly virtues. Melesias and Lysimachus propose to insure their sons' success by having them taught how to fight with armor. Two generals, Laches and Nicias, who symbolize the manly virtue of courage, are asked whether they agree that fighting with armor is a way to attain respect. Among the reasons he gives for learning to fight with armor, Nicias says:

> And I will not disdain to mention, what by some may be thought to be a small matter— he will have a more impressive appearance at the right time, that is to say, at the time when his appearance will strike terror into his enemies (*La.* 182 C).

Just as Achilles' armor itself symbolized his superior manly, heroic virtues and extraordinary fighting ability, so the physical appearance of a fifth-century Athenian fighting with armor would make him successful in battle.

Returning to *Protagoras*, these Homeric manly virtues are tacitly questioned by Protagoras when he abruptly changes his mode of discourse in the middle of the Great Speech and uses a discursive form of argument. In line with Sophistic discoveries about the nature of persuasive arguments and naturalistic, scientific discoveries about human life and psychology, Protagoras discards the older view of civic life characterized by mythic and traditional symbols, and turns to a purely naturalistic, behavioristic account of value and civic education. What is the meaning of Protagoras's shift in symbolic modes of presentation? The mythic worldview can be seen in the fable of Protagoras's Great Speech. Like the respected poets of the oral tradition, Protagoras employs familiar metaphors and symbols to interest and persuade his audience. For example, when the commonplace story of Prometheus is retold to serve Protagoras's evolutionary theory, the audience is more sympathetic than if a scientific treatise were presented.

After the audience is disarmed by these traditional mythic symbols, Protagoras can switch to a discursive mode, and the ideas presented in that latter mode will be reinterpreted by the audience within the older framework. Just as literacy and a written language created radical departures from the way oral poets expressed ideas, so Protagoras's discursive portion of the Great Speech is similarly different. The twofold technique of Protagoras's Great Speech becomes an ideal method to entertain and persuade his attentive listeners. In addition, through this twofold method Protagoras himself tacitly recognizes something else: that the discursive is not merely reinterpreted through the mythic paradigm, but that the mythic provides a means for the newer symbols in the discursive portion of the Speech to be introduced, understood, and accepted.

Socrates argues that the two ways implied by the mythic and discursive forms of discourse cannot provide a completely satisfactory education for civic life during a time of symbolic change. In the Great Speech, Protagoras had presented a social learning theory which assumed that civic education could be accomplished through modeling, reinforcement, and punishment and that the only standard of such education would be the agent's explicit behavior. Instead of wholly rejecting Protagoras's behavioristic program of social learning, Socrates sees this as only one aspect of early moral and civic education. On one side, Socrates asserts that Homeric and traditional symbols and values are no longer valid for fifth-century Athenian life and that they cannot be justified. Simultaneously, Socrates asserts that these earlier symbols only reveal external appearances and not the actual quality of a person's civic life and citizenship. What is paramount for Socrates is that education and civic life are not merely activity without thought, or thought and knowledge without activity, but a reflexive interaction and balance among thought, knowledge, and activity. This reflexive relationship is revealed by the method Socrates insists he and Protagoras use (*Prot.* 329B).

Through his dialectical method, interlocutors are required to search themselves and reveal how they interpret and understand symbolic systems. With this change in educational technique, Socrates insists that the student take an active role in the educational process. But, the Socratic method was necessary for another reason. The symbols accepted by society and required for civic life and citizenship were not wholly agreed upon or homogeneously uniform. Articulation and codification of radically changed symbolic systems had not yet been accomplished. In truth, scientific, artistic, and literary creativity for political and civic transformations required that such codification and articulation be suspended. Such suspension is also seen in the *aporia* endings of the Socratic dialogues. For Socrates is tacitly agreeing that during a time of radical social and political transformation, during a time that demands extensive modifications of civic life and education, there can be no closure in the way symbolic systems are conceptualized and understood. This was as true for classical Athens as it is for any other similarly cataclysmic period.

Symbolic Change in Contemporary Society

> Our sense of national community must be at its lowest ebb since the Civil War.
> —*Robert Nisbet*[9]

> That American society is disjointed is generally recognized, though there is disagreement whether this is a good thing or a bad thing. . . . Can it be put back together again, pluralistic but whole, or is it a matter of Humpty Dumpty revisited?
> —*Forrest McDonald*[10]

Is there a crisis in American political and social life, in democratic civic life, citizenship, and civic education? Are the people of the United States witnessing cataclysmic changes in democratic citizenship and the symbolic systems underlying our entire civic life that prevents the formation of social responsibility, roots, and connections with others? Are value, social, political, and intellectual changes occurring that prevent the formation of civic roots and connections to others, social responsibility and commitment, as in the case of Straight?

Some might argue that a reconstruction of civic life and education is unnecessary and, thus, tacitly deny the existence of cataclysmic changes in every aspect of life. Similarly, some say that traditional methods and symbols still guarantee a viable civic education. Radical thinkers, however, would claim that nothing traditional should be retained, that older types of civism or civic education must be destroyed and a totally new structure created. These antithetical views, the conservative or radical, the reactionary or anarchic, the traditional or revolutionary, must be rejected. Even if cataclysmic scientific, technological, and social changes affect civic life and education, society's traditional symbolic systems cannot be wholly destroyed. Just as a wave has a beginning and experiences steady accretion before crashing onto the distant shore, new symbolic systems do not spring into being *ex nihilo*. They are embedded within the older system, begin with tentative hesitation, and struggle to develop and be accepted.

Conservatives may long for bygone days and speak of old-fashioned, traditional values. They may even imagine a world which never existed. Their emotional nostalgia is not necessarily a realistic assessment of the ability to retain and implement traditional civic life in practice during the present period. Fear of an unknown future, the considerable problems facing contemporary society and government, and unrealistic memories and pictures of older communities cause some to look backwards and urge an education based on traditional civism.

Simultaneously, some radical thinkers claim that few remnants from the past should be saved. Accordingly, only through revolution and a totally new social structure can a truly humanistic democracy be created. Schools in their present form, it is argued, are unable to build a new social order, guarantee equality of opportunity, or transmit the revitalized values and skills for this democratic society. In particular, it is claimed that students' socioeconomic class determines the quality of their education. Children of upper-class and even middle-class professionals and entrepreneurs are assured admittance to prestigious colleges and economic success by being sent to private schools or public schools with private-school trappings. Lower-class children, on the other hand, attend crowded, urban schools where education is little more than baby sitting and training to accept passive social roles. Thus, critics argue that schools do not provide equal opportunity, but merely reproduce the social, political, and economic structure. Given this situation, public and private schools transmit unacceptable social and political values to children and adolescents. Though the wealthy and upper middle-class realize that they will be the leaders of society, even *their* introduction into democratic participation is far less than desirable. In school, lower-class students learn that they have little chance to participate in the governance of their community and society. Many radicals thus conclude that some form of revolutionary or structural social change is necessary. Democratic civic life and education, for these radical thinkers, can never occur in present schools. Only cataclysmic change is the answer.

Neither traditionalists nor radicals are correct in their assessment of the present and prescription for future civic life and education. Traditionalists and conservatives err in believing that change can be avoided and society can return to the values and symbols of an earlier historical period. Radicals err when assuming that a society's slate can be wiped clean and that, as with a Lockean infant, society can again begin with a *tabula rasa*. In place of these extremes, one must look to history as one might examine an early map. First, even an understanding of the present situation cannot be accomplished without an understanding of how it evolved. Second, and more important, symbolic systems never wholly disappear. Older symbols unexpectedly reappear within newer systems. If not understood and given their due within the newer systems, these older symbols haunt and destroy newer ways of life. Like recessive genes, consequences and offspring of older symbolic forms continually make their appearance. Thus, the issue is not merely whether to return to an older system or welcome a newer one, but how to integrate the old and the new. Only by examining and understanding these changes can we envisage a new future based on a new civism and civic education.

Radical Transformations and Concurrent Symbol Crises

> Those societies which cannot combine reverence to their symbols with freedom of revision, must ultimately decay either from anarchy, or from the slow atrophy of a life stifled by useless shadows.
> —*Alfred North Whitehead*[11]

> The prolongation of outworn forms of life means a slow decadence in which there is repetition without any fruit in the reaping of value. There may be high survival power. For decadence undisturbed by originality or by external forces, is a slow process. But the values of life are slowly ebbing.... There is an

alternative to this slow decline. . . . a quick period of transition may set in, which may or may not be accompanied by dislocations involving widespread unhappiness.

—*Alfred North Whitehead*[12]

Recent transformations in civic life are so overwhelming that contemporary scholars and critics have hardly articulated them or understood their nature. A greater difficulty is visualization of what directions future changes will take and their effects on other aspects of life. Fortune-tellers at present do not have cloudy crystal balls, but receive so many disparate pictures in such rapid succession that they cannot foretell any future.

The discovery of the memory chip and the advent of the personal microcomputer heralded the beginning of a new world which was as different from the world we knew as the world after the printing press differed from the earlier one.[13] The computer not only allows for the rapid processing of data but, because of the computer, different cognitive styles, different political and social structures and issues, different views of history, and intellectual problems will emerge. Have technological and scientific discoveries affected civic life and the various rights movements of the last three decades? This is difficult to answer, since one factor alone does not cause a radical change in civic life and citizenship. Just as an artist's many experiences; the conscious and unconscious; emotional and rational life; the use of different colors, brush strokes, textures, designs, and themes contribute to a painting; various interconnected components produce a particular age.

Someone may question whether technology and the computer should be given this preeminent role and, thus, provide a starting place for the examination of civic life. Two examples from the present era, I believe, indicate that we are living through a radical transformation in our symbolic systems and that technology is inevitably linked with social and civic evolution. First, the role of computer technology and, second, the recent feminist movement and its various scholarly studies, which attempt to delineate and explore differences between masculine and feminine morality and social interrelationships, have significant implications for our evolving symbolic systems in this era.

No one would question whether computers and technology are radically changing human life, though some would argue whether these changes are negative or positive. My only aim here is to examine how computers and technology must modify our symbolic systems, and then how this will influence civic life.

Just as the change from the archaic oral tradition to classical Greek literacy and from hand-written manuscripts to printed books radically transformed symbolic systems, computers must change the way the world is seen, what is known, how symbols are used, and the symbols themselves. For example, since the time of Socrates and Plato, philosophers and psychologists have posited theories and ideas which stressed methods and symbols which predominantly used the left hemisphere of the brain. The dynamic, interactive quality of the computer moves beyond this traditional way of using symbols and requires much greater reliance on the right hemisphere of the brain. Instead of seeing all problems through linear, logical programming, many dilemmas require considerable networking and the use of many symbolic systems simultaneously, e.g., graphics, statistical analyses, descriptive language, and artificial intelligence. In other words, I am arguing against those who picture the computer as merely requiring logical exactitude and instead asserting that the computer will change our way of approaching problems, processing ideas, and interacting with the world. These changes also allow maximum interaction between both hemispheres of the brain and require a new way of conceptualizing symbolic systems and their interrelationship.

Why must such new symbolic, interactive systems also change civic life? Computers and technology are not merely experienced passively or confined to one aspect of life, but rather influence every aspect of life. The ability to affect political decisions; have interactive town meetings and meetings between people with similar interests no matter their geographic location; acquire information; and solve complex, multidimensional problems has considerable impact on civic life. Instead of computer usage being limited to a narrow section of the population, all segments of society can have access to computers, e.g., through library acquisition of computer hardware, software, and dial-up facilities.

Images of Values/Images of Citizenship

> She was trying to catch hold of something, or to lay it bare so that she could look and define; for some time now she had been "trying on" ideas like so many dresses off a rack. She was letting words and phrases as worn as nursery rhymes slide around her tongue; for towards

> the crucial experiences custom allots certain attitudes, and they are pretty stereotyped.
> —*Doris Lessing*[14]

> The lights, the flowers, the music, the crowds, the splendid women, the jewels, the strangeness even of the universal murmur of a clever foreign tongue, were all a vivid symbol and assurance of his having grasped his purpose.
> —*Henry James*[15]

Engrained in the American imagery of success and social respect is the notion of the self-made person. Horatio Alger and Oliver Optic stories and the Protestant ethos extolled the personification of certain fundamental, traditional values. From Benjamin Franklin's diary, which tells how he acquired values, to contemporary literature, Americans continue to cherish these values. At the very time that such values are being challenged and rejected, they continually reappear. Values such as honesty, hard work, and diligence have been symbolic of the American way. Through competition and rugged individualism, it has been assumed, this country made its way from a wilderness to a sophisticated, materially comfortable, cultured society. Henry James in *The American* describes one such successful American:

> It must be admitted, rather nakedly, that Christopher Newman's sole aim in life had been to make money; what he had been placed in the world for was, to his own perception, simply to wrest a fortune, the bigger the better, from defiant opportunity. This idea completely filled his horizon and satisfied his imagination. . . . Life had been for him an open game, and he had played for high stakes. He had won at last and carried off his winnings.[16]

In every way, Christopher Newman is a symbol of the successful, respected American.

Theorists argue that fair play is basic for the American way of life. If life is a game, or more specifically, a competitive race, there must be rules and norms which victor and loser alike respect. Certain recent ethical theories and moral psychologies include these very elements, the rules and principles to insure that all competitors have equal rights and are treated justly. Civic life according to these theorists is a game with appropriate rules. No one can be excluded from playing, and all players must agree upon the rules—the justice and rights which control the game. To play the game, or even to accept the game, implies that players recognize and accept the rules. It is also granted that all players can use their own unique abilities in whichever ways conform to the game's basic principles.

Critics claim that the reality of American society is quite different from the theoretical paradigm. Extraneous characteristics often determine winners: the game is thus rigged and judged to be unfair and unjust. So much empirical research and critical commentary sustain this negative view that it does not need repetition here. The reality probably lies someplace between the ideal and real, the positive and negative, the theoretical and critical picture.

More interesting, however, is another view according to which both the theoretical and critical interpretations are correct. Victors manipulate and interpret the game's rules and play with great skill. Simultaneously, these players ignore the rules; for, by playing so well, they can bend the rules to serve their own purposes. In comparison with ordinary players, victors are superordinate players who remain precariously balanced on the boundary between the acceptable and unacceptable. By playing in the realm of the extreme; by intuiting newer, barely acceptable directions; by possessing style; these victors often experiment with untried and unrecognizable symbols.

No matter how it is interpreted, feminists assert that this American game of success is rigged against women, since women predominantly use a different paradigm to interpret life, relate to other human beings, resolve moral dilemmas, and conduct civic life in general. Instead of being players who picture other people as competitors in society's race for different goods, women construct help networks by which to sustain and assist each other. According to this view, qualities such as sharing, communication, dialogue, response, and caring are paramount.

These ideas have not merely been posited by a few theorists in limited fields or for narrow segments of life. Rather, theorists in many disciplines, e.g., those addressing problems in business management and university administration, have turned to similar categories. In business management, for example, it is asserted that the competitive paradigm might have been valid for an earlier age, but at present a new paradigm must be accepted. Instead of totally destroying the older model, the older view would have to be wholly refurbished with new qualities such as mutual sharing, dialogue, and caring integrated into the older model. This would not merely be additive, with new concerns added to older ones, but the new qualities would also require a reinterpretation of older categories.

How does this new way of viewing how people interact with each other and live and work within different institutions relate to symbolic systems and civic life? Some basic parts of our symbolic system are how we view each other and ourselves; what symbols and images are used to describe and think of men and women, employers and employees, colleagues and friends, clients and strangers; what dreams we have, and how our ideas and dreams are implemented in civic life. The two different paradigms, the older competitive and newer dialogical views, require radically different symbolic systems and civic lives.

The competitive paradigm fostered a symbolic system which included as main components winners and losers, those who were successful and those who failed, people able to compete and those who stood on the sideline and cheered the main players, those who played the game and those who were not allowed in the ballpark. The symbols of this civic life were as engrained in American novels and art as they were in the imagery and symbols, conscious and unconscious, of the general public. When Dreiser entitled a novel *The American Tragedy*, the title did not just refer to the actual, surface events of the novel, but to something much deeper. Instead of only presenting a tragedy in a civic leader's life, Dreiser revealed a greater problem. For, how society viewed women and men, their relationships with each other, their social class, their rights and responsibilities in society, the roles they were expected to play, and the values required by their lives were no longer valid. The tragedy was not merely one man's tragic fall from civic power and respect, but the impending disaster awaiting American society if its values and symbols were not changed.

The newer caring paradigm, on the other hand, is characteristic of family life and friendship. In actual life, what often occurs is not the acceptance of a single paradigm, but a dichotomy between the private and the public, with the caring paradigm used in private life and the competitive in public. Women now argue about the validity of this dichotomy and whether their quest for success in public life should require them to accept the conditions and consequences of different paradigms for different parts of life. What does this most complicated and difficult problem tell us? Not that one paradigm or the other must be chosen, but that a new paradigm and set of symbols is emerging.

Citizenship and Civic Education

> A nation won't get wisdom except by the love of it.[17]

> Culture is the knowledge of the best that has been said and done.... But such conceptions of culture, though true enough as far as they go, are defective. They are too static.[18]
>
> It takes the various forms of wonder, of curiosity, of reverence, of worship, of tumultuous desire for merging personality with something beyond itself. This sense of value imposes on life incredible labours, and apart from it life sinks back into the passivity of its lower types.
> —*Alfred North Whitehead*[19]

The rebuilding of civic life and education is not a simple undertaking. Though schools are usually charged with such responsibilities, no single institution can successfully change the course of American civic life. Children are not merely educated in schools, and schools are not untouched by the character of the larger society. The classical Greeks were correct when they used the term *paideia*, which we translate as *education*, to refer to the total of the experiences a person has in society. Not only did formal education by tutors and Sophists transmit civic values and skills, but so did seeing tragedies and comedies, talking in the agora, attending the gymnasium, serving on juries and making laws, being surrounded by classical architecture and sculpture, and taking part in the city-state's religious rituals.

Similarly, Americans do not acquire the symbolic structures necessary for active civic life in schools. Watching television; reading or not reading newspapers, literature, romantic and gothic novels, and magazines; meeting and talking with people in public places; working in offices, factories, retail stores, and garages; visiting a sick friend; sitting on a stoop or standing on a corner and watching the procession of humanity; being accepted or rejected by others; feeling popular, needed, or unwanted; teaching friends and children a skill, whether knitting, gardening, photography, cooking, or collecting stamps; shopping for food and clothing and being able or not able to purchase certain necessities or luxuries; playing games such as soccer, baseball, and bridge; attending a block party; and doing volunteer work—all these actions, events, and things contribute to a person's grasp of the society's and culture's interlocking symbolic systems.

Does the vast number of structures forming a person's symbolic life imply that schools can do very little to transmit symbolic systems or foster civic life and responsibility? Unquestionably, schools alone cannot change civic life. Unlike any other institution of society, however, schools are in a unique situation. For schools are the one institution that should intentionally struggle to transmit the symbolic systems of society and improve civic life. Other institutions either do not intentionally pay attention to these purposes and symbols, or have other primary, explicit, formal educational purposes. They only tacitly see the symbolic and civic as accomplishing other things, e.g., increasing profits, persuading the public to buy some product, changing fashions. The educational implications of such symbols are secondary.

Though numerous interest groups argue that schools should reinstate certain narrowly conceived traditional experiences and teach recognized symbols and experiences to assure citizenship, this too often leads to unthinking nationalism, or love of country. Some groups link repeating the "Pledge of Allegiance" each morning and singing the "Star-Spangled Banner" in an assembly with civic education. However, the rebuilding of civic education and civism has little to do with the maintenance of ritualistic habits and much more in common with the acquisition and use of symbolic systems which underlie the democratic process, social and communal activities, and knowledge and recognition of how the lasting ideas of democratic life reappear within and are transformed by newer symbolic systems.

Rather than merely stressing the ritualistic and habitual, schools need to attack citizenship and civic education on many fronts. For just as democratic life in general requires knowledge of complex, interrelated symbolic systems, ways of life, activities, and knowledge, so formal civic education is more than limited rituals or a single course. Though it seems too broad a statement to claim that every aspect of schooling relates to civic education, this is what must be claimed. With schooling as a whole being the basis of civic education, there will be a formation of roots and connections and the avoidance of the dislocation experienced by Straight and others. The problem educators confront is not how to teach or transmit a known set of symbolic systems, but how to prepare students to use and understand new systems. This does not require the rejection and mere destruction of older structures and symbols, but, rather, the use of the old to discover the new. It does require the recognition of the old in the new and even the new in the old. It does require an active involvement in the democratic civic life implied by these newer systems and structures. Passive knowledge and rituals alone can hardly answer the needs of society and the changes occurring. As argued throughout this essay, the issue educators and society must face is how, at a time of radical change, schools can provide students with the symbols, roots, and connections necessary for a dynamic, valid citizenship.

Notes

[1] Michael Straight, *After Long Silence* (New York: W. W. Norton & Co., 1983), 51, *cf.* 104-105.

[2] For another analysis of Aristotle's dichotomy, see Abraham Edel, "The Good Citizen, the Good Person, and the Good Society," *Citizenship and Education in Modern Society* (Proceedings of the Symposium on Citizenship and Education in Modern Society, 1980).

[3] For example, J. Cummings, "F.B.I. Cites Cash Woes As Motives," *New York Times*, 4 October 1984, 25A.

[4] For an argument about the impossibility of world communities, see Michael Walzer, *Spheres of Justice* (New York: Basic Books, Inc., 1983), 37 *ff.*

[5] Alfred North Whitehead, *Adventures of Ideas* (New York: Macmillan, 1935 [1933]), 23.

[6] M. I. Finley, *Economy and Society in Ancient Greece* (New York: Viking Press, 1982 [1953-1981]).

[7] Eric A. Havelock, *Preface to Plato* (Cambridge, Mass.: Harvard University Press, 1963).

[8] Herodotus, *The Histories*.

[9] Robert Nisbet, "Does America Still Exist?" *Harper's* 268 (1984): 52.

[10] Forrest McDonald in "Does America Still Exist?" 46-47.

[11] Alfred North Whitehead, *Symbolism: Its Meaning and Effect* (New York: Capricorn, 1955 [1927]), 88.

[12] Whitehead, *Adventures of Ideas*, 358-59.

[13] John G. Kemeny, "The Case for Computer Literacy," *Daedalus* 112 (1983): 212-230; Edward B. Fiske, "Computers in the Groves of Academe," *The New York Times Magazine* (May 13, 1984): 40*ff.*

[14] Doris Lessing, *The Summer Before the Dark* (London: Jonathan Cape, 1973), 7.

[15] Henry James, *The American in Novels 1871-1880* (New York: The Library of America, 1983), 727.

[16] *Ibid.*, 533.

[17] Alfred North Whitehead, "Education and Self-Education," in

Essays in Science and Philosophy (New York: Philosophical Library, 1947), 169.

[18] Alfred North Whitehead, "Historical Changes," in *Essays*, 201.

[19] Alfred North Whitehead, *The Aims of Education and Other Essays* (New York: The New American Library, 1949 [1929]), 49.

Bibliography

Selected Bibliography

By Susan Douglas Franzosa

Adams, F. "Highlander Folk School: Getting Information, Going Back and Teaching It." *Harvard Educational Review* 42, 4 (Fall 1972): 497-520.

Alder, Mortimer J. "Understanding the U.S.A." *Journal of Teacher Education* 34, 5 (November-December 1983): 35-37.

———. *The Paideia Proposal: An Educational Manifesto*. New York, NY: Macmillan, 1982.

Alexander, D., and Prideaux, D. "Citizenship Education as Ideology Transmission." *Curriculum Perspectives* 4, 1 (May 1984): 17-23.

Almond, G. A., and Verba, S. *The Civic Culture*. Boston, MA: Little, Brown and Co., 1945.

Anyon, Jean. "Ideology and United States History Text Books." *Harvard Educational Review* 49, 3 (August 1979): 361-86.

Arons, S. *Compelling Belief: The Culture of American Schooling*. New York, NY: McGraw-Hill, 1982.

Bagley, Ayers, ed. *Civic Learning in Teacher Education*. Minneapolis, MN: Society of Professors of Education, 1983.

Beard, Charles A. "Written History as an Act of Faith." *American Historical Review* 39 (1933-34): 219-29.

Belok, Michael V. "The Instructed Citizen: Civic Education in the United States During the Nineteenth Century." *Paedagogica Historica* 18, 2 (1978): 257-74.

Bowers, C. A. *The Promise of Theory: Education and the Politics of Cultural Change*. New York, NY: Longman, 1984.

Bragaw, Donald H., and Loew, Helene Z. "Social Studies and Language: A Partnership." *Social Education* 49, 2 (February 1985): 92-96.

Braverman, Mara. "An Overview of the Law in a Free Society

Project." *Peabody Journal of Education* 55, 1 (October 1977): 32-34.

Broudy, Harry S. *Truth and Credibility: The Citizen's Dilemma.* New York, NY: Longman, 1981.

Brown, Nancy C. "Student Citizenship Participation: Three Models." *Social Studies* 76, 1 (January-February 1985): 12-13.

Burstyn, Joan N. "The Civic Purpose of Education: Process and Product." *Journal of Teacher Education* 34, 6 (November-December 1983): 2-5.

Butts, R. Freeman. *The Revival of Civic Learning: A Rationale for Citizenship Education in American Schools.* Bloomington, IN: Phi Delta Kappa Educational Foundation, 1980.

_____. "The Revival of Civic Learning Requires a Prescribed Curriculum." *Liberal Education* 68, 4 (Fall 1982): 377-401.

Cadwallader, Mervyn L. "General, Liberal, or Political: The Need for Citizen Education." *Liberal Education* 68, 3 (Fall 1982): 249-58.

Childs, John Brown. "Concepts of Culture in African-American Political Thought, 1890-1920." *Social Text—Theory/Culture/Ideology* 2, 1 (1981): 28-43.

Citizenship and the New Federalism? New Roles for Citizens in the 80's? Conference Report on the Jennings Randolph Forum, Washington, DC, May 16-18, 1982.

Cohen, J., and Rogers, J. *On Democracy: Toward a Transformation of American Society.* New York, NY: Penguin Books, 1983.

Cohn, Ted. "Educational Knowledge Structures, Social/Political Education and the Legitimation Crisis: A Consideration of Recent Developments in Britain, West Germany and the U.S.A." *International Journal of Political Education* 4 (August 1981): 181-94.

_____. "Social Justice and Social/Political Education: A Theoretical Exploration." *International Journal of Political Education* 6, 1 (April 1983): 21-39.

Coles, Robert. "Civility and Psychology." *Daedalus* 109, 3 (Summer 1980): 129-43.

Cortes, Carlos E. "The Mass Media: Civic Education's Public Curriculum." *Journal of Teacher Education* 34, 5 (November-December 1983): 25-29.

Curtis, Charles K. "Relationships Among Certain Citizenship Variables." *Journal of Social Studies Research* 7, 2 (Fall 1983): 18-28.

DeBenedetti, Charles. "Peace History in the American Manner."

The History Teacher 18, 1 (November 1984): 75-110.

Derricott, Ray. "Social Studies in England: Perspectives, Problems and Reconsiderations." *International Journal of Political Education* 4 (December 1981): 287-303.

Dewey, John. *Moral Principles in Education.* Carbondale, IL: Southern Illinois University Press, 1909.

─────. *The Public and Its Problems.* New York, NY: Henry Holt, 1920.

Diorio, Joseph. "The Decline of History as a Tool of Moral Training." *History of Education Quarterly* 25, 1 & 2 (Spring-Summer 1985): 71-101.

Dynneson, Thomas L., and Gross, Richard E. "Citizenship Education and the Social Studies: Which is Which?" *Social Studies* 73, 5 (September-October 1982): 229-34.

Edel, Abraham. "The Good Citizen, the Good Person, and the Good Society." In *Citizenship and Education in Modern Society* (Proceedings of the Symposium on Citizenship and Education in Modern Society, 1980).

Egan, Kieran. "Social Studies and the Erosion of Education." *Curriculum Inquiry* 13 (1983): 198-217.

Ehman, L. "The American School in the Political Socialization Process." *Review of Educational Research* 50 (1980).

Ekman, Richard, and Strassburger, John. "Improving the Preparation of Teachers of Civic Education." *Social Studies Review* 24, 1 (Fall 1984): 83-88.

Elhstain, Jean Bethke. *Public Man, Private Woman: Women in Social and Political Thought.* Princeton, NJ: Princeton University Press, 1981.

Entwistle, Harold. *Antonio Gramsci: Conservative Schooling for Radical Politics.* London: Routledge and Kegan Paul, 1979.

Fenton, Edwin. "A Rationale and Set of Objectives for a Civic Education Social Studies Curriculum." *Social Studies Review* 19, 2 (Fall 1979): 49-55, 61.

Ferro, Marc. *The Use and Abuse of History or How the Past Is Taught.* London: Routledge and Kegan Paul, 1984.

Finkelstein, Barbara. "Thinking Publicly About Civic Learning: An Agenda for Education Reform in the 80s." *Civic Learning for Teachers: Capstone for Educational Reform.* Ann Arbor, MI: Prakken Publications, 1985.

Fontana, Lynn A. "A Guide to Sources in Citizenship Education." *Educational Leadership* 38, 1 (October 1980): 69-71.

Foster, Charles R. "Civic Education in the United States and the Federal Republic of Germany." *International Journal of Polit-*

ical Education 2, 1 (September 1977): 45-60.
Fox, Karen F. A., and Thompson, Jack. "To What End: The Aims of Two Centuries of American History Instruction." *Teachers College Record* 82 (1980): 31-46.
Frederickson, H. George. "The Recovery of Civism in Public Administration." *Liberal Education* 68, 4 (Winter 1982): 343-57.
Freire, Paulo. *The Politics of Education: Culture, Power, and Liberation*. South Hadley, MA: Bergin and Garvey, 1985.
Giroux, Henry. "Critical Theory and Rationality in Citizenship Education." *Curriculum Inquiry* 10, 4 (Winter 1980): 329-66.
―――――. *Ideology, Culture, and the Process of Schooling*. Philadelphia, PA: Temple University Press, 1981.
―――――. "Public Philosophy and the Crisis in Education." *Harvard Educational Review* 54, 2 (May 1984).
Golden, Kathleen. "The Relationship Between Voting Knowledge and Voting Attitudes of Selected Ninth and Tenth Grade Students." *Social Studies Journal* 14 (Spring 1985): 10-15.
Goodlad, John I. *A Place Called School: Prospects for the Future*. New York, NY: McGraw-Hill, 1984.
Gordon, Beverly M. "Toward Emancipation in Citizenship Education: The Case of African-American Cultural Knowledge." *Theory and Research in Social Education* 12, 4 (Winter 1985): 1-23.
Gowaskie, Joe. "The Teaching of World History: A Status Report." *The History Teacher* 18, 3 (May 1985): 366-76.
Graham, Duncan. "Attitudinal Change of a Radical Sort." *Independent School* 40, 1 (October 1980): 33-37.
Greene, Maxine. "Education and Disarmament." *Teachers College Record* 84, 1 (Fall 1982): 128-36.
Haavelsrud, Magnus. "Indoctrination or Politicization Through Textbook Content." *International Journal of Political Education* 3, 1 (March 1980): 67-84.
Hahn, Carole L. "Promise and Paradox: Challenges to Global Citizenship." *Social Education* 48, 4 (April 1984): 240-43, 297-99.
Hartoonian, H. Michael. "The Social Studies: Foundation for Citizenship Education in Our Democratic Republic." *Social Studies* 76, 1 (January-February 1985): 5-8.
Heater, D., and Gillespie, J., eds. *Political Education in Flux*. London: Sage Publications, 1981.
Hepburn, Mary A., and Richardson, Helen W. "The Improving Citizenship Education Project: A Change Model That Works." *Social Studies* 76, 1 (January-February 1985): 17-19.

Herndon, James. *Notes from a School Teacher.* New York, NY: Simon and Schuster, 1985.

Hickman, Faith M. "Education for Citizenship: Issues of Science and Society." *American Biology Teacher* 44, 6 (September 1982): 358-65, 367.

Howard, John A. "Reopening the Books on Ethics: The Role of Education in a Free Society." *American Education* 20, 8 (October 1984): 6-11.

Howlett, Charles. "The Pragmatist as Pacifist: John Dewey's Views on Peace Education." *Teachers College Record* 83, 3 (Spring 1982): 435-51.

Hull, Gloria T.; Scott, Patricia; and Smith, Barbara, eds. *All the Women Are White, All the Blacks Are Men, But Some of Us Are Brave.* Old Westbury, NY: Feminist Press, 1982.

Jackson, M. "Assessing a Political Skills Curriculum." *Teaching Political Science* 8 (1980).

Janowitz, Morris. "Toward a New Patriotism: Educating for Civic Consciousness." *Curriculum Review* 24, 4 (March-April 1985): 14-18.

Jones, Alan, ed. *Civic Learning for Teachers: Capstone for Educational Reform.* Ann Arbor, MI: Prakken Publications, 1985.

Jones-Wilson, Faustine C. "Schooling and Democracy: Editorial Comment." *Journal of Negro Education* 52, 2 (Spring 1983): 91-93.

―――――. "The Effect upon Minorities of the Civic Education of Teachers." *Journal of Teacher Education* 34, 6 (November-December 1983): 11-13.

Kammen, Michael, ed. *The Past Before Us: Contemporary Historical Writing in the United States.* Ithaca, NY: Cornell University Press, 1980.

Kane, Frank. "The Controversy Over Civic Education." *Social Studies Review* 22, 3 (Spring 1983): 4-8

Kite, R. Hayman. "The Future, Technology, and Citizen Power: A Challenge to Social Studies Teachers." *Social Studies* 76, 2 (March-April 1985): 53-58.

Kohl, Herbert. *Growing Minds: On Becoming a Teacher.* New York, NY: Harper and Row, 1984.

―――――. "Can the School Build a New Social Order?" *Journal of Education* 162, 3 (Summer 1980): 51-67.

Landy, Marc, and McWilliams, Wilson Carey. "Civic Education in an Uncivil Culture." *Society* 22, 3 (March-April 1985).

Larkins, A. Guy. "Citizenship Education as the Primary Goal of Social Studies: A Case for Teaching Democratic Values in the

Middle Grades." *Georgia Social Science Journal* 16, 1 (Winter 1985): 34-38.

Lawler, Peter Augustine. "Rhetoric as the Foundation for Political Education." *Journal of General Education* 34, 4 (1983): 330-48.

Leck, Glorianne M. "Teacher Burnout and the Extinguishing of Civic Education." *Teacher Education Quarterly* 11, 2 (Spring 1984): 19-34.

Lerner, Gerda. *The Majority Finds Its Past: Placing Women in History.* New York, NY: Oxford University Press, 1979.

Lightfoot, Sara Lawrence. *The Good High School: Portraits of Character and Culture.* New York, NY: Basic Books, 1983.

Lybarger, Michael. "Origins of the Modern Social Studies: 1900-1916." *History of Education Quarterly* 23, 4 (1983): 455-68.

Mar'enko, I. S., ed. "A Model Curriculum for the Social Upbringing of School Pupils." *Soviet Education* 25, 6 (April 1983): 1-103.

Markusen, Eric, and Harris, John B. "The Role of Education in Preventing Nuclear War." *Harvard Educational Review* 54, 3 (August 1984): 282-303.

Martin, Jane Roland. "Becoming Educated: A Journey of Alienation or Integration?" *Journal of Education* 167, 3 (1985): 71-84.

―――. *Reclaiming a Conversation: The Ideal of the Educated Woman.* New Haven, CT: Yale University Press, 1985.

Martin, Warren Bryan. "Education for Character, Career, and Society." *Change* 15, 2 (January-February 1983): 35-42.

Massey, Don, and Van Manen, Max. "Objectives for Citizen Education." *History and Social Science Teacher* 13, 2 (1978): 77-79.

McKelvey, Joyce. "Children's Recollections of the Falklands Crisis: A Small-Scale Exploration." *International Journal of Political Education* 6, 4 (March 1984): 315-30.

Morrill, Richard L. "Educating for Democratic Values." *Liberal Education* 68, 4 (1982): 365-76.

Morrison, Harriet B. "Some Implications in Rawls's Theory for Civic Education." *Journal of Negro Education* 53, 1 (Winter 1984): 78-84.

Mosher, A. "Civic Identity in the Juridical Society." *Political Theory* 11 (1983): 117-32.

Murchland, Bernard. "Citizenship in a Technological Society: Problems and Possibilities." *Journal of Teacher Education* 34, 6 (November-December 1983): 21-24.

Murphy, Paul L. "The Obligations of American Citizenship: A Historical Perspective." *Journal of Teacher Education* 34, 5 (November-December 1983): 8-10.

National Commission on Excellence in Education. *A Nation at Risk.*

Washington, DC: U.S. Department of Education, 1983.
Nelkin, Dorothy. "Science Education for Citizens: Perspectives and Issues. Science and Technology Policy and the Democratic Process." *Studies in Science Education* 9 (1982): 47-64.
Nisbet, Robert. "Does America Still Exist?" *Harper's* 268 (1984): 39-52.
Okin, Susan Mollar. *Women in Western Political Thought.* Princeton, NJ: Princeton University Press, 1979.
Olama, L. Tsoungui. "International Understanding and Civic Education in the UNESCO Associated Schools Project in Cameroon." *International Understanding at School* 33: 11-3.
Oliner, Pearl. "Putting 'Community' into Citizenship Education: The Need for Prosociality." *Theory and Research in Social Education* 11, 2 (Summer 1983): 65-81.
O'Neil, Robert M. "Civic Education and Constitutional Law." *Journal of Teacher Education* 34, 6 (November-December 1983): 14-16.
O'Neill, James R. "The Role of Political Science in the Social Studies." *Social Studies* 73, 5 (September-October 1982): 200-202.
Partington, Geoffrey. "What History Should We Teach?" *Oxford Review of Education* 6 (1980): 157-76.
Pateman, Carole. "The Disorder of Women: Women, Love and the Sense of Justice." *Ethics* 91 (1980): 20-34.
Pellicano, Roy R. "Global Education: A Macro Perspective for Citizenship Education." *Social Studies* 73, 3 (May-June 1982): 125-29.
Powell, Pearl M., and Powell, Jack W. "An Investigation of Political Apathy Among Selected High School Students." *Journal of Social Studies Research* 8, 2 (Fall 1984): 53-66.
Prewitt, Kenneth. "Civic Education and Scientific Illiteracy." *Journal of Teacher Education* 34, 6 (November-December 1983): 17-20.
Ravitch, Diane, et al. "The Paideia Proposal: A Symposium." *Harvard Educational Review* 53, 4 (November 1983): 377-411.
Raywid, Mary Ann; Tesconi, Charles; and Warren, Donald. *Pride and Promise: Schools of Excellence for All People.* Westbury, NY: American Educational Studies Association, 1984.
Remy, R.C. *Handbook of Citizen Competencies.* Washington, DC: Association for Supervision and Curriculum Development, 1980.
──────. "Criteria for Judging Citizenship Education Programs." *Educational Leadership* 38 (1980): 10-11.
Rice, Marion J. "Geography, Social Studies, and World Citizen-

ship." *Georgia Social Science Journal* 16, 1 (Winter 1985): 39-42.

Ross, Harry J., and Yashon, Julius R. "Using Examples of Inhumanity to Teach Responsible Citizenship." *Educational Leadership* 35, 1 (October 1980): 25-28.

Searle, Chris. *Classrooms of Resistance*. London: Writers and Readers Publishing Corp., 1975.

Shanley, Mary L. "Invisible Women: Thoughts on Teaching Political Philosophy." *News for Teachers of Political Science* 24 (1980).

Shaver, J. P., ed. *Building Rationales for Citizenship Education*. Arlington, VA: National Council for the Social Studies, 1977.

———. "Commitment to Values and the Study of Social Problems in Citizenship Education." *Social Education* 49, 3 (March 1985): 194-97.

Shermis, S. Samuel, and Barth, James L. "Teaching for Passive Citizenship: A Critique of Philosophical Assumptions." *Theory and Research in Social Education* 10, 4 (1982): 17-37.

———. "Indoctrination and the Study of Social Problems: A Re-Examination of the 1930s Debate in 'The Social Frontier.'" *Social Education* 49, 3 (March 1985): 190-93.

Shulman, Lee S., and Carey, Neil B. "Psychology and the Limitations of Individual Rationality: Implications for the Study of Reasoning and Civility." *Review of Educational Research* 54, 4 (Winter 1984): 501-24.

Sigel, R., and Hoskin, M. *The Political Involvement of Adolescents*. New Brunswick, NJ: Rutgers University Press, 1981.

Spender, Dale, ed. *Men's Studies Modified: The Impact of Feminism on the Disciplines*. New York, NY: Pergamon Press, 1981.

Stanley, Manfred. "How To Think Anew about Civic Education." *Journal of Teacher Education* 34, 6 (November-December 1983): 38-40.

———. "The Mystery of the Commons: On the Indispensability of Civic Rhetoric." *Social Research* 5, 4 (Winter 1983).

Stephens, Michael D. "Fashioning Americans: The Role of Education in the Development of the United States." *International Journal of Lifelong Education* 2, 3 (1983): 245-69.

Stevens, O. *Children Talking Politics*. Oxford: Martin Robertson and Co., 1982.

Stubblefield, Harold W. "Adult Civic Education in the Post-World War II Period." *Adult Education* 24, 3 (Spring 1974): 227-37.

Sullivan, William. *Reconstructing Public Philosophy*. Berkeley, CA:

University of California Press, 1982.
Sutherland, Margaret B. "The Impossibilities of Education for Citizenship: The 1981 Sera Lecture." *Scottish Educational Review* 13, 1 (May 1981): 5-11.
Thomas, Gordon R. "Commitment and Action: New Directions in Citizenship Education Research." *History and Social Science Teacher* 19, 4 (May 1984): 238-39.
Tjerandsen, Carl. "The Highlander Heritage: Education for Social Change." *Convergence* 16, 2 (1983): 10-22.
Torney, Judith V.; Oppenheim, A. N.; and Farnen, Russell F. *Civic Education in Ten Countries: An Empirical Study*. New York, NY: John Wiley and Sons, 1975.
Torney-Purta, Judith. "Psychological Perspectives on Enhancing Civic Education through the Education of Teachers." *Journal of Teacher Education* 34, 6 (November-December 1983): 30-34.
Walzer, Michael. *Spheres of Justice*. New York, NY: Basic Books, 1983.
Warren, Donald R. "Public Knowledge." *Journal of Thought* 18 (1983).
Weatherman, Donald V. "Civic Education: A Dying Art." *Improving College and University Teaching* 32, 1 (Winter 1984): 31-34.
Werner, Walter. "The Politics of Context." *History and Social Science Teacher* 18, 4 (May 1983): 201-4.
Wigginton, Elliot. *Sometimes a Shining Moment: The Foxfire Experience*. New York, NY: Anchor/Doubleday, 1985.
Wilen, William W. "Questioning, Thinking and Effective Citizenship." *Social Science Record* 22, 2 (Spring 1985): 4-6.
Wirsing, Marie E. "The Revival of Civic Learning: A Critique." *Journal of Teacher Education* 34, 6 (November-December 1983): 58-63.
Wolin, Sheldon. "The New Public Philosophy." *Democracy* 1, 4 (October 1981): 23-36.
Wood, George H. "The American Dream, Democracy, and Participatory Theory." *Georgia Social Science Journal* 14, 1 (1983): 4-8.
_____. "Schooling in a Democracy: Transformation or Reproduction?" *Educational Theory* 34, 3 (Summer 1984).
_____. "Education for Democratic Participation: Democratic Values and the Nuclear Freeze Campaign." *Theory and Research in Social Education* 12, 4 (Winter 1985): 39-56.
Woyach, Robert B., and Love, Janice. "Citizenship and World Affairs: The Impact of a Community-Based Approach to Glo-

bal Education." *Educational Research Quarterly* 8, 2 (1983): 36-47.

JOURNAL SPECIAL ISSUES

Brandt, Ronald S., ed. "Citizenship Education." *Educational Leadership* 38, 1 (October 1980).

Brown, Peggy Ann, ed. "Promoting Civic Literacy." *Forum for Liberal Education* 7, 4 (March 1985).

Butts, R. Freeman, ed. "The Civic Education of the American Teacher." *The Journal of Teacher Education* 34, 6 (November-December 1983).

"Civic Education." *Georgia Social Studies Review* 16, 1 (Winter 1985).

"Citizenship Education." *International Journal of Political Education* 6, 1 (April 1983).

"Educating for Citizenship." *Theory and Research in Social Education* 12, 4 (Winter 1985).

Frederickson, H. George, and Chandler, Ralph Clark, eds. "Citizenship and Public Administration." *Public Administration Review*, April 1983.

"Global Education," *Theory Into Practice* 21, 3 (Summer 1982).

Henry, Nelson B., ed. "Education for Citizenship." *56th Yearbook of the National Society for the Study of Education.* Chicago, IL: NSSE, 1957.

Hill, Barbara Ann, ed. "The Civic Purposes of Liberal Education." *Liberal Education* 68, 4 (Winter 1982).

Kress, Helen, ed. "Citizenship Education." *Social Studies* 76, 1 (January-February 1985).

Mar'enko, I. S., ed. "A Model Curriculum for the Social Upbringing of School Pupils." *Soviet Education* 25, 6 (April 1983).

Murchland, Bernard, ed. "Educating for Civic Virtue." *The Antaeus Report*, Spring 1984.

Rivera, Charles R., ed. "American Civic Education," *Social Education* 49, 3 (March 1985).

Contributors

Contributors

SUSAN DOUGLAS FRANZOSA is an Associate Professor of Education at the University of New Hampshire where she also serves as a member of the President's Commission on the Status of Women and chairs the University Committee for Equitable Educational Climate. Her scholarship includes work in the history of educational thought, educational equity, and women and education and has been published in *Educational Theory, Urban Education, The Journal of Education,* and *Vitae Scholasticae.* In her current research, she is investigating the social history of teaching and theories of feminist pedagogy.

JAMES M. GIARELLI is an Associate Professor in the Graduate School of Education, Rutgers University where he teaches philosophy and education. He is a member and officer of several national and regional scholarly societies and serves on the editorial boards of *Educational Theory* and the *Journal of Thought.* He has published articles and reviews in such journals as *Educational Theory, Educational Studies, Journal of Thought, Teachers College Record,* and *Ethics.* His current research projects include a book, *Public Philosophy and Education,* based on the "Social Frontier," and a special issue of the *Journal of Thought* (1987) devoted to ethics and education. During the 1985-86 academic year, he was the recipient of a John Dewey Senior Fellowship.

RONALD K. GOODENOW is a historian who has published extensively on the progressive education movement and urban, multicultural, and international education. Currently an Associate Professor in the Boston University School of Education, he is also co-director of the International Educational Relations Project, a multinational program of symposia and publications. An advisor to several urban studies programs in Britain, Goodenow is also assisting the development of a citizenship education project in England for the Brookline, Massachusetts schools.

CONTRIBUTORS

BEVERLY M. GORDON is an Assistant Professor in the curriculum and instructional development faculty at The Ohio State University. Her primary scholarly research focuses on curriculum theorizing, and she has also written in the areas of teacher education and African-American educational history. Gordon has published chapters in books and articles in journals, including *Journal of Education*, *Theory and Research in Social Education*, and *The Urban Review*, and has articles forthcoming in other national and international journals.

SANDRA L. PARKS-TRUSZ is a principal research associate with Tri-State Social Research Associates and director of social services for the Metropolitan Inter-Faith Association in Memphis, Tennessee. Her primary research interests focus on policy analysis for equity.

RICHARD PRATTE is Professor of Education at The Ohio State University. He is past president of the Philosophy of Education Society and is currently president of the Council of Learned Societies in Education. Among his books are *The Public School Movement* and *Pluralism in Education*. His major research interest in the past decade has been the study of social heterogeneity and pluralism.

BETTY A. SICHEL is Professor of Education at Long Island University, C.W. Post Campus, Greenvale, New York. Her major scholarly interests have been in the areas of classical Greek educational philosophy and moral education. She has published in *Educational Theory*; *Curriculum Inquiry*; *Journal of Moral Education*, *Philosophy and Phenomenological Research*; and other journals. At present, she is completing a book on the philosophy of moral education.

ANDREW R. TRUSZ is a principal research associate with Tri-State Social Research Associates in Memphis, Tennessee. His research interests focus on a comparative analysis of the history of educational provision and the sociological consequences of various forms of evaluation for educational equity.

DONALD R. WARREN is chairman of the Department of Education Policy, Planning, and Administration at The University of Maryland, College Park. He writes on the history of federal education policy in the United States and on the role of history in policy analysis. His most recent publication is *Pride and Promise: Schools of Excellence for All the People* (1984), co-authored with Mary Anne

Raywid and Charles A. Tesconi, Jr. He is a past president of the American Educational Studies Association and of the Council of Learned Societies in Education and currently serves as vice-president of the American Educational Research Association for the History and Historiography Division. He is a member of the Maryland Commission on Secondary Education.

GEORGE H. WOOD is Assistant Professor of Education at Ohio University and coordinator of the Institute for Democratic Education. His work has focused on democratic practices in the classroom and their relationship to the democratic empowerment of students. His work on education and democracy has appeared in *Educational Theory*, *Journal of Curriculum Theorizing*, and *Theory and Practice in Social Education*. He was recently named University Professor at Ohio University for outstanding undergraduate teaching.